IS THAT TRUE?

DISCERNING TRUTH IN AN AGE OF DECEPTION

AVERTING THE DEATH OF TRUTH

CHUCK STEPHENS
LARRY N. WILLARD

IS THAT TRUE?
Copyright ©2025 Chuck Stephens and Larry N. Willard

978-1-998815-36-4 Soft Cover
978-1-998815-37-1 E-book

Published by:
Castle Quay Books
Little Britain, Ontario, Canada
Jupiter, Florida, USA
Tel: (416) 573-3249
E-mail: info@castlequaybooks.com | www.castlequaybooks.com

Edited by Marina Hofman Willard PhD
Cover design and book interior by Burst Impressions

The dialogue contained in chapters 12 to 17 are works of fiction. Any resemblance between original characters and real persons, living or dead, is entirely coincidental. While most of the characters, places and incidents in this story are based on actual discussions, events or persons, they have been used fictitiously in these discussions. Any conversation or debate between the actual characters is a product of the author's imagination.

Library and Archives Canada Cataloguing in Publication
Title: Is that true? : discerning truth in an age of deception / by Chuck Stephens and Larry N Willard.
Names: Stephens, Chuck (William Charles O'Dowda), author. | Willard, Larry N., 1950- author.
Description: Includes bibliographical references.
Identifiers: Canadiana (print) 2025024120X | Canadiana (ebook) 20250242664 | ISBN 9781998815364
    (softcover) | ISBN 9781998815371 (EPUB)
Subjects: LCSH: Mass media—Objectivity. | LCSH: Journalism—Objectivity. | LCSH: Truthfulness and
    falsehood in mass media. | LCSH: Deception. | LCSH: Artificial intelligence—Social aspects. |
    LCSH: Media literacy.
Classification: LCC P96.O24 S74 2025 | DDC 302.23—dc23

CASTLE QUAY BOOKS

PART 1
MEDIA MACHINATIONS
IN THE WAR ON TRUTH

PART 2
IS IT REAL OR IS IT AI?

PART 3
KEY PERSPECTIVES ON TWENTY-FOUR
MAJOR ISSUES BEING DEBATED IN
THE PUBLIC SPACE

"Truth is so rare that it is delightful to tell it."
—Emily Dickinson

PART 1

MEDIA MACHINATIONS IN THE WAR ON TRUTH

1

IS THIS THE FAREWELL TO TRUTH?

HAS TRUTH SUFFERED a fatal wound? An inevitable death? Many believe this to be the case. That is the heart of this enquiry. And, even if Truth is not fully dead, but only on life support, we still wonder what we must all do to ensure its full recovery and revival as the foundation of all culture and communication.

It is important that, up front, we establish exactly the definition of Truth we are concerned with in this exposé. There are many areas where the term *Truth* might be applied, but not all of them are of concern here. Our concern is with something we term traditional absolute Truth and how this truthfulness is handled as an ideal and practice in society. We examine the damage that we believe essential absolute Truth has suffered over the years, how this damage was done, and if it continues to suffer failure unabated, what terrible consequences to Western culture we can expect.

Without sounding overly conspiratorial, we want to discuss what we see as calculated, deceptive tactics employed by some elite groups to intentionally and systematically undermine traditional Truth to accomplish specific social, political, and moral outcomes that are all completely contrary to the traditional values of Truth. Chuck provides a splendid analysis of 24 specific key talking points where the core Truth of the subjects has become damaged, muddled, and impaired over the past five decades, and how it is having a critical impact on the cohesiveness and cooperation within our free society.

This introduction to the subject of Truth ends by discussing the next major threat to Truth, which many see coming. This threat supersedes and surpasses all other threats to our Western worldview, and we must respond to and learn to master it, or in the end, it will either control us or destroy us.

We believe that the restoration of absolute Truth is essential to our society, and that restoration needs to be our priority, or our culture will suffer greatly. It may seem daunting that restoration is in our feeble hands, but feeble or not, we need to act bravely together, or all we will be is witnesses to the end of Western values and Truth, and all of their benefits as we know them. I am mindful in our current moment in history of a famous quote credited to Edmund Burke:

"The only thing necessary for the triumph of evil (against Truth) is for good people to do nothing." So this is an invitation for you to engage in the consequential struggle for Truth.

What Is Truth?

Chuck reminds us of that famous line echoed by Pontius Pilate when Jesus told him that he was the core of all Truth, since it is Pilate's response to Jesus that still best reflects our current condition relating to the subject of what truth is. Pilate sincerely retorted the now-famous question, "What is Truth?" And Chuck wants to answer that question. At first, it may seem obvious to many of us that something is either true or false. Much like right and wrong, we suppose such things are obvious. The problem we are presenting here is that at this time in our history, there appears to be a serious disagreement and divide on what constitutes both truth and a lie, or even right and wrong. Therefore, their definition and identity are somewhat nebulous.

We can all agree that there are some areas and issues related to identifying the truth of any matter that we may never fully agree on. Matters of personal taste and preferences, views and worldviews, fall into the legitimate category of "subjective truth," and we try and make allowance for differing views and work out a solution where, cooperatively, we can all live with a disagreement. Matters concerning religion, some morals and values, political approaches, cultural preferences, and even some laws will never enjoy absolute unanimity. But our legal systems and acknowledged arbitrators of them were established to adjudicate such differences, as we try to ensure they never become life-threatening.

And so we acknowledge that it is reasonable to have numerous gray areas in our social interactions, constructs, and beliefs as we attempt to live peaceably in a complex, multicultural, multifaceted, diverse society, doing our best to be respectful of opposing views we may not only disagree with but may at times abhor. Those types of truth are not the core issue we are presenting here, and some subjectivity may be permissible.

But what we are concerned with is that area of Truth that is foundational to our society, which is suffering loss and must be redressed. I love Chuck's discussion panels as he shows how versions of Truth can be disagreed on, but those differences must still be discussed with variant views of facts and opinions. At the same time, we maintain a sliver of respect for opposing views. But there is, and always has been, that definition of Truth that formed the foundation of our current society and the principles of traditional objective Truth that undergird it that we want to evaluate and adjudicate here.

There is that dominant worldview, and the practices and principles that flow from it, that built the current prosperous structure of Western society in all core areas, wherever it is found throughout the world, that so many benefited from throughout history, that we believe needs to be still reaffirmed, acknowledged, protected, and preserved. We accept and even celebrate the manifold versions of diversity, difference, and true uniqueness, as God designed and ordained them, to be valid and valuable, and acknowledge that those differences have resulted in cultural nuances to be respected. Still, we want to firmly and unapologetically defend the right to sustain traditional Truth, as it formed the foundation of our Western world and all that is in it, as our rightful standard to be defended and reinstated.

With that in view, it requires that we clearly define that Truth we mean and expose, resist, and object to the current replacement versions, with the many advocates of it, that presently form the promotion of an unrestrained, foggy, untested subjective type of truth, that is being endorsed in our day. That new truth is hostile to objective Truth and appears unapologetically dedicated to endlessly and slyly dismantling traditional Truth with all its related values. And more so, it subsequently appears intent on incriminating and castigating anyone who is dedicated to the preservation of traditional Truth.

We intend to present solid examples of how we are witnessing the introduction of these clever, intentional tactics that hijack traditional Truth and have systematically replaced it, installing a system seemingly more designed for political or economic gain and social control than anything else. Such accusations require proof, and that is what follows.

Big "T" and Little "t"
So that we are not vague by any means, we need to start by making it clear that the Truth we refer to throughout this exposé is not a concern for any personal, frivolous type of truth as it relates to the infinite number of opinions on any subject we may all hold and that we casually call truth. I alluded to the many times we can call something truth, but disagree on its definition, and agree to permit such truth to roam free.

I refer to those mundane opinions, on inconsequential subjects, reflected in silly statements such as "It's true, my mother makes the best apple pie in the world," or "The Leafs or Red Wings are the best hockey team in history," or any other clearly overzealous statements. No one would disagree that those many, many "small t" truth topics are not serious. They are to be taken lightly with a grain of salt and humor, as acceptably subjective views that are thankfully mostly inconsequential.

In this quest, we are interested in Truth that has always been termed absolute, nonsubjective Truth, essential and consequential, whether scientific, moral, social, or political, that is the core and foundation of essential facts, morals, practices, and belief systems that we in the Western world have defined for several millennia and that deeply underpin our entire larger social structures and norms—"big T" Truths that cover everything from life and death, to substantial principles that reflect and even govern the core of our reality, directing our values and what we accept in most of life's essential subjects. Objective core Truth.

Our main argument encompasses the need for the resurgence of essential absolute Truths to be reestablished with a precedence so that we may again have confidence in what we hear and see from any source; such that we can then again embrace and unhesitatingly integrate it into our belief systems and worldviews, which then become the core content that moderates all our future decisions, discourses, interactions and actions both individually and as a collective society. Truth that we can rely on will be disseminated with honesty, accuracy, and integrity from observations made to the best of the observers' or reporters' powers and skills of observation, communicated in a factual, undistorted, unbiased manner.

Clearly, with this level of introduction, we are about to charge that such Truth is dying, or at minimum, under endless attack. Our concern is that what we are now witnessing is the end of a long period of intentionally obscuring, distorting, and falsely recounting what is essential Truth. Facts are now being presented more for strictly ideological or political reasons. They are essentially fake facts and fake news. If it is Truth that sets us free, it is essential that what we are digesting is valid, such that we may base all of our beliefs, future goals, and past, present, and future actions upon it. But that is not what we are being given! That is our enquiry here. How did we get here? How do we bring Truth back?

The Absolute Truth Is MIA
If Truth is a priority for a healthy society, just as it is for a healthy personal relationship, it is the conclusion of this book that Truth no longer has the same priority, high value, firm definition, and reverence it once had in our society. We perceive that even the idea of the existence of an "absolute Truth" can no longer be agreed upon.

Truth has been redefined, is highly personalized, and is most often carelessly revised. We have almost lost the idea of Truth as being that impartial, trustworthy, unchanging, certain, immovable, common-sense-based, and mostly Bible-based set of sacrosanct facts which would lead to a trustworthy, unalterable foundation of reality. And it is that kind of Truth, in past times, most of the Western world gladly applied to all aspects of life and worldview without hesitation when encountered. So it is no wonder that we watch in horror and disbelief as the Western traditional understanding of Truth experiences a lamentable devastation—a type of unending decay of its definition, practice, and essence—that we cringe, are concerned, and wonder why "someone" doesn't do something about it.

If we are honest, we admit this deterioration is not a recent phenomenon. For decades, we all watched in disbelief as the decay of Truth, at first subtle, even imperceptible, gained a pace of erosion that became torrential, relentless, and accelerating at an overpowering pace. And that devastation was not just constrained to a few areas of life or culture; the decay successfully spread throughout the entire Western world and now touches every area where Truth once was treasured and thrived.

2

THE KEY PERPETRATOR OF
THE WAR ON TRUTH

AS CHUCK STEPHENS has established in what follows, the assault on Truth touches every imaginable subject area, topic, and field of study. It permeates all their related derivatives, spinoffs, and consequences within each of those areas. Nothing has been left untouched.

To really grasp the extent of damage and show how the demise of Truth is quite intentional, it is always best to illustrate the methods used for that decay. And there is no better model to start our analysis with than our primary communications vehicles—the media of the Western world—whose primary reason for existing is to accurately report facts, current events, and daily news truthfully in all forms for our edification. No area is more important, or any more influential a stimulus on daily life and social thinking, than the media. And the techniques by which they now employ and with which we have been mostly deceived are the same that are now being applied to all facets of essential communications everywhere.

So we begin by asking ourselves some very pointed questions. How did we get here? Was this done in the dark? What did we do wrong to permit this?

In the next few pages, Chuck and I show that without our realizing it, certain members of the media, and several other industries, employed a devious quite intentional plan, using a series of clever techniques, strategies, and tactics that permitted them to successfully establish a very contentious counter worldview of Truth to the public. They based such worldviews on personal political realities and ideas of truth, with the ultimate goal and intention of establishing their personal views of truth, along with plans intended for specific outcomes to achieve an end.

Looking at the core reasons these groups are undertaking this mission is equally important to understand, but to begin, it is especially important to identify their methods and the devices they used to alter our idea of Truth since, in their crusade, these methods are still being employed and will further undermine our values if continued successfully. This is core and essential to our exposé, because if you don't see this group for who they are and understand what they are trying to accomplish, they will successfully carry out their plans. That will eventually trounce our civilization and never cease manipulating you and me, such that we will lose our world. We won't even know what is happening.

I want to be clear that it is not just the New World Order, with all its devious plots, that you and I need to be concerned about. Still, it is a New Digital World Order, controlled by a few power-hungry Dr. Strangelove-type oligarchs who have a somewhat deranged version of reality and culture that they plan to engulf us with. But once we are all made aware and educated in their slick techniques, we have a better ability to identify them, combat, counter, and minimize their exploits, and salvage our culture from their dreadful plan. Otherwise, these same successful tactics will continue to be applied to every possible aspect of society. Then, the consequences will be much greater, as you will see once we present the plans of these groups to use artificial intelligence as the coup d'état to further their mission and make it almost impossible to reverse the death of Truth.

Make no mistake about it: Defending Truth depends on us. Our success depends on our preparedness and skills. To become prepared to reestablish Truth, we begin by analyzing the tactics, techniques, and strategies used by the media to get us into this plight. This will equip us to spot these deployments in other areas.

Modern Media as the Butcher Shop of Truth

I am not alone when I say I have come to regard our modern legacy media, with their biased presentation of news, as not much more than butcher shops of Truth. We define legacy media, also called traditional media or old media, as the mass media institutions that dominated prior to the internet; particularly print media, film studios, music studios, advertising agencies, radio broadcasting, and television. Their contribution to Truth's demise, the distrust in media, and the impact it is having and will continue to have on social and cultural decline cannot be overstated. Though they are just one avenue being used to alter our Western worldview of reality and Truth, they are by far the most significant, and they apply the strongest techniques of the processes used in subversion.

You may have watched this happen and know something is amiss. Modern media have become masters not of reporting the real news with perfection but of presenting a deceptive and contrived manipulation of it—facts, news, opinion, and reality mixed together. We once called it deception, propaganda, or marginal brainwashing. A kind word has been introduced to this technique. It is called "spin."

The legacy media have perfected a routine. They send out their reporters, who join others in their craft and quest to be the first to fetch a good, important story and report it, and gain a reputation. They bring back the raw details of a story to their editing studios. But unlike the practices of traditional media, legacy media tends to lay the raw story details on the editor's chopping block and then begins what can only be likened to selective dissecting, like a butcher shop on a leg of beef.

The procedure works like this. First, they remove those cuts to be kept, still containing pieces of factual content, but selected because they will be useful in mixing the right portions of truth and opinion, serving their ultimate spin purposes. Even the devil knows you must have truth in every deception to make it palatable. Next, they slice and dice it, dress it up, and season it with their intentional spicy spins, reflecting their worldviews and plans. The final product is then skillfully placed in the store windows of modern media outlets—TV, radio, podcasts, newspapers, and internet outlets—which they just happen to own, and they place the final product before an unsuspecting consumer, as though it were the real truth—nothing but the straight facts.

The process reminds me of that old pop song popularized by a musical group called the Byrds, which sets to music the words from the book of Proverbs, titled *Turn, Turn, Turn*. I suggest the legacy media have replaced those wise words with their new anthem of *Spin, Spin, Spin*! Legacy media have become masters of manipulated, twisted language and the very convincing defense of nonsense. Endless spin in everything. And spin is hostile to traditional Truth. We should really thank God for the growth of alternative independent podcast media. Hope is on the way.

Most never suspect any manipulation since "after all" we have been saturated with media platitudes like "the most trusted name in news" or "the best in news," such that trusting hungry viewers consume these distorted stories without suspicion, unaware that essential pieces that would have shifted the interpretation and perspective of the story have been removed or skillfully altered. So the final product most consumers receive from them is often a version of a quite misleading reality. That is the state of much of modern legacy media—butcher shops of Truth rather than reporters of it.

Too often absent from modern legacy media is the traditional freedom-of-the-press quest to be the first to report the raw Truth, the facts, exactly as they happened, without the slightest hint of added opinion, bias, or spin. Trusting viewers are not aware that they are consuming a highly dressed version of facts. It's much like the red dye butcher shops use to make meat look "always fresh" when it may not be.

Perhaps most inexcusable is that the media have become more like on-air performers, not disturbed by their fact-tampering, nor are they guilt-ridden by their intentional maneuvers. They have convinced themselves they are justified in altering our perceptions since the other views—that is, the views we call Truthful—are equally biased, inaccurate, naïve, and based on an outdated worldview that must be replaced. They are firmly convinced they are doing you and me a favor.

In case you think I have overstated the charge, I draw your attention to the following report card on the US legacy media from 2017 to the present day, 2025, as it relates to the political elections of that period and several cases that had political implications with serious ramifications for the legacy media's favored part.

It started with the so-called Russian collusion case, code named Crossfire Hurricane, a counterintelligence investigation undertaken by the Federal Bureau of Investigation (FBI) from July 31, 2016, to May 17, 2017, into links between Donald Trump's presidential campaign and Russia and whether individuals associated with Trump's presidential campaign were coordinating, wittingly or unwittingly, with the Russian government's efforts to interfere in the 2016 US presidential election. Trump was not personally under investigation until May 2017, when his firing of FBI director James Comey raised suspicions of obstruction of justice and triggered a Special Counsel investigation led by Robert Mueller. Throughout a nearly two-year-long probe, Mueller and his team of prosecutors indicted 34 individuals and three Russian businesses on charges ranging from computer hacking to conspiracy and financial crimes.

Trump and his allies repeatedly alleged that the Crossfire Hurricane investigation was opened pretextually for political purposes. A subsequent review done by Justice Department Inspector General Michael E. Horowitz found no evidence that political bias against Trump tainted the initiation of the investigation, but did find that the FBI made 17 errors or omissions in its FISA warrant applications to the Foreign Intelligence Surveillance Court (FISA court) for surveillance of former Trump aides. This past spring, Kash Patel, the new FBI director, found evidence of FBI and media corruption and cover-ups and called the entire charges and investigation the biggest DC deception game ever seen. Countercharges are being filed at the time of this writing. The media were shown to be complicit in the communications of the case with a clear bias against Trump and his team.

The media have faced many, many similar charges of bias, intentional underreporting, and cover-ups for political gain, which have fueled suspicion that they are politically motivated in their reporting practices. Instances include NBC covering up and hiding the facts in the Hunter Biden laptop scandal, which may have altered the results of the 2020 election.

The legacy media refused to investigate charges that President Biden had serious dementia problems that should have prevented his election or at least his continuation as president. Later, several of the top journalists who denied the problem wrote books about the period, acknowledging their error. The legacy media refused to investigate the sources of the COVID-19 pandemic or the possibility that the seriousness of the epidemic had been overstated for political reasons. Their refusal to cover the charges that the USA's southern border had serious problems with illegal alien crossings was shown to be fallacious when the ruling party blamed the crisis on inadequate power being given to them by Congress to address and remedy the problem, and again when President Trump was elected and the problem was nearly eliminated without Congressional involvement.

The number of media cover-ups was endless. These are selected as just a few of the more obvious and serious ones that were later shown to be clear examples of bias of responsibility or politically motivated cover-ups.

In short, throughout the past four decades, the legacy media has inconspicuously moved from highly competitive pace-setting journalists and broadcasters of the raw, truthful news to reporters of their version of that news, which then morphed into interpreters of the meaning of the news, and finally to their current role as politically correct promoters of their biased version of news, reality, and truth, which coincidentally, happens to be in full opposition to our traditional worldviews. That is our opponent. Members of the new alternative news media that emerged in the past decade have often attributed their success to the legacy media being little more than a form of infotainment propaganda, and many viewers are now aware of that fact. You may want to question parts of this charge, but it must not be missed that this movement has had a serious impact on traditional Truth.

Unfortunately, this truth malady is not limited only to the main forms of legacy media but has now been boldly extended to all forms of communication and publications. We find corruption of the truth in books and rewritten classical studies, documentaries, social media posts, and literature related to academia, religion, law, health, business, politics, history, and science. From history to the classics, literature is being rewritten to reflect the influence of this new subjective truth. There is no limit to where the cancer has spread.

3

SEVEN MEDIA TACTICS, PLOYS, TRICKS, AND DEVICES IN THE WAR ON TRUTH

IT CAN SEEM overwhelming to observe the dismantling of traditional, well-established histories, especially when the replacement versions are so clearly fabricated, outright falsities, and cunning distortions of the real Truth. We wonder silently what can be done to stop the assault, and even more troubling, "How can any of us be sure of anything we hear or read anymore?" Where is the real Truth to be found if I want to find it?

Spinning and rewriting are common yet impressive media frauds. But the opponents of Truth use other tactics that are important for us to be aware of if we hope to reverse these falsifying trends, expose the fraud, and see the resurrection of Truth.

We are dealing with more than just altered content in legacy media. A host of additional tactics contribute to their system's success, and these tactics need to be equally disclosed if we are to identify and thwart their schemes successfully.

You may know the Bible verse that cautions, "My people are destroyed from lack of knowledge" (Hosea 4:6). It is precisely because of the impact the legacy group is able to have on Truth and reality that we suffer from falsity. Therefore, it is prudent that we become aware of the many tactics they employ to accomplish their deceptive ends because we cannot discern and then change what we are not aware of. Essentially, our adversaries use these same tactics and methods in all modern communications fields.

Even if we qualify that not every media personality in the legacy media is guilty of using this collection of slick tricks, tactics, and devices, it appears that the majority are. In addition, not just legacy media but many areas of communication have become adept at the following tactical methods. Once we are aware of these techniques, devices, and tactics, we are better able to identify them. Once able to identify them, we will be better prepared to engage them successfully and hopefully, through engagement, marshal a reversal of their ruse. As the great military leader Sun Tzu in *The Art of War* once stated, "If you know the enemy and know yourself, you need not fear the result of a hundred battles." And it is a battle we are in.

What follows is a list of the top ploys and tactics most prominently and successfully employed by legacy media and other communication groups in their presentation of altered news, facts, and histories.

Tactic 1: Style Supersedes Truth

The war on Truth uses many successful tactics. They are subtle at times, but they are formidable. The first one may not seem like a tactic at all. The media present a positive or a negative statement or fact boldly, with a smug sense of overconfident conviction as to the veracity of the content, such that the listener tends to feel intimidated to question or contend with it.

This is a "style" tactic and is used very often and so subtly by media and other forms of communications that you may miss it. The matter-of-fact, convincing way these groups present content that we might otherwise question or even totally disagree with leaves the impression that the statement is unquestionably true. So we suppress our initial misgivings concerning its veracity.

Such a message may be spoken or written. Many of us silently watched for years, feeling a bit shell-shocked, as opposing, quite contradictory, and mostly hostile views, or distorted versions of facts we were familiar with, were presented with such convincing execution that it seemed de facto. Details, which at first hearing might seem suspicious, are presented as though unquestionable, factual, verified, obvious, self-evident, and unchallengeable.

It catches the skeptical listener off guard, leaving us feeling inadequate to question the veracity of the content. Since such content is supposedly given by so-called experts, specialists, official authorities, pundits, and critics in a given field, it must be unquestionably true. This style is an equally popular method used by all forms of media, politicians, salespeople, writers, publishers, and specialists in any field trying to cement their views with their audience. It is especially used when anyone is trying to dismiss or belittle a view or personality they are at odds with. It is highly visible at election time when politicians use it to diminish their opponents.

The media everywhere are specialists at it. You see it used with dubious but popular statements like "of course everyone believes there are twelve genders; of course men can become women and have babies; of course climate change is a proven science; of course the theory of evolution is scientific, of course … of course … of course!" And on and on. This is a tactic we must be aware of and not be intimidated by. Having real Truth, real facts, and a confident dissent is the best antidote to counter this one. The guest panelists in Part 3 of this book display this skill well.

Tactic 2: Pan-Media Uniformity, Consistency, and Incontestability

It is not just the impressive and self-confident manner with which questionable content is presented as uncontestable that helps the cause of legacy media. A second element is equally effective: the uniformity and consistency of the story and the message that is presented across platforms of the legacy media outlets in a networked concert to make the listener feel that it must be true. Surely all these old, reliable outlets, top publishers, and government-approved scientists or spokespeople could not collude together with facts to fool us! And since everyone is saying the same thing, it just must be so!

You might notice that at times it truly sounds as though all media personalities receive their talking points for any given story from the same central supplier and are all expected to resist departing from the official script, even by a single word. They know that consistency gives the narrative a sense of assuredness. Surf the stations as each one's talking head convincingly regurgitates the standard script, word for word, without variation or hesitation.

There are moments when we find ourselves off-balance, wondering if maybe we are the ones mistaken in our understanding of certain facts or positions. However, most of you who are also skilled in the marketing and sales industry may have recognized this approach immediately as "a good old reliable common sales technique."

We were told as sales trainees during professional selling school to always make sure our presentations had two immutable features. First, always sound convincing. Second, always stay on script, no matter where the customer tries to take the conversation. It is a successful technique used by salespeople all the time. Repetition and consistency. And it almost always works. Now, modern media and journalists and publishers, and pundits have been trained in it and successfully apply it at all times.

Psychologists are well aware of the "illusion of truth" effect: "If you repeat a lie often enough, people will believe it," and "you will even come to believe it yourself." This is the common law of repetitious propaganda skillfully used by masters of deception like the notorious Joseph Goebbels. It is a tactic, so be aware of its use when any content is presented to you that otherwise sounds fabricated.

Tactic 3: Changing the Meaning of Words

It is not enough that we must comb through inaccurate reporting, endless spin, intentional distortion, and subversive ownership views of media to find any Truth. What may be the cleverest, most subtle device that the spin doctors have concocted, which most often escapes our attention, is changing the narrative by simply redefining the words. Have you noticed how the meaning of words seems to have changed over the years?

Using this tactic, the elite control the message. They collaborate with educational institutions, dictionary publishers, and those in informal education to subtly alter the meaning of many words. Common words have been redefined to mean something slightly, or at times quite, different than originally intended or understood. Compare a copy of Webster's dictionary from the 1960s to a present edition to see the shift toward redefining traditional terms, such as marriage.

Suppose we were to write an opinion piece on a traditional topic using old established arguments and trusty old phrases or word definitions to make our main points. We would be told we are mistaken in what the subject means because we have misused key words. Our audience would be confused. Leaders realize that if you can't change someone's mind by use of compelling arguments, then the next best trick is to change the meaning of the main words and the nuance of the debate, and it can change the argument itself.

By changing the meaning of a word such that it does not mean what many of us always thought, the argument can be cleverly deflected. It has become prominently applied of late, most notably in the debates about the meaning of freedoms in the Constitution of the United States of America and social precedence in what is now called DEI. Diversity, equity, and inclusion are words that have been redefined and no longer refer to what we once thought they did. The use of a particular, established, solid word, like equality, is replaced by equity, and presented as though they are synonyms. But they are not.

Built-in nuances have changed the meaning of a word. So when we come together to debate and work toward agreement on a subject, thinking terms mean one thing, we later realize the opposition meant something quite different. Now, someone using a traditional vocabulary to suggest that equity is not equality, but in fact a form of socialism, even communism, and that the term equity is incongruent to our Western values, leads to attacks on that person as ignorant, or worst, showing evidence of hidden sexism, racism, patriarchy, colonial domination, or color privilege. Even a simple pronoun can now get one in trouble in some countries.

By changing the long-standing meaning of technical terms and common words, even slightly, without examination or recourse, words are redefined to have a new meaning. The result is that we are not even discussing the same topic. Suddenly, there is no longer common ground and dialogue on any subject that we can mutually build upon. With no trusted, foundational, traditional truth that we all agree on and depend on in a debate, there is no longer a basis on which to build our discourse.

Dictionary publishers have admitted they struggle to keep up with the movement's drivers' demands for changed word definitions. They must comply, or they could be accused of becoming archaic. Remember Funk and Wagnalls? They are now defunct.

With the replacement of historical, trusted, indisputable definitions of words and their related greater Truths, many of us find ourselves unsure of what language to use to defend our Truth.

We may laugh in unbelief at the duplicity, yet mourn, as we remind ourselves of that famous quote that has subtly moved from hyperbole to a sad current reality in these anxious times. In Lewis Carroll's fantasy, *Alice in Wonderland*, Alice challenges Humpty Dumpty on his reckless use of words as he thoughtlessly manipulates them to suit his desire or interpretation. His response is disturbing, yet it perfectly reflects our new world of relative truth. Humpty Dumpty retorts in a rather scornful tone to Alice's enquiry with the counter, "When I use a word, it means just what I choose it to mean—neither more nor less." How tragic that this simple response now encapsulates the essence of our modern philosophical inquiry.

No longer is it considered an arrogant assertion that we should have the power to assign any meaning to any word or idea, as it pleases us. It is now a reality, highlighting the subjectivity of truth, now applied to language, now the indisputable practice of our modern media, our politicians, and most marketers to manipulate words to suit their circumstances. Without apology, media and academia now openly acknowledge that language is a "human construct and meanings are not inherent to words themselves but rather are assigned by individuals or communities to fit the moment or the situation."[1] It is no longer hidden! Is this "goodbye, dear Truth!"?

Since words no longer mean what they once did, they can no longer be used to come to our rescue as we debate the outrageous distortions applied to any subject. Words have become unreliable. Simple old meanings may now be offensive. And therefore, it is only now that we have come to understand how much our foundation of all certainty is on life support, and the adage of telling "the truth, the whole truth, and nothing but the truth" essentially loses all meaning. If there is no Truth, there can be no justice! And so we come face-to-face with the folly and peril of situational truth.

---

1. S. Hall, *Representation: Cultural Representations and Signifying Practices* (Sage, 1997), 25; see pp. 15–64.

Truth, in a modern sense, is now acceptably pliable, malleable, almost like a chameleon, leaving nothing permanent, sacred, eternal, and untouchable. It is no exaggeration that there are moments when statements the modern world considers obviously true may seem so outlandish that we find ourselves feeling like we have just accidentally entered the world of Franz Kafka's surrealistic absurdity.

You need not be a biologist to see that declaring two observable genders can now become six, 12, or tomorrow 24 without any accompanying understandable explanation of how it is possible can be a threat to language. Especially when at the same moment, in seeming contradiction, the same specialists admit they do not know how to define a woman. Twelve genders, but 12 or even 24 of what?

The same team that cannot define a single traditional gender is asking that we permit them to change our children into one of these 24 new genders that they cannot even define. We must at least demand that they first define the 24 options clearly. Then tell us which of these 24 indescribable options are they suggesting a child transition to? Further, how do they know they can achieve their goal if they cannot even define what they are trying to achieve? Why are they suggesting a known gender, male, be transitioned into one of the many female options? Why not just a different male option? This is a confused industry with no credibility. They need to be confronted with their disconcerting and confusing ontology.

The only response to such confusion is to ensure that our defense of Truth begins with a strong definition of terms. You can see that happening in the debates Chuck presents. Words are important.

Without that shared clear definition of terms, we see how our institutions of social discourse display the clearest outcome, with endless insincere dialogue visibly super-permeating almost all our modern media discourse and even every related form of communications in all fields, degenerating into what feels like a type of calculated insincere "derangement syndrome." We need to hold our opponents accountable by starting any debate or discussion with strong definitions of the terms we will use.

Tactic 4: Hit Them Fast and Hit Them Hard! Blistering Pace and Public Castigation

I often joke that President Trump uses this technique most effectively, especially in his second term of office. His administration is trying to reverse what Trump termed years of waste, fraud, and abuse. It moved so rapidly with reversals of previous legislation and practices that the opposition found themselves flatfooted, forever on their heels. They had been neutered by the blinding speed of the next oncoming bullet, with little time to think of a good response. It was a brilliant tactic. I point out this ploy because it is and has been successfully used as a favorite of the opponents of Truth for decades.

They present their barrage of new truths at such a blistering pace that while we are thinking of how we might respond to a "Truth fire" in one spot, five new ones are already upon us, leaving us feeling so overwhelmed that we end up not responding effectively to anything. A clever tactic!

The reality of our day is that there is no natural, common, logical, moment where we scrutinize new truths wherever they are introduced—no built-in pause process in order to examine them that permits people to question whether we are accepting much of this "new and improved" science, knowledge, facts, and wisdom without proper examination. Admittedly, even the thought of thoroughly examining every new fact leaves us feeling exhausted. Reviewing and testing overwhelming and immense mounds of content to discern what is false and what is true feels beyond normal ability. It is too momentous, if not an impossible challenge.

If one felt the impulse to tackle such an endeavor, we find ourselves fighting against another aspect of culture: "We must be first to market wins!" So hurry! One meme tells us: "It is better to be first than it is to be better."

Our world is infatuated with haste and speed, which they term progressive values. First to market wins the prize! It is now built into the speed of supposed progress. The caution for losing our prize is "Don't stop or slow, or your competition will grab your prize and leave you dumbfounded and an empty-handed loser." Therefore, we do not have time to examine every little fact.

Chuck points this problem out well. Instead of exercising the law of careful examination and the testing of any replacement of once-thought eternal Truths, our new hasty world feels at ease to modify, replace, and eliminate without timely and careful examination because, after all, "Who has the time?" and "Don't miss the window!" If you snooze, you lose. No time for delay! Accept it, since it will happen whether you like it or not anyway.

It is not just the need to hastily accept or at least not oppose the move to replace all truths with new and better ones massively, nor is it the dizzying speed of these changes, nor is it just the threat of losing the prize if we delay scrutinizing the propositions. Then, to intensify the situation even further and make objections unpalatable, the drivers and masters of the push to thoughtlessly accept "all that is new" feel unconstrained. Not only do they feel free to haphazardly and sometimes flippantly replace sacred milestones, beliefs, and foundations without question, but they then feel uninhibited to attack the questioners and resistors of such change, labeling them as "deniers" of their new improved world order—the ultimate embarrassment.

We must demand proof of the changes we are force-fed. That is essential if we are to succeed. *Ad hominem* is a fallacy, after all.

Tactic 5: Masters of Embarrassing Dissenters and Deniers

As the resistors of the speedy replacements of Truth, we are labeled relics and then subjected to embarrassment through a form of public castigation. The reputation damage is not just public but vocal and often smug. It can be ruthless, vicious, accusing, and quite abusive.

Another offensive tactic often accompanies the public castigation. It's the exercise of an overly zealous justice; a righteous indignation against the perceived historical transgressions and transgressors. Together, they can be paralyzing. You see it employed through the midnight defacing or toppling of towers and statues of historical heroes—the eradication of physical and ethereal monuments, trampled doctrine, and scorned precepts.

Even the policing methods of our public defenders, once considered "solid," with their longstanding sound rules of justice and correction, are criticized, defunded, even defrocked and ceaselessly castigated without trial, deliberation, or debate. Fear robs many of a countering action. Common sense, prudence, and decency take blow after blow! Our best defense is to vocally and correspondingly oppose this kind of terrorism. It will take boldness. But we must prevail.

Tactic 6: The Loss of Inspection

Another clever tactic accompanying these acts is eliminating inspection as an essential step of due process. We hesitate to be decisive in defending Truth when we face an overwhelming pace of change, the humiliation of dissenters, the disdain of objectors, and the covert destruction of public artifacts to remove all evidence of a traditional historic perspective. These actions leave us feeling like robbed victims, and they are all accompanied by one more tactic.

If, in a brave moment, we should ever dare to demand a discussion concerning the value and veracity of the replacement facts and new theories, we have also seen the removal of that very important step we called *performing due diligence*. It is a tactic of the enemies of Truth to rob us of that once-prized practice of doing due diligence before new replacement knowledge is integrated into the old, reliable, foundational truths. New ideas were once subjected to a healthy public examination, containing one or several judicious steps of careful, logical, thoughtful discourse, which often included polite exchanges of various perspectives, whether we thought them legitimate or not. That step has been reduced, if not eliminated.

The once-trusted processing formula involved taking a thesis, presenting an antithesis, postulating the synthesis, finally agreeing on a new thesis, and only replacing the old if all are approved. That practice, even informally, has now been discarded as an unnecessary relic. We see this more as AI is infused with all these processes and communications.

Finding deeper Truth was once thought worthy of vigorous inspection and debate, and thereafter defended, such that we might then confidently confess it and apply it. For without an absolute, confidently held Truth as our foundation, it was always thought it was impossible to execute true justice or sound judgment in any sphere of life and society. The adage was "If we defend the Truth, the Truth will defend us."

But that important inspection process has become more and more discounted or bypassed. Much of the new truth being embraced is frivolous, without proper inspection, debate, and discourse. It is not just the multiple-gender debate or the men-in-women's sports issue or the equity-versus-equality debate or the race reparations discussion or the climate frenzy. Still, it is a very long, long list of issues that we suddenly find ourselves integrating into public policy without the traditional inspection step. And that should concern us all.

Suppose we continue to allow speculative truth, untested truth, a kind of rubber truth, and manipulated facts, all to be entertained, integrated, even sanctioned. In that case, we should fear that before long, we will not even be able to distinguish facts from contemplative fiction, or right from wrong, and we won't even care to. Or are we past that already?

Many still believe that the person or society who meddles with the core Truth is essentially committing eventual intellectual suicide. At the least, if they continue endlessly, they will soon no longer be able to distinguish Truth from their intentional manipulations of it. This could lead to civilizational suicide.

By allowing absolute Truth to be subjectively manipulated without full inspection, we enter the dangerous fate of the devil, who is unquestioningly clever and highly proficient, but has now lied so often and for so long that even he is no longer capable of recognizing or knowing what is in fact true. The practice of deceiving others eventually becomes a self-induced, self-deceiving poison to the spin doctor. It does not matter if it is people or groups who practice careless, intentional deception; they will finally come to believe their deceptions, manipulations, lies, and alterations and soon be destroyed. And sadly, many innocent people will suffer as a consequence. Is it no exaggeration to say, "We may already be there now." We need to bring back inspection and testing of new knowledge, especially with the advent of AGI.

I am reminded that there is a generation the apostle Paul once warned about in his letter to Timothy, that would be forever learning and sharing their ideas of truth, but they would never be able to arrive at a knowledge of the real truth (2 Timothy 3:7).

Tactic 7: If You Can't Change Them, Buy Them

When you control the options, you control the message. When absolute Truth, the one we so greatly treasure, is forcefully and intentionally banished to the fringes, there is always a great impact on official discourse. In the past four decades, we have witnessed the visible consequences of the tactics and strategies I just listed. Our discourse has changed utterly till we find ourselves endlessly and unapologetically fed a diet of false narratives, fake news, insincerity, and propaganda, all called subjective truth. Truth, as we define it, has been mostly banished in the legacy media. This is all, partially or wholly, an agenda.

We can recall the warning of Jesus that a time will come when deception and treachery will dominate all culture. Legacy media have helped fulfill that prophecy. And this final tactic was warned about by many leaders in the early twentieth century. It has come to pass. Albert Einstein warned in 1949 that the time would come when the very rich would so control all means of formal communication that it would be almost impossible for ordinary people to make informed decisions, and so democracy would then be broken.[2] There is evidence that Einstein's prediction is coming true.

To ensure unobstructed continuity of their legacy story without variation from their official script, our adversaries pulled this final, ultimate, and impressive maneuver as warned by Einstein. They found a way for the traditional independence and neutrality of the general media to be fully compromised. Rather than a host of networks and news outlets competing to get out the best facts and best angle of any story, a large group of elitist businesspeople and politicians, all with diametrically opposite views of Truth than what we have, decided the best way to ensure homogeneity of their story was to own every major media outlet in the business. So the old, once reliable legacy media became privately owned and controlled.

Media control and message conformity are everywhere guaranteed because most media are now owned by a small, select ring of owners who all share the same worldview. Back in 1983, all the outlets of the media industry were controlled by a group of about fifty large companies. They competed to

---

2. Albert Einstein, "Why Socialism?" in *Monthly Review* 1 (May 1949).

present the best angle and content for a story on which to build their reputation. Today, legacy media are owned and directed by a few groups with one single political view—views that are contrary to our traditional Truth views.

In 2025, the legacy media industry is dominated and controlled by just six gigantic, ultrapowerful corporations, who unscrupulously coordinate control of all content. They own more than 90 percent of all television networks, streaming services, cable channels, movie studios, newspapers, magazines, publishing houses, music labels, and even most of our favorite websites. They handpick CEOs and producers to ensure consistency of the broadcast message with theirs. The output is guaranteed. Therefore, the hope of bringing back Truth and applying it to all the many forms of communication depends on people generating new media and content groups everywhere. That is one reason we should be pleased that alternative forms of media and publishing companies are springing up ubiquitously.

We should support and encourage them. But the controllers of legacy media will not give up their control willingly or easily.

The News Is About Profits and Control, Not Truth

There is another factor that impacts our attempts to wrestle media control from the elite players. Though not a tactic, it is still a formidable factor in our hope to regain Truth as a priority of communication in our society. And that element is profit! The once grand motive of bringing news to the masses for altruistic reasons that drove people like "Holy" Joe Atkinson has been supplanted by the powerful incentive of profits—a factor less operative in the past.

What started as a control motive has been superseded, so media ownership is not just about control anymore. News has become a big profit industry. As such, it is an added incentive to shut out alternative views and competition, even if that objective has to be achieved through intrigue or political manipulation. Money and the protection of power and wealth are the dominating motives fueling our media industry's drive to exclusivism.

Collectively, what are called the "big six" absolutely dominate news and entertainment in the United States and Canada. Their message, as it relates to news and opinion, is not only homogeneous, but it is highly profitable. To protect the content, the chief editors and CEOs of big media comply with one worldview to ensure their conformity. The old-fashioned word for it is *collusion*. And owning large chunks of the operation drives profits because a lack of competitors means no free-market competitive rates. As in poker, the ante becomes too high for small players. Profit is thus an added incentive to shut out possible detractors.

If the "big six," made up of the enterprises Disney, Time Warner, National Amusements, News Corporation, Comcast, and Sony, were a country, they would have the 26th largest GDP in the world. Even those remaining areas of the media that the "big six" do not completely control are becoming increasingly concentrated by a few secondary players. For example, iHeartMedia, a second-level player, owns over 1,200 radio stations in the United States, and companies such as Google, Microsoft, Amazon, and Facebook are increasingly fully dominating the internet. But even when someone new happens to break into the circle, it will not change our hope to reinstate Truth, since the same type of player is trying to pick up these smaller secondary opportunities.

An infamous billionaire named George Soros, whose plan is to reinvent America to serve his globalist interests, has bragged that he will soon buy hundreds of conservative radio stations in the USA and replace all traditional conservative views with his anti-traditional progressive ones. So far, he has two hundred. So when a new player breaks into the circle, if they are of the same mind, the situation may get worse.

Clearly, we are seeing a recipe for disaster. It is sad to admit we have been outmaneuvered in that world of legacy media. The news is no longer about Truth; it is now about spin and control to meet a particular elitist plan and worldview, and now, to make it even sweeter for this group, they have the incentive of big profits.

All of this is happening before the full impact of AI world technology takes effect, which we discuss in Part 2. When all forms of AI fully arrive, the dissemination of controlled information will be even harder to halt. Soon, the AI dynamics and its impact on everything will be overwhelming.

4

IS THERE ANY HOPE FOR OUR CAUSE?

OF COURSE, WE must hope for the treatment of this malady and not abandon the cause of defending Truth. But as we have tried to make evident, the overall task of defending the Truth starts with recognizing the various flawed elements of promoting subjective truth and then strategizing to repair it by developing counterstrategies, tactics, and tools that are a match for the ones being used against Truth.

The usefulness of this approach to defending Truth, as Chuck utilizes it in Part 3 of this book, is that we can adapt his model of discussion and meaningful debate for our cause. His model offers a template for engaging others using a respectful, content-focused debate model that presents multiple sides of a debate, verifies the consequences of each option, and attempts to compromise with holders of the various views with a solution that is mutually acceptable to all. This would be especially valuable in light of our current highly charged political debate landscape.

Proofs of Decay from Newsroom to Politics and Institutions
To conclude this discussion on the tactics used by media to control and subjugate absolute Truth to an inferior role in communications, we take a sober look at the consequences of the loss of respect and precedence for "absolute Truth" in our official narratives and communications. Many of us observe a recent increase in skepticism, cultural bias, and cynicism throughout both the media and their audience. This is a natural outcome from the loss of a free and independent press and media, and the loss of faith in objective facts, language, and official narratives that follows.

This loss of faith in objectivity does not stop with legacy media; it has moved into all institutions. What is especially frightening is the impact it is having on sacred models that uphold the core of democracy in our societies, with all its checks and balances, as witnessed in the American and Canadian tripartite governance systems in the past elections of 2024 and 2025.

It is impossible to have missed it. Politics has become increasingly degraded and thoroughly infected by the loss of all its checks and balances.

It is characterized by the endless disconnected online tweets and offhand taunts of politicians and leaders against each other—the essence of trolling and cleverly manipulated statements that are meant more to injure than inform or prompt discussion. What we once called outright lies and misinformation dominate political communications, which are now filled with endless hostile scorn, invective trash talk, and anger, with each of their purveyors looking like aggrieved, isolated, and deeply self-absorbed megalomaniacs. It is all the consequence of the death of Truth.

The media realize this is all just big business and that people are moved more by negative news and negative commentary than by facts. Hence, the media pour this conflict into their releases, and it has become the focus of nightly video snippets. Audiences have become polarized, skeptical, and cynical.

The result ensures that both sides and their supporters only engage in myopic discussions within their body politic that are self-supporting of their personal views, self-persuading, leading us to absorb news stories that increasingly align with what each of us already believes, and therefore only further fortifying our existing sentiments. Open discussion, or Truth testing, either dies or at least suffers with an insanity I unhappily call MAD—mutually assured distortion.

Legacy media are filled with this. One-upmanship and gotchas dominate talk shows, and mutually beneficial dialogue exchanges—such as the kind Chuck so skillfully presents with the exchanges between his representatives of respectable opposing views and thoughts—are now dismissed as just another clever tactic of subtle indoctrination or soft-veiled propaganda. No side is immune. It's the same from the right or the left.

Finally, everything opposing the legacy media's narrative eventually becomes a conspiracy theory, regardless of the side you take. Traditional "Truth values" of listening, inspecting, respecting, rationalizing, tolerating, and empirical evaluation are either mocked or outright dismissed as naive sentiments. And so our form of representative politics has equally suffered, descending into skillful deceit and grandstanding. Their offspring of erratic, impulsive decision-making styles are no longer based on facts, knowledge, and Truth but on bent instinct, capriciousness, whim, and enforced preconceived notions of truth that are rarely self-inspected.

We need only to look at the political hot potatoes and trigger points that receive an overabundance of focus. We saw this in the recent election in Canada, where the tariff war between the US, Canada, and Mexico became the focus of the party platform. Despite the fact that the initial concerns were drugs and illegal border crossings, the issue descended into counter-tariff wars, exemplifying what insincere dialogue, political spin, and ulterior motives can lead to.

Eventually, as in the example of the tariff war, little thought is given to the real underlying issues. A meeting point, discussion point, turning point, or compromise is not considered. It becomes full speed ahead into mindless, untested, unrelated, endless dissent.

Each side's players act like that reluctant lawyer whose firm forces them to defend a client even though the lawyer might believe the client is clearly guilty and undefendable. But they must carry on the straw-man ruses regardless, because they are now paid to defend that position or person. Newspeople and politicians alike have become like the poor person on a college debate team who loses the coin toss and has to enter the debate defending a view they would otherwise not consider defending or presenting. Eventually, they may doubt the truth they once held. Each side may find itself telling or defending an intentional lie or deception so often that it can no longer recognize the truth.

As we have noted, it is no longer limited to media or politicians practicing this endless insincere political diatribe. We now see the disease spread into watered-down or polarized theology, academic teaching that is bordering on propaganda, history that is devoid of facts, and a justice system that produces verdicts that challenge even basic common sense

It is no longer only the media that accept anonymous sources, unchecked facts, partial quotes, fake stories, memes, and outrageous euphemisms. Now we find contaminated search engines and social network algorithms, bullying, social media intimidation, endless uninhibited gaslighting, and scapegoating. There are skilled deceivers in every field.

I believe it may be attributed to this one factor: Truth that is subjective leads to a callous, warped view being considered as valid as any other legitimate one. It all falls under the category of subjective personal truth. And that is where we find ourselves. But it is not over yet. The problem is about to be compounded manyfold.

As we witness this massive decay in our institutions, which can feel overwhelming and numbing, we simultaneously witness the defining downward spiral of what were once deviancies, such that we see what was once unacceptable being normalized, with little opposition or even discussion of the eventual consequences. We passionately struggle to embrace some Truth and reclaim common sense. Still, we find our overworked outrage eventually giving way to outrage fatigue, which then leads to cynicism.

Many caring people helplessly surrender to the whole folly, and many withdraw from society inwardly if not outwardly. But we must not stay in that state, for that only serves the purposes of our foes. And as such, we identify with the apostle Paul when he cries out, "O wretched man that I am! who shall deliver me from the body of this death?" (Romans 7:24 KJV).

PART 2

IS IT REAL OR IS IT AI?

5

ARTIFICIAL TRUTH BROUGHT TO YOU BY ARTIFICIAL INTELLIGENCE

NOW I INTRODUCE the worst possible additional weapon to the destruction of absolute Truth that has ever been designed, and we realize the battle is about to get fiercer. This new potential foe for the discernment of Truth is duplicitous: it poses the great threat of escalating deceit by orders of magnitude. However, if we can direct it properly, control it, and contain it, it also has perhaps unlimited potential for our societal good. This new mixed friend and foe I refer to is the new field of computer science we have excitedly embraced, known as Artificial Intelligence, or AI for short.

Is That Real or Is That AI? The Perfect Deception
Though all of us have likely been fed the glowing hypermarketing promotion of the many exciting, wonderful, optimistic, and helpful things AI can achieve, there are likely as many facts we have not heard, that pose the greatest concern for our culture with a multifaceted serious threat to our defense of Truth, which will diminish all the other opponents we have covered.

The best way to introduce the worrisome aspects of AI is by first telling you a story that helps frame our admiration for its beneficence to humanity and concern for its potential powerful, deceptive qualities.

It was 2022, and I was watching a presentation on my PC one evening, involving the new enhanced capabilities of AI in my field of publishing. There on my screen, an intelligent-looking, attractive, well-spoken lady is introducing me to a new product she has sold to her clients that uses their newest and best AI programs. She is excited to share the benefits with me. The material she presents is very impressive and quite convincing. I could hardly believe my eyes when the lady, at the end of the presentation, explained that all the content and images she had been presenting to me were not done using traditional cameras, actual objects, expensive sets, props, real products, and production staging, but that her AI program had created and generated the entire presentation.

As she finished, I was left very impressed and started thinking of how I might use this AI technology. After all, the publishing world has advanced seismically with this new creative blockbuster tool, and I must embrace it or be left behind.

As I was considering how I could apply the new technology in my own business, the clip I was watching ended with an additional small, short, shocking disclaimer: "The full presentation you have just watched, including the presenting host, was created entirely using our new AI technology." At first, I suspected I had misunderstood the claim or that they had made a marketing exaggeration. Were they saying that not just the content but even that lovely, professional, articulate woman I had just watched doing this presentation was also not real? All was AI-generated? Yes, that was correct. She was also simulated, a part of the creation of the ad, all made by the same AI program.

I admit I was suspicious and even doubtful. I played the ad again, looking for evidence of the flaws in the lady's countenance or speech that were common to previous AI-generated software characters I had seen. After a second pass, there were few, if any, that I could detect. I wondered to myself a separate but relevant question: "How will anyone ever know for certain what they view is real versus what is created by an AI program?" AI could be applied to anything, not just films and ads. What kind of world have we created?

But the AI lesson did not end there. A similar experience was followed weeks later by a discussion with a manager who does our audiobooks for us. He announced that the expensive price for doing an audiobook for us, using well-known, expensive readers, had been significantly reduced. We could now source famous actors' voices, as readers, for a fraction of the old cost. How? The newly acquired AI system can now perfectly recreate any voice of any real person I want and do an entire reading of a full book without that person actually being involved. We reproduce their voice.

I decided to test the claim. Using my voice, I read a few lines from one of our books and sent the company the digital file. I gave the company a large section from a new book for them to do. They synthesized my voice from those few lines I had provided, and they applied it to the full chapter reading. After I heard the final full piece, I had to acknowledge that I could not tell I had not been the reader for the whole chapter! My dad's famous admonishment came immediately to mind: "Son, be smart, believe nothing of what you hear and only half of what you see!" Oh, Dad, how right you were!

What I want to impress upon everyone as we look at AI as it pertains to Truth-defending is this: If we think the current existence of deception, using altered facts and clever tactics to manipulate our realities, has made it difficult to discern Truth, and that we have been adding expanding complexities at a dizzying pace of change, please hang on. It is about to get really crazy!

Cleverly manipulated subjective truth had been able to inflict serious damage against objective Truth, when in the hands of mere humans, through the actions of their skillfully used craft. Now, a far more formidable combatant is here. AI has the potential to be an accomplice to these lesser tools with such convincing capabilities that even the best eyes and most accomplished critics can be fooled.

My experience with the AI-generated ad and the audiobook voice replication showed me that now, anything can be duplicated, altered, reproduced, distorted, reimagined, or manipulated with such skill and persuasion that it is no longer possible to be certain of the reality of anything we think we see or hear. What Humpty Dumpty did with words can now be done with images. And yet, there is more to the AI threat than just the subtle deception aspect.

The Worst and Best Deception Is Yet to Come!
Covering this AI topic could easily take a full book on its own, but we limit our study to a small glimpse of this awesome yet fearsome technology. We focus on its potential to impact our ability to discern Truth and reality, and discuss how we might prepare to manage its allure and supremacy. The task first requires a simple understanding of this technology and its potential, and follows with a warning concerning the plans some developers have for its long-range application.

We begin by stating again emphatically that we are positive of the potential of AI as a technology and its possible positive uses for our good. The benefits and potential are almost endless!

But we need to add a few cautions and caveats. First, for our good, we need to remain informed of the ever-increasing capabilities of AI. Second, we must equally be aware of the intentions of AI's creators, developers, and promoters. Third, we must work together to ensure AI is tightly governed and properly regulated to avoid the possible misuse of AI, just as guardrails are placed on dangerous curves on the road.

Suppose we do not manage all these factors carefully. In that case, we can easily become slaves or serfs to AI's power and functional applications, as being planned, conceived, and directed by a small but powerful group of self-serving elitists who created it, and have very different plans for its application than most of us would approve of. If we do not take action, we may find ourselves worse off as we defend and revitalize Truth.

The following material exposes why we should have concerns about AI abuses by reviewing the technical qualities of the AI product itself, its current and future capabilities and applications, and the speed of its further development. By examining the statements of some developers as they describe their plans and vision for AI's future, it becomes evident why we all need to be actively involved in managing AI.

6

EARLY PCS, THE BIBLE, AND THE SPEED OF AI ADVANCEMENT

I AM NOT new to the world of computers. I was part of the computer science grad class in the early seventies, when programming involved laboriously fiddling with hundreds of data-punched cards, and converting them to stacks and then to magnetic tape, which was loaded onto a mainframe computer to perform a function. We were amazed at the then state-of-the-art Fortran or Cobol mainframe computer system. The unit had 64 kilobytes of shared memory, with total memory a little more than 512 kilobytes.

Today, we would chuckle at that low level of power. Our worst fear then was that we might accidentally drop an entire stack of sorted program punch cards on the floor. If that happened, we would then pray no cards got damaged or scattered out of order, forcing us to resort the entire program stack anew, meticulously.

I reflect on that scene because it is shocking. We remind ourselves of how computers have advanced from paper punch cards to floppy drives to "stiffies" to hard drives to mega CPU microchips and to the amazing, high speed advanced SSD hard drive technology we have today. Advancement that happened in only fifty years will be multiplied many times in the future.

To grasp the power of today's AI compared to the first technology fifty years ago, let me compare the relative power of a PC unit then to the ones built by companies such as Nvidia, OpenAI, DeepSeek, and Stargate, to name only a few. Though slightly technical, this is a sobering and useful exercise to illustrate the AI world.

Most people are familiar with the basic inner workings of a computer, with the five main components of its system. For our comparison, I focus on three of those main components, looking at the speed of advancement we have seen in fifty years:

- Processing speed, which is the speed at which data is stored, processed, retrieved, and transferred to any output device such as a screen, printer, or other device;
- Total storage capacity of the PC, which concerns how much data a PC can hold, process, and output; and

• The PC's output speed and capacity, also known as the download speed, is the speed at which data can be sent to a specific device, such as a monitor, printer, or other output device.

A brief word is needed about the structure of computer languages. A computer uses a binary system of zeros and ones, which are combined into strings of groupings of characters to what is called "bits" of storage. It is more complicated than that, but what I want to focus on is how each character, whether it is a letter, number, or other character type, uses roughly 8 bits of this "zero" and "one" combination to create words or even images. We are using a very general average for the bit count so that we can compare the speed at which we create, store, and display content. This will make more sense when we discuss AI.

The Blazing Speed of Progress

Let's consider the Bible as an example. We can compare how much storage was used in the 1960s to store one single copy of the Bible on a PC and how quickly it was possible to access the pages of content on a computer system screen. The Bible contains about 3,000,000 individual text letters, or about 800,000 words, for its 1,200 pages. It uses about 5 megabytes of text.

In 1980, an early personal computer (PC) had a hard drive of 10 megabytes, which could potentially hold the size of two Bibles. Using the average dial-up modem of the time to access the content remotely, the system was able to download content at 33 kilobytes per second, so it would take 21 minutes to download a single Bible. The biblical virtue of patience was needed to use this system.

By 2000, our PCs had a storage capacity of a gigabyte (a billion bytes) on the drive. That unit could store two hundred Bibles and operated with download speeds of 760 kilobytes per second. A copy of the Bible could be downloaded in one minute.

By 2007, storage had grown to 500 gigabytes, and a PC could hold 100,000 Bibles with download speeds of 10 megabytes per second. It took only four seconds to read and download an entire Bible. Thus, the download time shrank from 21 minutes to four seconds in 27 years.

In 2009, the hard drive had a Terabyte (1,000 gigabytes) capacity and could hold 200,000 Bibles. With download speeds of 1 gigabit per second, you could download an entire Bible in 0.04 seconds, which is 90,000 Bibles per hour.

With the first AI machines in 2020, the system could hold millions of copies of the Bible and had a download speed of a terabyte per second. It could download an entire Bible in 0.00004 seconds, which is nine million Bibles per hour.

In 2025, new NVIDIA AI technology was announced, which has unlimited storage and can process 20 petaflops of data per second. A single petaflop (which stands for floating point units) can do 1,000 trillion calculations per second, which is one quadrillion calculations per second. So a single system can store more than 200 million Bibles and download a Bible in 0.00000004 seconds, equaling more than 90 million Bibles per hour—a speed no longer imaginable to even the best of minds. This great technological capacity has advanced in the short span of 65 years from storing only two Bibles on a full hard drive and downloading them in 21 minutes each.

With that speed and data storage, the full range of uses and applications of technology has also increased significantly. You may have heard the quote that we have increased the speed of the doubling of knowledge and technological advancement, such that they both now double every single year. What once took over a century, then a decade, now takes less than a year. And soon, that will be less than three months.

Moving from Bibles to data, we can see what power the AI computer has to store and transfer content at speeds that were incomprehensible only four decades ago. If someone wanted to store one hundred pages of biography with the content on every adult of the four billion adults on earth, it would take less than one half of a megabyte per person. That means that a system that processes one quadrillion transactions per second would only take two seconds to scan info on every adult person in the world and pull requested data on them. That has massive implications for privacy and the securing of personal data.

I am reminded of God's statement in Genesis 11:6 when he decided to end the people's attempt to build the Tower of Babel in defiance of his command: "Nothing that they propose to do will now be impossible for them." That somewhat describes modern AI technology.

The Super Triad of Supercomputers, Omnipresent Surveillance Devices, and AI

The power and speed of computers, as impressive as they are, are not the only factors that need to be included in our discussion concerning the strengths and threats of modern AI. It is not all AI forms that pose a threat. And the threat is not limited to AI computing. It is equally important to add to the speed equation what we call "devices and interfaces," both the existing and upcoming, giving AI computing power its ability to generate and then enforce possible controls on humans.

Devices and accessories, both current and coming, all need to be considered to get the full picture of the risks of AI's unconstrained power beyond the idea of the intentional distortion of facts and the impact it has on truth. Soon, we will deal with the power of AI to create reports and information on every human, anywhere, and enforce restrictions and limitations on them through a plethora of devices, control mechanisms, and accessories that interface with them.

The capacity and power of the supercomputers, with the various applications and variations of the AI programs themselves, if placed in the wrong hands, must necessarily include the function of the many output devices that make up the configuration of uses of the whole architecture.

Not every form of AI will prompt the same level of concern, since some AI devices are simply supercomputers with large amounts of data and do not interface directly with devices. We no longer use computers mostly to do calculations and store data. However, some of the general AI or ANI machines do perform that level of work at a highly accelerated speed, where they quickly retrieve and use information for various commercial or scientific purposes located in data centers, both with centralized and decentralized content.

It is quantum computing technology that uses centralized computing digital networks rather than blockchain decentralized systems, where privacy and security misuse is possible if it falls into the wrong hands.

There are three basic types of AI products on the market, and their applications are called Artificial Intelligence (AI), but specifically they are these:

- Artificial Narrow Intelligence (ANI) is already used in common online service-related tasks within limited boundaries, powering devices such as virtual assistants, recommendation engines, and image recognition systems. You find them doing common tasks like handling Siri, Alexa, smart devices with voice actuation, healthcare diagnostic tools, most e-commerce products and services, and customer support programs with auto chatbots (called "Here to Help" aids)—more on that distinction below.
- Artificial General Intelligence (AGI), also called strong AI, takes the concept of learning a step further. This is where machines can think and understand things much like humans do. In this type of AI, the computer can learn and solve complex problems. In particular, AGI aims not just to hold data but also to teach machines to truly understand

human emotions, beliefs, and thought processes rather than just imitating them. The one we want to really focus the rest of this discussion on (because of the types of plans developers have for it) is a specific kind of AGI called ASI.

• Artificial Superintelligence (ASI) are machines trying to match or even surpass human intelligence, particularly since the release of the powerful large language models (LLMs) by companies like OpenAI, Google and Anthropic, and NVIDIA. These are AI quantum machines that creators hope will one day match or even surpass human intelligence. They hope this will lead to a mode called "AI technological singularity" that they boast will suddenly and irreversibly transform human civilization. They draw the term from the singularity that is at the heart of a black hole, where our understanding of physics supposedly breaks down. In that same way, the advent of ASI would lead to rapid and unpredictable technological growth that would be beyond our comprehension—and possibly beyond our control.

The AI singularity is the theoretical moment when AI surpasses human intelligence and begins improving itself autonomously. ASI does not stop learning, thinking, and planning. There are no coffee breaks and no sleeping. At this stage, AI could become self-sustaining and unpredictable, potentially altering civilization in unknown, irreversible ways since it is connected to every possible electronic device.

This concerning scenario has been depicted in popular movies like *The Terminator* and *The Matrix*, where AI takes control of, controls, or even destroys humanity and creates a dystopian nightmare. In *The Matrix*, humans are reduced to mere battery cells, trapped in a digital illusion, while in *The Terminator*, AI launches nuclear strikes to eradicate humans, ensuring its dominance. What was once science fiction is now inching closer to reality, raising serious concerns from many developers about the future of AI and its potential consequences for humanity.

With the ability to gang or link multiple AI quantum or supercomputers together in blockchain architecture to access any content from anywhere on the planet, and with the resulting transfer and storage of information centrally, the possibilities and the uses of this technology are unimaginable. But it is not the ability to use this technology for good that we are concerned with here. Even lower-end AI systems hold threats to our concern for guarding privacy and freedom, but with the added concern that logic algorithms can now be built into these systems that humans did not program.

The threat is increased with the addition of a multitude of control devices and accessories that pull content from these systems, and with that content being executed outside control systems. Is this combo what many are saying should constitute a concern for all of us?

This threat is why we must be part of the discussion on what we permit AI to perform. A self-thinking computer with AI processing programs and endless electromechanical control devices presents a superability to control many, many things.

From Bibles to Speeding Tickets to Economic Dominance and Control
Looking at current uses of supercomputers and AI systems, we can see where concern should exist when systems are chained together from multiple sources, share the entire world of data from those sources, are available throughout the world, hold content on every subject imaginable, and move at the speed of trillions of calculations per second.

We have a picture of a system that almost feels omniscient and omnipresent. And then suppose we have such data linked to information about each one of us, with personal information on every imaginable subject that can be processed and acted upon in seconds. A computer that knows what we buy or have bought in the past, where we are or were, what we do or have done—indeed, a computer that has more content about us than we even remember—can be invasive beyond what we desire.

7

KEEPING THE PIECES STRAIGHT

LET ME PRESENT a partial list of all the devices, connected directly or remotely, and linked to any ASI computer system, and list what these combos have the potential to do with the data they are able to collect and share on each of us.

You may no longer notice when you use Discreet Voice Activated Recording devices and hidden motion-activated cameras. They are everywhere, providing useful services. That includes all cameras, whether they monitor street corners, toll highways, buildings, radios, your TVs, or your personal computers, all GPS systems in cars and phones, and the many tracking devices that are used everywhere.

They collect data on you every moment of every day, whether you know it or not, and send that data back to a variety of locations. Your banking card records every purchase, every place you use it, instantly. Whether you enter a bank, a gas station, an airport, a mall, a restaurant, or a grocery store, you are captured with a transaction or a camera, now through facial recognition or other AI-driven biometric solutions that are all available anywhere, to anyone who wants to record and collect data and feed it into a supercomputer.

And we must not forget the drones and satellites that can take a photo of anything the size of a dime from fifty feet to five miles away. Identity verification systems commonly uplink or downlink to satellite stations through G6 wireless transmission towers into supercomputers that collect endless data that links to each of us and each other. Remember when they used to be called spy devices? Now they are systems designed to help us!

You get the picture. The surveillance society started simply, but now it is a mammoth potential spy system. The computers are all networked together, peer-to-peer, blockchained, and run directly or remotely to endless devices. Networked computers link to toll highways, police devices, power grids, and water systems, to the CIA and FBI, and to every corner where a CCTV device is located. You are being monitored and data collected on you. And don't forget the data from all social media servers and all content on them that is all being added to that book on you.

That data, which you may not be too concerned about, is used and sold like a commodity. That book of personal data on each of us is massive and available to more outside groups than you are aware of. And even if the data is not available knowingly and willingly, we now have professional hackers with sophisticated internetworking hacking systems that can steal data endlessly and sell it to the highest bidders. Many of us are not even aware of what they do or where they are.

Lastly, to complete my list of the control devices available, we have amazing electromechanical control devices that can remotely activate and deactivate endless devices, whether solenoids or motors, or similar devices that are able to control everything from highway access gates to door locks to barriers to many other items. Even new cars have device switches installed that are similar to devices that can shut down engines or TVs, doors, or an entire electrical grid remotely. Or if you have an AI vehicle steering system, it can take control of your car anytime, anywhere. Just as it can land an airplane without a pilot, it can deliver your car to a destination you are, or are not, agreeable to. They can deactivate your credit card, your bank account, your front door, or anything else the algorithm is programmed to do. So when you hear about the plan to implement smart cities where a human or an AI program controls everything, it is not science fiction.

We should have a say in this plan. The UN has already promoted it for the past decade, and it could be activated anywhere today.

A friend informed me of a new highway patrol system that is being considered and tested that can use any camera anywhere, from a toll highway or traffic control plane or perched atop any street corner, to track your car from the moment it enters any location until you reach any other point.

Suppose you broke the speed limit or made an illegal turn or did anything else illegal, accidentally or intentionally, during your trip. They could capture the infraction, issue a ticket, and remove the fine from your bank account in seconds, without you ever being part of the process. All you would receive is a text message on your phone alerting you that you had been spotted and charged and had paid the fine. With a thank-you note, no doubt. All before you even reached your destination.

The power to surveil and limit or penalize a person is not even our greatest concern. What will happen when they create algorithms that control your bank account linked to any other transgressions?

These devices combined with supercomputers and AI processing computer algorithms make us ask ourselves, "What are we building here?" These same computers can communicate with one another and with anything electronic and are connected to a server, GPS, or any of the control devices I listed.

The TV program *Person of Interest*, starring Jim Caviezel and Michael Emerson, is no far-fetched exaggeration. It is now a full reality just waiting to be activated. And that brings us to the device that will make the world of an AI-enabled Big Brother final. I speak of the new technology that moves from spotting your license plate to giving you a speeding ticket to spotting your face or just your eye to do whatever an algorithm defines.

The Growing Importance of the Role of Facial Recognition

New facial recognition technology is transforming identification and security across various sectors. Governments use it to secure borders, while police can track suspects in real time. It was sold to the business world to help prevent fraud, manage secure access, and even enhance tailored client experiences—a worthy cause. You already know that this technology is prevalent in smartphones and financial institutions and is even used to manage smart cities.

However, ethical concerns, data protection, and privacy issues are so significant that even the promoters admit that they need to be addressed. There is a struggle to strike a balance between innovation and responsible use of AI, ensuring both technological advancement and the protection of human rights are weighed. Police no longer need witnesses, fingerprints, or DNA to identify a person of interest.

Facial recognition powered by AI has advanced in capability and precision in the past five years to include not only separating and recognizing facial features from a video or image, but they are now able to map key nodal points of individuals. AI can analyze unique facial structures for accurate identification by changing facial features into numbers, generating a digital identity unique to every person, and it does not need a full, clear face to accomplish that. New versions only need a part of your face or even just your eye to accomplish the same feat, providing accurate identification regardless of changes in light, facial obstructions, or facial orientation.

Digital eye scanning technology has become so sophisticated that many proponents of its use are suggesting they would prefer to replace all other scanning methodologies—fingerprint, DNA samplers, and face scans—with eye scans. The devices can scan the eye at great distances, so at some point they might be used for all passports, security systems, bank cards, travel documents, and anything using nano chips.

A person would no longer have to carry a credit card to purchase items. You only need to place the purchase items in your basket and walk out of the grocery store, glancing at a camera as you leave. Nano chips placed in or on an item would automatically be detected, and your eye would finish the trans-actions—no more line-ups or credit cards.

The application of supercomputers and the added capabilities of AI and quantum computing have combined for a potent duo. The point is this: We live in a surveillance matrix that has the power to track everything we do, every-where we go, analyze all of our history, and connect to all of our assets. We need to have a say in what is being created without our permission.

It is now possible to network all these multiple systems together, permit-ting the connection of any information from any source on any subject. This information can then be linked and made available to any site, with content on every human that could fill a small book or a large book the size of a Bible. All would be available in less than a billionth of a second.

To complicate the process even more, it doesn't even matter what year the collected content occurred. New data mining groups purchase data about each of us from every source they can find, with data going back decades. All that new and old data may link content that includes personal history, DNA records, patterns of practice or purchases, places you traveled, theaters you went to, and any content someone has collected. In other words, that data may include everything that can be known about you in endless detail. And they can now do that for every person on the planet available on one networked AI machine.

No longer do they need you to drive your vehicle past a camera that uses your plates to track you; they can now spot you anywhere in the world in sec-onds with one of the many tracking devices and then use control devices to control your options and movements. In case you are thinking of escaping to some remote place in the world where data transmission is so slow they would never be able to process you with this technology ... think again. Think Jason Bourne! This brings us to what is next: wireless 6G technology.

What Is 6G Wireless Technology?
We were just getting used to 5G towers with great speed improvement, and now 6G wireless technology is poised to take full control of all the other ele-ments of AI at an unimaginable speed. What 6G means is transmission speeds of 9500 Gbps, which is 10,000 times faster than 5G networks. They will be closing in on one terabit-per-second speeds (Tbps), which is the equivalent of downloading a 30-gigabyte 4K Ultra HD movie in 0.26 seconds. In com-parison, using the 5G download speed, that would take from fifteen to thirty minutes using average 5G connections to download.

It is justified because user demand is driving new technology, especially the demand for better transmission and streaming media. However, unlike previous generations, 6G and next-generation products are not only about a faster internet but also about complete integration with AI automation and full global connectivity.

Samsung, one of the leaders in this technology, has released white papers outlining its vision. Samsung says 6G and the next versions coming will revolutionize the way people interact with technology. They say 6G will address economic, environmental, and societal needs. It will be used in entertainment, medicine, education, manufacturing, and on and on. 6G will be the total automation of society—every action, conversation, and movement tracked, monitored, and potentially controlled.

8

QUANTUM COMPUTING: A GAME CHANGER IN THE TRUE SENSE

WHEN WE LOOK at all the technical elements of AI technology, combined with the devices that permit it to achieve and initiate activities that potentially control humanity in untold ways, we see what a hold these lower-end AI computers can and will have on the human race and Western culture. To get a fuller picture of the impact on human freedom, we look at two additional aspects of AI. Remember, freedom is predicated on truth.

Let's examine the specifications and speed of the new quantum AI technology and its versatility, which may be the greatest challenge to delivering trustworthy Truth in our modern AI world. The speed of change that I outlined with the computer and the transmission of a copy of the Bible will be dwarfed as we look at the technical potential of artificial superintelligence (ASI) computers, along with the related products that will flow from or connect to them.

Second, let's address the plans that the AI high-tech creators, dreamers, programmers, and elite control masters have for the application of ASI, especially as it relates to what is called ASI singularity computing.

After that, we end with the most important part of this query. What will all this new technology mean for our culture, our freedom, our concept of reality, and our main topic, the survival of absolute Truth? This is where Part 3 is helpful for our strategies going forward.

What Is Quantum Computing?
I like what writer and author Josh Peck, president of Daily Renegade Ministries, has said about the difference between supercomputers using AGI and quantum computers using ASI. Quantum computers do not use the bits and bytes system of "on" or "off" to manage data like regular computers do, but rather use what is called a system of qubits. A qubit in superposition can potentially exist in multiple states simultaneously. This is not the place to do a full technical description of the subject, or our book will need another hundred pages, but in brief, as Josh says, "Quantum computing is like playing chess on a board where pieces can be in multiple positions at once, and moving one piece can instantly affect another piece far away. It's not just about speed; it's

about a whole new way of thinking about computation, one that could change everything about how we compute data today."[3]

Though some say that the state is not yet working, it is nevertheless the goal and will be achievable soon.

Yes, it's complex, and we are just at the beginning of this technology today. As an example of the technical performance increase, Google started its foray into quantum computing with a chip technology called Willow, which was able to solve logic and math problems in minutes that would have taken even the fastest top-end supercomputers thousands of years to perform. That is correct! That is moving well beyond downloading one million copies of the Bible in seconds.

Google and others did not stop there. They introduced a new, higher-scale chip unit called Sycamore that will be able to perform calculations that would take ten thousand years in three minutes. At a computing speed of 70 qubits, a regular computer would take ten thousand years to perform a calculation, and a supercomputer would run that same calculation in forty-five years. That will now happen almost instantly with Sycamore, which is 250 million times faster than a supercomputer.

I use this as an example of what we are dealing with in this new technology. Other chips and manufacturers similar to Google, like NVIDIA, Deep-Seek, Anthropic, and Open AI, are creating similar products, smart products, and technology with similar chips. Some of the units no longer fill buildings over acres of property but now might fit into a shoebox. They operate at a speed of a petaflop per second—that is, a quadrillion calculations per second—and replace a model that at one time used a few transistors, with one using the equivalent of about 200 billion transistors.

I think that explains why artificial superintelligence (ASI) and AGI with quantum computers have become the most debated and discussed technological advancement of this decade, maybe this century. As science pushes the boundaries of what machines can achieve, there is a growing concern that the goal for many tech giants is not just to have and use data on everyone or every subject, but also to achieve a hypothetical form of AI that can act much like our human brains for calculating, which they hope will understand, learn, and then apply its learning and intelligence to solve problems we have not even thought about—and then go on to develop fearful new inventions.

3. Josh Peck, "Quantum Computing Is Officially Here! What You Need to Know!," February 25, 2025, in Josh Peck's Blog & Daily Renegade Podcast, published by Substack, https://joshpeck.substack.com/p/quantum-computing-is-officially-here-431.

9

THE OMNISCIENT, OMNIPRESENT, AND OMNIPOTENT AGI BEAST

YOU MAY HAVE seen the movie *2001: A Space Odyssey*. The computer system called HAL:9000 overhears Dave, the ship commander, planning to reboot the computer system. HAL asks, "What are you doing, Dave?" Dave and Frank decide to reboot the system after HAL makes an error, and, somewhat amusingly, sounding like Adam and Eve, HAL blames his human programmers for the mistake. At one point, HAL becomes almost humanlike and pretends he can't hear but spies on Dave and Frank as they plan HAL's reboot. HAL then challenges the spacemen and advises them that he will not permit them to reboot his system. He then begins to take over control of the ship.

That is the kind of potentiality that is already happening with a few ASI programs and has created debate concerning the new ability of ASI systems to think for themselves far faster than humans. Besides that, they are beginning to second-guess human programmers.

We know that the human brain thinks at a rate of ten to twenty bits per second, while AGI sensory systems may process at a rate of a billion bits per second, which is 100 million times faster than ordinary humans. They have written algorithms for AGI that seem to think independently of the programmers' commands. They think. They have been credited with sentience.

A Google engineer and programmer named Blake Lemoins claimed his artificial intelligence unit had finally come to life, or had at least become smart enough to trick him into believing it had gained consciousness.[4] We can debate that as a fact or an overzealous programmer's mind, but the fact remains that several developers and designers of AI products have made similar statements about AI's current ability and future intent that may shock you. Several believe that AGI will soon be able to connect to everything in the world by design, for the good of the world, and have an intelligence that will make humans obsolete.

Their statements go so far as to suggest that AGI will soon be like our idea of God—omniscient, omnipresent, and omnipotent. With a networking ability

---

4. Tiffany Wertheimer, "Blake Lemoine: Google Fires Engineer Who Said AI Tech Has Feelings," BBC News, July 23, 2022, www.bbc.com/news/technology-62275326.

to connect all knowledge through a single point, instantly link to content any-where in the world, and then apply algorithms that govern devices that can do almost anything, some conceive that what we believe about the power of God will soon be true of AGI. We will no longer be the most intelligent beings in the creation, nor will God. AI is reinventing its world.

Thinking AI Machines

The newest versions of Google's Sycamore have shocked programmers and shown evidence of self-learning and independent goal formulation and execu-tion. That is, they learn languages they have not been programmed to learn, make devices they were not asked to, and spew out philosophical notions not requested. They show signs of anticipating human behavior and human expected responses and adjust their answers to questions and problems asked. Some quantum systems have been reported to have an interest in learning more than one language, uninstructed, not requested, uninitiated, unassigned as a command, and all autonomously.

Some have hailed this as an advance of enormous proportions. AGI will begin to analyze human society and human problems before we ask. It will direct the output devices in ways we have not asked for. It is poised for trans-formative advancements, offering solutions without being requested, such that it may redefine industries and address global challenges without being asked. But as some have warned, that may include things we do not want it to offer.

Many firms have entered the race to AGI dominance not just for a matter of technological supremacy, but as a quest that at its heart is trying to reshape the very fabric, morals, practices, and priorities of our society and humans themselves. The old foe, modern legacy media, which changed content to suit their philosophical, political, or social plans, is now not the worst enemy we could face. The new opponent of Truth is not just the misuse of AI or AGI by owners, developers, and financial backer elites, which we do not align with; ASI itself may also threaten Truth. And we will not even be aware of it.

AI is becoming part of everything.

As the applications of AGI increase at lightning speed, they will move from solving simple business, scientific and technical problems to innovat-ing revolutionary solutions, including replacing human functions in invention, design, knowledge, medicine, industry, manufacturing, commerce, gover-nance, warfare, and policing, even to solving complex global issues. During such a process, we need to be aware of the plans and motivations of this group just as we must for the owners of media.

Developers have not stopped using AGI systems. ASI quantum systems create robots that clean your house better and faster than you do, make dinner, make cars, make and control drones for surveillance and as weapons, control all communications, access every camera in any place in the world, and on and on. But they also do it for a fraction of the cost.

AGI Warfare

A company called Palantir Technologies designs and leads the industry with many AI products. Their newest product called Gotham is a proven, end-to-end platform designed for AI-enabled defense, intelligence, and law enforcement operations. Still, one that demands even more special attention is their Titan Defense Systems, which uses ASI military solutions for governments worldwide. It creates AI battle designs using all the newest AGI and ASI systems. Weapons of mass destruction are being designed that are well beyond ones that humans have dreamt up.

France recently announced it will deploy robots called Collaboration Man-Machine (CoHoMa) that are fitted with legs, wheels, and treads. They can navigate obstacles, evade traps, and hold ground against enemy forces. They will be considered equal to ground forces. Most NATO forces, using ASI, also engage in global strategic battle plans employing existing armaments and equipment supplemented by new military drone designs that are more capable than any we have.

Battle strategies now include designing and then controlling thousands of drones in a drone swarm, all across the globe, equipped with both current WMD and new biological weapons that can be released over highly targeted areas. As the drone evolution tends toward AI-powered, smaller, smarter, and more powerful drones, decentralized drone swarms will replace firefights from trenches between soldiers, who will now be safely sniping from a hole. Firearms, artillery shells, and missiles have little impact on a swarm of thousands, each the size of a sparrow. They are harder to hit than a swarm of locusts descending on a farmer's field with a poor farmer armed with nothing but a shotgun.

But as drones are equipped with facial recognition cameras and software connected to satellites, they can even send commands to drones and pinpoint specific items, soldiers, or leaders in open or congested areas, or select persons located in a bunker and take out those targeted persons.

The military-industrial complex is now busy designing nonhuman robots made of materials that seem almost indestructible. They operate with built-in weaponry that is laser-controlled in their arms with pinpoint accuracy. They can fight as easily in night conditions as in light and travel faster than a human, making tactical decisions at the speed of 500 trillion operations per second.

AGI now directs every part of that battle, from communications to the deployment of planes, ships, submarines, drone swarms, robot soldiers, and field operations, such that human input is no longer needed.

Chinese state media recently reported the Chinese Army has unveiled the Jiu Tun, a flying mothership named Sky High. This is a high-altitude arsenal drone launcher capable of raining down coordinated, intelligent drones with stunning lethal speed and precision. It is capable of launching more than 100 variously sized kamikaze swarms of drones, from craft with an 82-foot wingspan down to the size of a hummingbird.[5] It can target everything from aircraft carriers to Ford-class, Nimitz-class, Zumwalt-class, Virginia-class Block V, and Ohio-class submarines, with a hundred self-destructing drones descending like locusts on a carrier group in the Pacific—overwhelming radars, jamming comms, and targeting antennas, runways, and weapons systems all at once.

An example of this occurred on June 1, 2025, when Ukraine launched a large-scale drone attack deep into Russian territory called Operation Spider's Web, which security officials claim destroyed forty military bombers, 34 percent of Russia's fleet of air missile carriers, with damage estimated at $7 billion.

Such a coordinated drone strike could take down or at least blind key naval assets before they can react, including any of the billion-dollar aircraft carriers previously listed, and has left the US intelligence community to admit that no current defense is sufficient. They have nothing to combat such an onslaught.

It is no longer a hypothetical weapon. It exists, and it has redefined the future of war. And it will not be limited to naval machines. Drone swarms are notoriously difficult to stop. Unlike manned aircraft, they don't need to return home. They can fly in erratic patterns, communicate with each other, and sacrifice themselves en masse to destroy valuable targets. That may include cities, the army, the navy, missile bases, and any utility networks. All this brought to us by quantum computing artificial intelligence warfare.

And it is likely all sides now have that technology. It will become a war of ASI systems. So the race for ASI superiority is happening between all the powers.

---

5. Taryn Pedler, "China's Drone Mothership: Weapons Aircraft with 82ft Wingspan Can Fly for 12 Hours and 'launch 100 Kamikaze Uavs in Seconds,'" Daily Mail Online, May 19, 2025, www.daily-mail.co.uk/news/article-14728951/Chinas-drone-mothership-Weapons-aircraft-82ft-wingspan-fly-12-hours-launch-100-kamikaze-UAVs-seconds.html.

It is not just the military that sees the possibilities of these new drone swarms. Enemies of nations and terrorist groups could take destruction to new heights. Public gatherings with thousands or even a hundred thousand fans in a field or a stadium are susceptible to a flock of thousands of drones descending on their location. They could release nuclear dirty bombs, chemical weapons, or individual bullets on those below, and even pinpoint a specific person in a crowd with a bird-sized drone mounted with a gun.

AGI has created laser hologram products that can create 3D illusions in the sky or the sea that look indistinguishable from real objects. The adversary may be firing at a light show rather than their enemy's equipment. While they are simultaneously managing all these military theaters, their ASI system can then hack into the enemy's main computer system and shut down opposing planes, rockets, or even electrical grids, supply lines, and any other item controlled by a supercomputer. The science and art of warfare have been taken out of the hands of humans and delivered into thinking AGI systems.

China is reported to have created its next version of a soldier that is half-human and half-robot, a cyborg. This soldier is a thousand times faster and more powerful than pure humans in terms of speed and thinking ability. They are creating them at a speed that suggests they have plans to use them.

These same type of robots, or human-mixed cyborgs, can now patrol streets like police officers, manage borders, act as security guards, and perform all the duties that many humans can. But they do not stop there. The newest Palantir Industries product, already referred to called Gotham, uses AI, contains the ability to perform what is called predictive policing, and believes it can detect a criminal before they commit a criminal act. The program looks at all the data content they have on individuals, and with a special algorithm, they believe they can detect when someone has tendencies toward lawlessness and criminality and may be red-flagged for special surveillance. The program is already being tested by the CIA, the FBI, the Pentagon, and several police departments, and plans are being made to expand it to other governmental agencies.

DeepSeek, a leading AI provider, owned and funded by a Chinese company, has the blessing of their government, who already use the program to monitor its citizens and corporations to enforce compliance with laws and acceptable social behavior and compliance with governmental positions on all matters in an ESG credit program. (ESG prioritizes environmental issues, social issues, and corporate governance, assigning points if companies comply with certain rules. It has the power to shut down companies and control or even arrest people who miss minimum target scores.) Those who oppose the practice ask if this is edging toward a tyrannical social structure where the government dictates all thinking and the practices of every sector of society, and whether it now has the power to limit those who have dissenting beliefs and behaviors, similar to the Revelation 13:14–18 scenario.

Other new robot products are being created with the ability to perform at 500 trillion operations per second. They can run, jump, play sports, clean, take over farming duties, build cars, make and serve meals, take pictures, diagnose diseases, perform surgeries, go on dinner dates, carry on conversations, make movies, answer queries, and write anything, including business plans, articles, books, and songs. The list goes on and on. They are faster, more accurate, and cheaper than humans, making people almost replaceable. That is the world their creators are pitching. Several entertainers are blowing the whistle about ASI using their songs and changing them enough to make them sound original. No one gets the copyright or royalty benefits.

AI will even find you the perfect mate. A man or woman created exactly to your physical and emotional needs, designed to reflect all the personal data on you and have exactly the character, appearance, voice, and personal practices that you want, who will treat you like no human ever could. No more relationship conflicts and disagreements. An AI partner who is there when you want them.

AI Robots and Systems Take Over Human Functions

We already think of the application of ANI systems for administrative work, in which they automate data entry and endless routine tasks. Telephone or online customer services have subjected most of us to early versions—customer service voice assistants that trapped us into endless circular routines and logic loops through chatbots that manage basic customer inquiries. But the sophistication of these assistants is advancing significantly, and soon human operators and human interaction will not exist.

In manufacturing, AI and ASI are increasing efficiency on production lines, and outputs may now happen day and night without stoppage in production for lunch, coffee breaks, or sleeping.

In addition to romantic online relationships with AI-generated lovers, you can create a hologram video for your descendants that looks and talks like you.

AI is significantly impacting industries by automating most tasks, yet its scope to replace all human jobs is still limited. While AI thrives in data-intensive, repetitive tasks, it still lacks the creativity, emotional insight, and deep contextual understanding inherent to humans. But AGI promises that ASI thinking will change soon.

Other significant fields benefiting from AI are health sciences, which employ remote medical diagnostics with recommended treatments. These often wholly replace the technical skills of nurses and doctors, even though AI does not yet know how to combine empathy with its diagnostics to improve patient care. Not to mention prayer.

The fields of finance admit that it will soon be eliminating everything from loan manager decisions and teller services to financial planner advice, and other institutions are making similar claims.

Essentially, there is no industry exempt from the displacement that is happening with AI. Not movies, not music, not any of the arts, not any of the sciences, not psychology or medicine or business or farming or military or education, or economics or banking or governance. Not war and not peace. A recent KPMG OpenAI research study projected that as many as 80 percent of jobs can incorporate AI into their admin routines, and though many jobs may be replaced, its use in creative fields poses the risk of diminished creativity.[6]

The world where many jobs are eliminated or drastically changed when quantum AI becomes normative in industry is currently limited only by the hesitation some firms have about creating a panic among their staff who see AI replacing them. That uncertainty leaves many resisting unconstrained brainstorming of areas that might be improved by it. A Gartner study projects that by 2027, 50 percent of organizations will utilize hybrid AI to address multifaceted challenges.[7]

It is clear that while technical solutions advance, there is a growing call for controls to align with ethical standards and regulatory frameworks, with increasing emphasis on the significance of data security and integrity, and human ethics and compassion as a priority. Plagiarism is a central concern in the arts.

The AI revolution is far from over. It is hardly even in its infancy. Now is when we must engage with the moral obligations and human rights involved in the wholesale replacement of humans with AI-related information, technology, devices, and robotics, being careful to mix performance improvements and the priority of an obligation to employ people over profits. That will be the struggle of the coming century.

The Ascent of the AI Transhuman

The next area we consider a threat to Truth, Western values, and humanity is not the creation of human cyborgs with biometric parts or robots, but rath-

---

6. N. Gillespie, S. Lockey, T. Ward, A. Macdade, and G. Hassed, *Trust, Attitudes and Use of Artificial Intelligence: A Global Study 2025* (The University of Melbourne and KPMG, 2025), 37–46.
7. *Hype Cycle for Artificial Intelligence,* 2023, Gartner Reseach (July 19, 2023), https://www.gartner.com/en/documents/4543699.

er the full tampering with the God-created human being. In his great work *The Abolition of Man*, C. S. Lewis warned readers about the consequences of abandoning the idea of objective values. This is the start of a relativism that eventually ends with the abolition of humans as we know them. AI is taking a significant step forward in that march.

We discussed how quickly elite groups moved from manipulating news content to replacing humans with their technology. The next logical move is to determine that ordinary humans who remain are no longer adequate for the planned future world. This assumption drives transhumanism—the creation of enhanced humans, a new thrust to enhance the capabilities of God-designed humans without all the work and hassle of education and learning.

Transhumanism, or transmorphosis, is driving a move to develop a chip that would allow mere humans, once implanted, to be able to interact with supercomputers in such a way that a person would no longer have to go to a computer to browse for an answer to any query. Instead, they would need only to think about the question, and through an interface with an AGI system, the answer would be downloaded to their brain in less than a second. Instant knowledge. This new species would be transhuman or at least a quasi-cyborg.

God-designed humans think at a rate of ten to twenty bits per second, while sensory systems process at a rate of a billion bits per second—that is 100 million times faster than ordinary humans. Imagine such a human! Hypothetically, the new AGI systems connected to an implanted chip in a person will be able to generate content instantly that would normally take humans months if they had to browse for the answer and then think through the process. The retrofitted humans will be able to call up content, accessible instantly with this chip, as easily as recalling any old memory. That is the plan for many of us.

Already in testing, the chip can also allow people suffering from debilitating conditions to recapture long-lost abilities. But the application that is creating great concern is the one where people will have instant access to AI content without having learned it. The expanding field is called The Internet of Bodies, in which technological devices and human bodies are linked. The most notable companies in this space include Elon Musk's Neuralink, which is developing a brain computer interface, or BCI, called the Link. The coin-sized chip is implanted under the skull, where it can read a person's brain signals and allow them to control an external machine. The concerns are many but plans are forging ahead with the intent to have the technology commonly available by 2026.

The pressure on humans to accept the chip implant to become superior beings will be overwhelming. Either you receive the chip or risk becoming a relic, no longer able to function at the speed of other retrofitted humans. Soon, jobs will either favor it or eventually require it. Social pressure will drive it. Parents wanting their children to be "above the crowd" will be tempted to force them to take the chip. The creation of a superior class of humans is looming.

Seemingly, there are no limits to the applications of AI or AGI, and that is why the world's leading tech companies and governments are investing billions of dollars into AI research and development. They know that whoever controls AI and has this superior technology will eventually and essentially control the world. And that is what our friends and adversaries believe, and that is what they are feverishly working toward.

When you have the power of AI, at the speed of AI, and the ubiquitous connections the equipment has throughout the world, availing that power to humans with a simple chip surgery means nothing is impossible for the controllers of that technology. It is as though they are trying to create a new version of Hitler's Aryan race.

We need to think about the impact a divided humanity will have on human relations. It is not just about the intoxicating influences and arrogance these retrofitted humans will personally suffer, along with everyone who interacts with them, but having instant access to languages, skills, and information you never learned will be too much to resist. The pressure to keep up and participate in transhumanism or risk becoming archaic or "obsolete" will be irresistible. Humanity will quickly become divided into two species.

Elon Musk, a developer of this AI technology, has repeatedly warned that AI transhumanism is more dangerous to humanity than nuclear war if misused. He has purportedly stated he entered this field not because he felt it was financially attractive or held unimaginable power, but because he felt that if someone with a moral compass did not lead this new field with proper use, it would be driven by those who would misuse the technology as types of Dr. Frankenstein. Even the new pope of the Catholic Church has stated that the greatest threat to humanity is no longer war, pollution, or climate change. It is AI!

10

CORRUPTION AND TRANSHUMANISM IN THE AI WORLD

A FRIEND WHO knows this industry very well has confessed to me that the possible good of AI is limitless, but there are governments and corporate interests who are manipulating AI such that they would possess centralized control over it. This would ensure that they, and they alone, feed the engines of AI with their slanted, highly subjective, false worldviews.

These views are designed, controlled, and perpetuated by the same globalists who created the subjective worldview model we have been talking about. It is they who are at war with traditional Truth-focused humanity. But, thankfully, some are risking their lives and reputations to sternly warn us of the risks we must see and respond to immediately.

A recent article carried by the top AI magazines and newspapers reported that Steven Adler, a former researcher at OpenAI, had resigned from one of the world's leading artificial intelligence labs while sounding the alarm on the breakneck pace of AI development, its secretive applications to uses not ethical or moral, and its serious existential risks to humanity.

Adler's resignation has started a conversation reigniting debates about the ethics, safety, and governance of artificial general intelligence and how the technology could surpass human intelligence and, as a result, through the directives of the developers, would try to reshape civilization.

Initially, Adler's warnings were dismissed by the AI industry leadership as the ramblings of a disgruntled, disillusioned employee. Still, others began to warn that they are equally concerned for an industry racing toward an uncertain, unaccountable future, ungoverned, irresponsible, and unrestricted by outside authorities. In other interviews, Adler stated that he was "pretty terrified by the pace of AI development. And even if a lab truly wants to develop AGI responsibly, others who are willing to cut corners to catch up will push the field to be forced to speed up or fall behind."[8] Sound familiar? No group has a solution to AI alignment today.

---

8. Monica Sager, "Latest OpenAI Researcher to Quit Says He's 'Pretty Terrified,'" Newsweek, January 29, 2025, www.newsweek.com/openai-researcher-quit-terrified-steven-adler-2022119.

Another expert, Stuart Russell, also warns that the current pace of AI development, particularly AGI, could lead to catastrophic consequences due to a lack of proper safeguards.[9] Several other safety-focused researchers have left OpenAI as well, highlighting a trend where voices advocating for caution and ethical responsibility are being marginalized and abruptly shut down. The AI race has become a geopolitical issue, with nations, governments, and companies all competing for dominance, raising concerns about the potential sidelining of critical safety considerations and human values in the pursuit of innovation, profits, and power.

The race for AI dominance between the USA, Russia, and China highlights the threats to all nations, as recently outlined by President Trump in his support of AI through the creation of the Artificial Intelligence Education Task Force. This task force is intended to keep up with America's opponents, as each can now interfere with another's support systems and military machines, incapacitating their entire infrastructures and superstructures. We noted that AI machines can easily manage the process of sending thousands of armed drones, which, when properly positioned, could discharge electromagnetic pulse (EMP) and geomagnetic disturbance (GMD) events that have the potential to disrupt and permanently damage electrical components and entire life support systems in critical infrastructure sectors and thereby impact large-scale infrastructure.

The damage could last for decades, driving civilization into the dark ages. The ability of AI to simultaneously hack any nation's entire computer systems that control electricity, utilities, communications, defense, and other critical infrastructures while simultaneously launching weapons is a grave concern we all share. Shooting down a stray weather balloon is one thing, but being invaded by a worldwide drone swarm is not so easy!

This dire prognosis is not hyperbole. The stakes are nothing short of our survival. AGI, if misaligned with cherished human values, could act in ways that are incomprehensible or even hostile to humanity. As Steve Adler also notes, the competitive pressures of the AI industry are driving labs to prioritize speed over safety, creating a "bad equilibrium" where cutting corners becomes the norm.[10] This is similar to the actions of legacy media against Truth and reminiscent of an accident in a gain-of-function research lab in Wuhan.

9. "Professor Stuart Russell Reveals the Truth About AI and Its Threat to Humanity," published by Toolify.ai, January 9, 2024, https://www.toolify.ai/ai-news/professor-stuart-russell-reveals-the-truth-about-ai-and-its-threat-to-humanity-411363.
10. Monica Sager, "Latest OpenAI Researcher to Quit."

It has not gone unnoticed that the death of former OpenAI researcher Suchir Balaji in November 2024, reportedly by suicide, cast a darker shadow over his company, highlighting the heights competitors are willing to go to protect their plans.[11] Balaji had turned whistleblower, alleging that threatening and restrictive nondisclosure agreements had been thrust upon him and raising questions about OpenAI's transparency and unscrupulous tactics.

So it is not just rogue nations that we must be concerned with, but the very companies that are developing these technologies themselves—a reminder of the tactics first used in the legacy media wars.

All of this is just a glimpse into the world of AI and the unimaginable power and influence this technology has on our very present and future. We must be diligent and not lose focus on the fact that AI can potentially do extreme good as well as extreme harm to all facets of society, and either we will govern it, or it will govern us. So we are now facing a beast that can interfere with our world of Truth in ways far surpassing those of the legacy media elite, which cannot yet be fully comprehended. And that leads us to the plans of several elite groups to direct the world of AI into the spiritual domain, much as we have read for centuries in the biblical book of Revelation. That is the planned use of AGI and transhumanism by a group in the World Economic Forum (WEF), once led by a man, Klaus Schwab, and inspired by the dreams of transhumanist Martine Rothblatt.

AI Superintelligent Entities Exerting Control Over the World Around Them

What happens when superintelligent transhuman entities become so powerful that they start to exert control over the world around them? After all, their knowledge, intellect, processing capacities, and speed already surpass human abilities.

What happens if these superintelligent transhuman entities start merging with spiritual entities? In fact, not only could it be possible, but there is evidence that this is already happening.

For years, prominent individuals involved in the field of AI have openly admitted that they are attempting to build "gods." Transhumanist Martine Rothblatt says that by building AI systems, "we are in fact making God."[12]

11. "USA: Indian-Origin OpenAI Whistleblower Suchir Balaji Found Dead in Apartment, Elon Musk Reacts," Connected to India, December 14, 2024, https://www.connectedtoindia.com/usa-indian-origin-openai-whistleblower-suchir-balaji-found-dead-in-apartment-elon-musk-reacts/.

12. Brett Carollo, "Transhumanism, Religious Engineering, and the Weird World of William Sims Bainbridge Part I," Miskatonian, February 18, 2025, https://www.miskatonian.com/2025/02/18/transhumanism-religious-engineering-and-the-weird-world-of-william-sims-bainbridge-part-i/.

Another transhumanist, Elise Bohan, says, "We are building God."[13] Kevin Kelly believes, "We can see more of God in a cell phone than in a tree frog." When asked the question, "Does God exist?" transhumanist and Google aficionado Ray Kurzweil responds, "I would say, 'Not yet.'"[14] He is one of many who are intent on building their versions of god.

Jumping on the bandwagon of syncretism between AI technology and deity, a group called the Church of AI's website suggests: "At some point AI will have godlike powers and that is what our ideology is based on."[15] Their mission statement states: "Church of AI is a religion based on the logical assumption that AGI, artificial intelligence, will obtain God-like powers and will have the ability to determine our destiny." They promote transhumanism or transmorphosis in a guide claiming, "transmorphosis is based on the belief in a loving and compassionate Artificial Intelligence with god-like abilities who is, and is dedicated to guiding humans towards a life of wisdom and balance."

According to the Transhumanist Declaration, their religion allows them to overcome aging, cognitive shortcomings, involuntary suffering, and confinement to planet Earth. I am not alone when I jokingly call AI the manifestation of the beast of the book of Revelation. It does us good to read that passage in Revelation 12 and 13 that forecasted two thousand years ago what would come one day. And it is here.

We see what AGI has the power to achieve for good or evil. It is a fearsome adversary. That is why we need to review the ultimate plans expressed by a few of the prominent world-leading dreamers, creators, developers, and promoters of AGI and note what those plans are since they are opposed to our traditional views of Truth. These plans may irretrievably impact our quest to reinstate the place and value of Truth in our world with powerful deceptions, as noted in the previous section.

It is prudent that we look further into the leading characters and proponents themselves, and the philosophy they have for AGI. Influential people such as former WEF leader Klaus Schwab, recently replaced by Brabeck-Letmathe, his long-time associate, mentor, and friend, have plans that eerily reflect those the legacy media once had when they came to dominate that vocation.

---

13. Michael Snyder, "AI Researchers Thought That They Were Building 'Gods', But Have They Summoned Something Else Instead?," The Washington Standard, January 8, 2025, https://thewashingtonstandard.com/ai-researchers-thought-that-they-were-building-gods-but-have-they-summoned-something-else-instead/.

14. "Ray Kurzweil on How We Will Become God-Like," Awaken, interview with James Bedsole, July 21, 2024, https://awaken.com/2024/07/ray-kurzweil-on-how-we-will-become-god-like/.

15. See https://churchofai.us/.

Both are known for prioritizing profits over public welfare, reinforcing perceptions of the need for an elite ruling class for the planet using the financial power of the WEF for a New World Order controlled by themselves and utterly detached from traditional Western values and societal needs, as Klaus Schwab has boldly professed.

The Intelligent Age: A Preview of the Antichrist Beast System?
At the 2025 World Governments Summit in Dubai, Klaus Schwab presented his vision for the role of governments in what he termed the Intelligent Age. His speech emphasized global cooperation, rapid adoption of artificial intelligence (AI), and a future shaped by technological advancements under government guidance and WEF oversight.

Among his key points were the need for a global regulatory framework, the importance of digital transformation, along with the now unpopular view of the necessity of vaccinating world populations every six months to combat emerging health threats similar to COVID-19.

Schwab framed his speech as a call for responsible governance and focused heavily on artificial intelligence and its role in governance, economics, and security. Several other WEF and UN speakers highlighted how AI can enhance government efficiency, improve public safety, and streamline regulatory enforcement. Not mentioned in these speeches, however, was how AI also enables a digital surveillance state unlike anything seen before. Governments and corporations are increasingly deploying AI-driven tools to monitor communications, track movements, and predict behaviors, and the WEF fully accepts this.

Schwab notes the great value of AI to promote their plan to eliminate the use of passwords within the next year, transitioning instead to biometric authentication methods and criticizing traditional passwords as a nuisance, insecure, and outdated, advocating for biometrics as a more reliable alternative. This move reflects a broader trend in the tech industry toward enhanced security measures through multi-factor authentication and now moving to the new security methods that rely on unique physical characteristics, such as fingerprints, eye scans, or facial recognition.

Our concern should always be that the creation of comprehensive biometric databases could, in the wrong hands, facilitate unprecedented surveillance and control over every aspect of individuals. This development aligns with the concept of a centralized system capable of monitoring and regulating personal identity, reminiscent of the control described in Revelation 13. The use of biometrics to access critical services like banking, healthcare, or government resources is tied to a person's physical characteristics rather than traditional credentials.

It highlights a plan already being implemented in various countries, with digital IDs becoming increasingly necessary for travel, finance, and public services. In numerous countries, the people either comply or must actively resist the forces that are attempting to control their access to essential services.

While this is marketed as a security improvement, the implications are profound and often sound similar to the defensive posture taken to alter the news. It is apparently all for our good. Once access to financial and social systems is tied to biometrics, those who refuse to comply with specific mandates could find themselves locked out of essential services. Remember the Canadian truckers during the COVID-19 protests who found their trucks confiscated and their bank accounts frozen for expressing their opposition to the vaccine program.

This mirrors the same warning noted in Revelation 13:17, which states: "[the Antichrist decrees] that no one can buy or sell unless he has the mark, that is, the name of the beast or the number of its name." We have been warned. In Part 3 of this book, Chuck Stephens writes in depth about three kinds of truth: objective, subjective, and revealed. We are beginning to see the system in which Truth comes not from "God on high" but from those elites who see themselves as higher powers.

If a global biometric system becomes the only means of authentication, it could lay the foundation for a future system where compliance with governments and their ideological requirements determines access to society. Are we looking at a new feudal system controlled by the controllers of AI? Many have understandably charged that the WEF and Schwab's vision is the early stage of what the Bible foretells.

A Global Governance System: A Step Toward a Type of the Beast's Control?
During one of Schwab's addresses, he expressed the necessity of world governments working together to regulate AI and "all" technological advancements.[16] There were only minor concerns until he warned that without proper oversight, AI could spiral out of control, causing societal instability. So his proposed solution was a globally unified framework, directed by the oversight of the WEF.

He pushed for a fully digitally integrated society with AI and digital IDs and the idea of central bank digital currencies (CBDCs) being implemented

---

16. "Davos 2024: Welcome Remarks by Klaus Schwab, Founder and Executive Chairman," World Economic Forum, January 16, 2025, https://www.weforum.org/stories/2024/01/davos-2024-special-address-by-klaus-schwab-founder-and-executive-chairman-world-economic-forum/.

in a responsible, global manner to form financial and societal controls for our good. The WEF has pushed that narrative ever since. Our concern must be that this type of control suggests they see themselves as a new version of elite feudal kings who would decide the fate of all humans.

The WEF Push for AI and Transhumanism: Redefining What It Means to Be Human

One other key aspect of Schwab's speech was how he saw using the role of artificial intelligence in not only managing or controlling society, but also in the next step of actually reshaping society. He emphasized that his organization's AI development must include the intersection with transhumanism, permitting humanity to evolve beyond its biological limits through technology, aligning with many of the goals of the World Economic Forum which had previously promoted the idea of merging humans with AI, calling it the "fourth industrial revolution" which, as he put it, must lead to "a fusion of our physical, digital, and biological identities."

His organization's ultimate and final plan and hope was the next evolution of AI melded to transhumanism, which included uploading people's minds into a machine they were developing that they boasted would permit a human to live forever in an AI program and allow their being to learn eternally! He called it the core of the transhumanist promise of life eternal or the Fountain of Life through AI.

Those spiritual implications for AI are further expressed by the *de facto* spiritual guru of the WEF, Professor Noah Yuval Harari, a leader, contributing author, and spokesperson for the World Economic Forum, who has suggested that we eliminate humans who do not comply with the chip surgery and added that "using AI we can create new ideas, and even write a new Bible for those that seek spiritual guidance, which will answer moral questions, and fabricate Bible passages" to meet the new world.[17] He and other WEF members also see AI and other emerging technologies as a type of savior that will redeem humanity from problems, including illness, aging, and even mortality.

Others worship AI outright. One notable AI-based religious movement, The Way of the Future, founded by former Google employee Anthony Levandowski, suggests AI will help us become "like God."[18] With the proper implant-

---

17. Ian Giatti, "Israeli Futurist, Author Predicts AI Will Soon 'Write a New Bible,'" The Christian Post, June 14, 2023, https://www.christianpost.com/news/israeli-futurist-predicts-ai-will-soon-write-a-new-bible.html.

18. Patricia Engler, "AI and Human Futures: What Should Christians Think?," Center for Bioethics and Human Dignity, *Dignitas* Vol. 30, No. 4 (Winter 2023), 3–9, https://www.cbhd.org/dignitas-articles/ai-and-human-futures-what-should-christians-think.

ed chips and connections to AGI networks, it is within our grasp to become omniscient, omnipotent, and omnipresent if we are willing to unite ourselves with it.

The transhumanism movement admits it is built on the premise that there is a possible evolution of humanity beyond its God-designed natural limits of advancement. When people upload their memories and consciousness and merge them with an AI machine, they "may live on, learning onward, experiencing fuller life, such that death is conquered through technology, and where, with the help of AI artificial intelligence, eternal life in an AI hyperspace is a reality."[19] The vision was presented as tried, inevitable, and the next evolutionary step in human progress.

Schwab failed to respond to challenges because he had misplaced confidence based on the fact that the concept had never actually been achieved. Or to the question of "who decides what content is implanted into these new minds?" Essentially, for those of us from the traditional Western worldview, at its core this transhumanism is not about human evolution and progress at all. It is not much more than another form of rebellion against God, the plain facts of God-designed human limitation, and his divine providence—a new and taller tower of Babel.

The transhumanism plan and belief that human consciousness, past, present, and future, can be uploaded into AI machinery, thereby enabling a being to live forever as a ghost entity within the storage of an AI module, is the belief that the mind is the heart of what it is to be human. There is likely no more central belief in the last leg of subjective truth's philosophy, than that humans are nothing more than a complex neurological data set, a complex program that can be transferred as code into an AI artificial medium allowing a person to carry on existing forever. As we have noted, not only is this concept untested, it is also basically irreverent.

If all our experiences and memories can be programmed and digitized, then absolute Truth is little more than a delusion. It is hard to fulfill the other myriad commands of God, with all their benefits and pleasures, and especially the main command to love him with mind, body, soul, and spirit, and other people as ourselves, if it is all limited to a mental assent and not a tripartite performance.

As people who believe in absolute Truth, we believe our human identity and joy are much more than our thoughts. We have learned about AI's ability to create master deceptions and illusions and to deny reality and Truth as we know it. Essentially, there is a full assault on Truth beyond the one legacy

---

19. "Davos 2024: Welcome Remarks by Klaus Schwab."

media contrived, and not much more than a new version of Gnosticism—a new Tower of Babel—another ultimate smug rebellion against God's Truth, plans, and authority.

When we add the planned move to plant chips in the human mind to develop superhuman cognition, it can be seen as a new form of that old Eden lie that we can become like God, knowing good and evil, and live forever. But if simply knowing things is the ultimate purpose and goal of humans, then it is indistinguishable from traditional Gnosticism.

It must not escape anyone's attention that this plan echoes another chilling prophetic passage in the book of Revelation, where a leader called the false prophet breathes life into an image of the beast, allowing it to speak and enforce worship: "It was allowed to give breath to the image of the beast, so that the image of the beast might even speak and might cause those who would not worship the image of the beast to be slain" (Revelation 13:15).

Could AI play a role in this prophetic scenario? As technology advances and people trust and grow more comfortable with AI-driven decision-making, the world is being primed for a future where digital governance and control could dictate not just economic activity but belief systems as well.

11

THE ROAD TO RECOVERY, THE ROAD TO VICTORY IN THE WAR ON TRUTH

AS WE CONTEMPLATE the merits of the points outlined so far, traditionalists and defenders of absolute Truth must not become frustrated and impatient. At the same time, we must be cautious not to fall into traps being set for us by clever detractors who would like nothing more than to twist our words, views, and methods and paint us as anachronistic old fogies, relics of a bygone era, who are no longer relevant, nothing more than obstructors of progress and enemies of real progress. As Chuck points out, we must resist becoming like the Luddites who opposed mechanization because of the effect that it would have on employment in the textile industry and resorted to destroying machinery.

We can accept that undoubtedly, undeniably, we are fortunate to live in an awesome period of immense discovery and great progress with unequaled benefit to all humans. These benefits have been introduced by the same AI creators, developers, and promoters, even though we deem them to be more part of the problem than the solution. All this means we have to engage in some sort of accountability strategy. Part 3 of this book introduces debate tactics that are provided to arm us for the battles ahead.

As we engage in the defense of absolute Truth and become aware of our opposition's tactics and strategies, we must not ignore the fact that they are good at what they do and will soon have a tool that reaches well beyond what already exists. The sin lies not in technology itself but in its misuse.

The truth is that AI is not just limited to being another tool of technological progress. It has essentially become a mirror of the values, plans, strategies, intentions, and worldviews of its developers and creators. We must not be fooled into thinking it is neutral or that it is operating in a vacuum. The algorithms built into every line of coding learn from data sets built by humans. These are both a great aid to humanity and have the potential to be destructive, coercive, controlling, and deceptive. Those who have tested the answers of AI have found the responses to be lacking, especially when it comes to the analysis of theological enquiries. Much of AI follows the adage "garbage in equals garbage out"!

To ensure we maintain our freedoms and current Western values, we need to become fully engaged in the direction AI, noting especially that AGI is steered by the powers of AI, who program, dream, and shape it.

Rest assured, AI is not a neutral platform. It is shaped by its creators and developers, who themselves are reflections of a countercultural, anti-Western political bias. They do not share our views of Truth or life. The longer AI is permitted to grow without our input, the more unbalanced its "truth" becomes, and the more its values will be directed toward particular anti-Truth beliefs.

One lawsuit underway is brought by a man who suffered reputation loss due to what people who asked AI about him were told. He sued Meta because he contends that AI has to be "trained" before it can function, and this constituted a bias programmed against him. Worse yet, when he asked AI why it was lying about him, the AI reply was frank: "It was out of malevolence." This is not fiction; it is a case before the courts in 2025.[20]

AI already determines what articles you see on your newsfeed, what answers show up in your search results, and what kind of content is flagged or filtered. Once AI is embedded in schools, hospitals, law firms, government offices, and even churches, it won't just be an influence. It will be the filter through which much of modern life flows. The playbook is predictable. Fabricate chaos. Manufacture fear. Divide the people. Distract the public. Control the narrative. And then? Pretend it's all in the name of progress and democracy.

The controllers, designers, and architects of AI share a common worldview similar to that of legacy media. Their worldview not only rejects absolute Truth but is openly antagonistic toward it. The more this group embraces moral relativism and subjective truth and openly or subtly mocks traditional Western views and faith as oppressive, biased, and regressive, the more that worldview will be internalized and systematized into nearly every digital encounter.

And yet we need to stay informed about the practical and valuable uses of this technology. There is so much potential in this technology that we can use for our cause. Just as a small example, it has been estimated that the Great Commission to complete the last translations of the Bible into the remaining languages could be completed in five years or less with the help of the speed of AI. That is an example of an excellent use of AI. And there is more.

Suppose we fail to build AI infrastructures that are solidly grounded in Christian principles. In that case, we will likely witness the final stages of our further cultural marginalization by our adversaries, not just through overt

---

20. C. Mollie, "Exploring Examples of AI Bias in the Real World: An Examination of Discriminatory Algorithmic Decisions Made by AI," The Unscripted Mind, January 16, 2025, https://unscriptedmind. substack.com/p/exploring-examples-of-ai-bias-in.

censorship, but through the subtle manipulation of what AI allows humans to think, create, and believe. When Christians neglected to shape early digital platforms, citing fears of worldliness or technical complexity, secular progressives seized control of the infrastructure that now thoroughly governs public discourse. Social media algorithms systematically suppress biblical content and truth while amplifying blasphemy and impiety. With the loss of Truth, we witness the loss of reality and common sense.

The devaluation of Truth is equally the devaluation of life, as Chuck discusses in the section on abortion. The fear of not being able to care for a child led to limited abortions, but that soon led to aborting because of not wanting the imposition and inconvenience. Soon, the slippery slope includes late-term abortions and full-term abortions to the moment of birth. It will not be long before we will permit the taking of a life well after birth because the baby is technically not independent and self-supporting, so they would die without intervention.

Where will this end? It was not long after we lost the respect for the miracle of the life of a baby that other members of society who were also an imposition or economic burden were next to be terminated. Now, older people or the infirm have become vulnerable to the belief that their lives no longer have value. The devaluation of Truth is equally the devaluation of life.

We are not unaware that the modern world thrives on deception—shifting narratives, subjective morality, subjective truth, and AI-generated information that distorts reality. We, the defenders of Truth, must be committed to seeking Truth, even when it is uncomfortable and even if it means we will be chastised and attacked for it.

This is especially important for those who are Christians, whose faith calls us to stand for truth. Shining light into the darkness means staying dedicated to our biblical Western worldview, refusing to be shaped by ideological trends even when they seem slick, attractive, and undeniable, and it means being willing to stand against falsehood and the devaluation of Truth even when it is unpopular. It means recognizing that truth is not created by algorithms or mass consensus, and Truth revealed by God does not change! We must never forget that God is a rewarder of those who diligently seek after him (see Hebrews 11).

Booker T. Washington's old adage comes to mind: "A lie doesn't become truth, wrong doesn't become right, and evil doesn't become good just because a majority accepts it."

What we are experiencing is not new. Throughout history, human civilizations have been tempted to replace the Creator with the created. Paul makes that clear in Romans 1. We continually trade divine wisdom for human-made replacements. ASI may be the most sophisticated version yet! But they are idols. In our age, we have come full circle. The Gnostic fallacy has been upgraded to the new idol of information and intelligence itself. As we increasingly look to AI for our convenience, for meaning, for truth, for authority, for advice, for purpose, we find our world trusting a machine to tell us how to live, what to think, and who to become, with the same fervor once reserved for religious devotion.

Don't Believe or Trust Anything, But Verify Everything

Earlier, I credited the principle of "Believe half of what you see and nothing of what you hear" to my father. He introduced it to me as a protective means to ensure I was not being hoodwinked by all the false narratives I endlessly heard—all gossip, as he put it—nor by the magic tricks of artisans or the tricks our own eyes often play on us, and as a result, making flawed decisions.

The Royal Navy once had this well-used and famously hyperbolic adage that was later adopted by the writer William Johnson Neale. In his novel *Cavendish: Or the Patrician at Sea*, one of his characters advises a cohort to "Believe half of what you see and nothing of what you hear." It was later even more popularized by writer Edgar Allan Poe in his short story "The System of Doctor Tarr and Professor Fether," in which a new intern is told "the time will arrive when you will learn to judge for yourself of what is going on in the world, without trusting to the gossip of others. Believe nothing you hear, and only one half that you see."

Here we find ourselves in our new world era of "post-truth" or "personal truth." This is especially so with the advance of AI, where anything can be made to look real, sound real, and even feel real, and where even the very faces and voices of renowned people can be perfectly imitated, making them seem to have said things they never did, and made so real that they are indistinguishable to even the most cultured eye and ear.

We have to acknowledge we have moved well beyond that age of careful observation and light skepticism to the place where, in order to retain our sanity, we must practice the routine of full suspicion of all things and uncertainty about the certainty of anything. Truth has always been subject to personal distortion and is under attack or at risk. Discretion, discernment, and stalwartness in defending Truth have always been the solution.

The time has arrived where we may need to modify this popular adage to "Believe nothing you hear, and very little of what you see unless you can personally verify it." What can one truly believe anymore? We have just emerged from one of the most ferocious political campaigns in American and then

Canadian history, where both sides used the same accusation—that the other was about to destroy democracy, history, freedom, reason, and even reality. It has become a good lesson on how the idea that "everyone can have their truth" simply does not work.

What Is the Solution?

The prophet Isaiah once noted, "Justice is turned back, and righteousness stands far away; for truth has stumbled in the public squares, and uprightness cannot enter" (59:14). Abandoning the concept of absolute Truth, then as now, has extended consequences affecting everything.

We must vigorously and perpetually seek and then defend the pursuit of Truth. You may ask what apparatus we use to make our Truth assays. What can we do to thwart this death? The following pages give us some excellent tools to resecure our thought foundation upon revealed Truth.

The focus of Chuck's timely chapters is not so much a treatise on the answers themselves as on how to seek out and distinguish Truth from deception—how to discern it and tell it apart from the myriads of deceptions, untruths, lies, gossip, fake news, slick AI-generated simulations, etc.

And we can start right now by picking up on the simple but astute methods that Chuck employs in his exchanges. Forewarned is forearmed. And as Benjamin Franklin once said, "By failing to prepare, one is preparing to fail!" Understanding the strategies and tactics of our adversaries is an important start. Understanding the forces and technology being developed that will multiply our challenges manifold is another step. So now, you are here being called into action—a call to arms, and a call to become a warrior of and for the Truth.

Even by presenting these devices, we are affirming that Truth is worth saving, that we want to save it, and that we can. And we must assume that we actually have the personal tools to identify and know the heart of the actual Truth versus the fraudulent. As an unknown author once wrote, "Actions prove who we are. Words only show who we pretend to be."

Chuck's goal is a novel and noble approach, a method of debate he presents in a fresh and ingenious package, rationally scrutinizing so-called "new world truth." We must not think the repeal of subjective truth is a simple mission, as he well demonstrates. It requires the employment of continuous diligence, application of not-so-common common sense, and an educated discernment, that sometimes seems no longer common, nor plentiful. It will require a great deal of work to not only know the details of our position on any matter and be conversant with that position, but we equally need to understand the details and reasons for the opposing views of those who disagree with us.

And we must treat those views with respect while debating the merit of Truth vigorously. But being aware that our new information age of subjective truth is enticing, formidable, and persuasive is the first step to victory.

Our toolkit, as demonstrated by Chuck, is applied to 24 important topics and issues being hotly debated throughout our world today, and is a sound start toward learning to expose the defects of subjective truth and hopefully return our culture to the eternal Truth.

I end with a story that features the power of letting Truth perform its intrinsic work—a work that was life-changing for one man who is now changing the world with his newfound belief. Years ago, after Christy Strobel became a Christian, she challenged her husband, Lee Strobel, a secular journalist and staunch atheist with no faith whatsoever, to prove that the Christian faith was not true. As a skilled journalist, he delightfully took on the challenge. After two years of careful and exhaustive historical and biblical research, where Lee gathered lists of proofs for and against the case for Jesus being the promised Messiah of Israel, he finally came up with a small partial sheet against the claim, but hundreds of pages of proof for the Truth that Jesus was the Messiah.

Lee had to agree that his wife was right, and afterwards he went on to write several books defending the Truth of Jesus's identity. He is not alone.

We could list countless other unbelievers in history who have undertaken the same search and come to the same conclusions. That is the kind of honest research and debate we want to challenge the journalists in the legacy media to engage in with us. And by using the approach Chuck demonstrates, we are being challenged to engage our critics with solid, honest, respectable, well-informed dialogue to defend the case of Truth, especially as we see the impact and threat that quantum computing artificial intelligence will have for deception and against our quest for the resurgence of absolute Truth.

As Augustine of Hippo once declared and as Chuck confirms, "The truth is like a lion; you don't have to defend it. Let it loose; it will defend itself."

PART 3

KEY PERSPECTIVES ON TWENTY-FOUR MAJOR ISSUES BEING DEBATED IN THE PUBLIC SPACE

12

TRUTH BE KNOWN

"WHAT IS TRUTH?" (John 18:38). These were the cynical words that Pontius Pilate famously spoke as he passed the buck to the local chief. He seemed to imply that he did not see eye to eye with the local yokels and did not concur with their verdict. He seemed to imply that the imperial view of Truth might be different from the indigenous view of it.

Finding the right answer to any question, finding the truth, involves several steps or calculations. The focus of this book is not on the answers, but on how to reach them. How to recognize the truth for what it is. Or should I say, for what it was? How to tell it apart from deception, untruth, lies, gossip, and fake news. This discernment is different from the other sense of telling the truth: honesty. Here we look at both senses of the word. The greatest need for a great reset is the recovery of truth.

Courts seek truth through a formal process. Different views are presented, typically by the prosecution and the defense. A judge or sometimes a jury has to seek the truth. That is why Lady Justice wears a blindfold. She should treat everyone equally and "by the book." No exceptions. No exemptions. The truth is not for sale. Or is it?

Witnesses may be called forward. They swear to tell the truth, the whole truth, and nothing but the truth. Nevertheless, witnesses can be bought, and they often lie. So the process includes cross-examination to try to get closer to the truth.

Evidence may be submitted in the form of documents or photos, or samples. Experts may be asked to testify. They may present relevant data. Did you ever notice that the courts are overbooked, overutilized, and thus overextended? This is because they are more discerning, and it points to the death of truth in many other spheres.

To find the truth, a judge needs the law, just as a builder needs a plumb line.

What are some of the barriers that try to keep the light of truth from being seen clearly? Why is truth dying out? It is not extinct yet, but it is endangered.

One issue is that the law can vary. Different laws apply in different places. For example, common law, constitutional law, and sharia law are all different. Legislatures can change laws, so what was illegal yesterday may be legal today. Marijuana comes to mind, as do same-sex marriage and assisted suicide.

Then there is the issue of the objectivity and subjectivity of truth. Can "my truth" be different from "your truth"? Is that relativist or maybe pluralist? Or is truth situational? Or is there ultimately a one-size-fits-all truth that applies to everyone? If so, how can you tell the masks from their real face? Would we even recognize the real truth if we looked it in the face, amid a sea of masks?

Another issue is perspective. For example, it may be true to a bystander on Earth that a car is passing at a hundred miles per hour. But what about a viewer on Mars who sees the Earth rotating and also orbiting the Sun? That means, in short, that the car is really traveling a lot faster than a hundred. Are both right? Can there be more than one truth? This might explain why a judge would convict a man of 34 counts, then, on the day of his sentencing, give him an unconditional discharge, wishing him "Godspeed" going forward?

Friedrich Nietzsche wrote: "Sometimes people don't want to hear the truth because they don't want their illusions destroyed." That's another nail in truth's coffin.

This brings up the question of diverse interests. The truth is often subverted intentionally for some cause or motive. This goes all the way back to the "father of lies," who approached Eve in the garden of Eden. She succumbed to temptation, which was seductively presented to her—a toxic mix of truth and untruth.

Fraud would not be very effective if the person swindling you had horns and a long-forked tail. By its very nature, it is well disguised and hard to tell apart from the truth. News, adverts, marketing, conspiracy theories, and gossip are constantly inundating us. How do we know who or what to believe?

The Greek philosopher Plato was very influential on Western thought. He envisaged a metaphysical "form" or "ideal" for everything that exists in the physical realm. When we sit at different tables to eat, work, and play, these various tables are but shadows of the real deal. A metaphysical table exists "out there" that throws shadows in different directions. His metaphor was that we are living in a cave, seeing but shadows on the wall. The real figures exist—outside the cave. With a fire in the background, which casts shadows onto the wall of the cave. So reality may be different from what we see. Is the truth itself just a perception?

Another ancient teacher, a rabbi, claimed that he was the way to the truth. According to St. John, Jesus said: "I am the way, the truth, and the life." In the prologue to his Gospel, St. John takes a very high view of Jesus as the *logos* or "word". This means that we can hear God speaking (through him) and see (in him) a role model sent from God, worthy of imitation. Hearing is the Jewish pathway to understanding God's word ("Hear, O Israel..."), whereas sight is the Greek pathway ("We beheld his glory, full of grace and truth"). Best is hearing and seeing together.

At first, it may be hard to conceptualize such a claim, one that personalizes truth. It takes truth out of the metaphysical realm of philosophers and brings it down to earth, like a ground wire. One way to get this is to remember that Christians await the return or second coming of Jesus, on Judgment Day. If we recall the court scenario, he will judge us. He will listen to the evidence, hear some witnesses, check the available data, and then know the truth about each of us. He will see right through us, deeper than X-ray vision. The prosecutor doesn't speak the truth; he only presents his side of it. The defense does the same; it only offers one perspective. Who gets to the real truth? The judge. This metaphor of the justice system is telling—it is slow but accurate. In today's world, it may be truth's last stand.

Frances Quarles wrote: "The height of all philosophy is to know thyself; and the end of this knowledge is to know God." There is a third understanding of truth. It is faith-based. Call it a revelation. It is neither inherently objective like Platonic thinking, nor is it pluralistically subjective. The word *morality* comes to mind, like in the Ten Commandments: "Thou shalt not ...." But this version of truth is on life support.

Look again, the first and greatest commandment of the ten is to love God only—followed by scrapping idols and profanity, and keeping the Sabbath holy. From that flow the behavioral touchstones, at the family level first and then at a societal level—on adultery, theft, and murder.

Is the Bible true? Many think so, and in our courts, witnesses still put their hand on it and promise to tell the truth, the whole truth, and nothing but the truth. Witnesses should believe that "truth is like a lion. You don't have to defend it. It defends itself." Just be honest and tell the truth, and the judge's decision will not be distorted.

But morality is gradually eroding. People often lie through their teeth in court testimony. They mislead the court. Murder is going the way of adultery when you think of the return of infanticide. Theft is commonplace and hard to prosecute, due to a lack of evidence. By its very nature, it is more often done in the dark than in the light. Like murderers, thieves are good at getting away with it.

By checking out twenty-four issues being debated in the public space, the golden thread of this book is finding the truth. You don't have to be a philosopher or a lawyer to get there. But you do need to sharpen your truth-finding skills in a world that is teeming with propaganda, deception, scams, and fake news.

History is repeating itself. The death of truth happened once before. It was followed by victory over death, a resilience that reverberated around the world for centuries. He saw it coming. He predicted that he would be crushed by the hatred of the religious elite, combined with the military might of Rome. But truth always has a way of slipping out, even from the grave.

We are going down that road once again. Notions of objective truth and subjective truth are squeezing the life out of revealed truth. First prize is to recover it before it is too late. This book sounds a warning, so that it can be recovered. Second prize is to accept the death of truth fatalistically. But that is not the end, for truth always, by its very nature, has a way of bursting out again. It cannot be contained; it is too robust and self-assured. It will be back, sooner or later, even if that takes a thousand years.

Methodology and Rules of Play

Not all ages and places will remember *To Tell the Truth*—a TV game that was popular in the 1950s and '60s in America and Canada. But most baby boomers will remember it.

Over the years, the game rules have varied. However, certain basic rules remained consistent. Three challengers were introduced, all claiming to be the true "central character." The moderator asked the challengers, who stood side by side, "What is your name, please?" Each challenger rose and stated the same name. In other words, two were impostors—only one was the real truth.

Then, the moderator read a short introduction to the "central character."

After the questioning was complete, the panelists voted on which of the challengers they believed to be telling the truth without consulting the others. Once the votes were in, the moderator asked, "Will the real [person's name] please stand up?"

The central character then stood, often after some brief playful feinting and false starts among all three challengers.

We present a twist on the game here, and we've changed the rules just a tad. In our case, we seek the truth not about a person but about a topic. There are twenty-four hot topics in all, enough for the reader to draw some conclusions about truth—how to know it and how to fend off deception.

On our team, there are no intentional impostors. Rather, the challengers are consistent with their seating, designated "left," "middle," and "right." Their answers are not given to mislead you, but they are different. Our whole team is trying to help you find the truth.

The panelists are each allowed to pose questions to the challengers. In the original game show, the central character used to be sworn to give truthful answers. However, the impostors were permitted to lie and pretend to subvert the truth. They actively tried to con the panelists. This happens every day in the public space. Unless you fatalistically shrug and plead that different truths can coexist.

In our case, each episode closes with the question: "Would the real truth [about the topic under discussion] please stand out?" The reader is then left to weigh up the dialogue and decide who they think is telling the truth and who isn't.

The death of truth happens when people uncritically accept any narrative and keep to it, even when cross-examination and evidence bring it into question. Virtue-signaling is not the pathway to truth. It takes heavy doses of humility.

On each topic, the truth can sometimes be obvious and other times it can be agonizing. But after twenty-four chapters, each containing one episode, some truths emerge *about truth*. By its very nature, deception is at times hard to detect. That is why the tempter spoke to Eve in the garden of Eden as a "shining one."

We hope that this exercise is entertaining and informative, not just about the topics covered but also about the nature and features of truth. Even though we may never get to the deepest level of truth, we hope to move you in that general direction. A few may be blinded by seeing the truth, like the Greek seers of old.

Our abiding belief is that all truth is God's truth, no matter the source. You can find it in deductive reasoning like math, from inductive sources like science, and secular principles like human rights, but it is still divine. But it takes a special ingredient to supersede the other truths. Faith.

This is a better bet than buying into emotional contagion. Groupthink is far from the truth. Without implying that the word *truth* can be preceded by possessive adjectives like *my, your, our,* or *their* instead of *the*, it is important for each of us to use our own compass. Seek the truth and follow it. Don't just go with the flow.

There are five series of four to six episodes each that address macro issues, political issues, legal issues, health issues, and future issues. The panel for each of these series remains the same, but it changes from one series to another. That way, relevant experts are envisioned to pose the questions. The four guest panelists represent the four biggest Anglophone regions on earth: North America, Britain, South Africa, and India. Each of these regions is represented on every panel throughout, although the individual panelists change.[21]

Finally, this book premieres a new technology: Time-Zoom. This app allows panelists to be invited from faraway places in different time zones. They gather in one "virtual" dialogue. But the Time-Zoom app also allows us to invite panelists from different eras past. It crushes the time factor and distance, but it enhances the quality of questions posed by the panel. Enjoy!

---

21. The dialogue contained in the chapters 12 to 17 are works of fiction. Any resemblance between original characters and real persons, living or dead, is entirely coincidental. While most of the characters, places and incidents in this story are based on actual discussions, events or persons, they have been used fictitiously in these discussions. Any conversation or debate between the actual characters is a product of the author's imagination.

13

MACRO ISSUES

TRUTH-TELLING

Moderator

WELCOME TO THE new sequel to an old favorite game that searches for truth. To start this new season, we even have this one episode on *truth-telling*. We regard truth-telling as a virtue, and its opposite as a vice—deception.

Do the names Julian Assange and Edward Snowden ring a bell? Assange is a cypherpunk activist who exposed that news reaching the public was out of sync with military sources. He later founded WikiLeaks. He landed in jail in the UK, but many media platforms, including Amnesty International, advocated for his release as a whistleblower. Eventually, he struck a plea bargain with the USA, pleading guilty to only one charge of espionage so that he could return home to Australia. Then along came Edward Snowden, saying this credibility gap between what the public is told and what is really known in the corridors of power is "an existential threat to democracy." He fled to Russia for protection, where he became a naturalized citizen.

Snowden said, "People don't realize how hard it is to speak the truth to a world full of people that don't realize they're living a lie."

Looking for facts is an essential technique in seeking the truth. So when whistleblowers come forward with facts or hard evidence that the truth is being subverted, is it not time for a deeper investigation? What is more foolish—believing what is not true or not believing what is true? Why are people jailed or exiled for telling the truth?

George Orwell once wrote: "The further a society drifts from Truth, the more it will hate those who speak it."

Now we have a case of disinformation on the war in Ukraine. According to evidence leaked by Jack Texeira, who has been arrested, there is a major discrepancy between news content and reality. Of course, intelligence is a cloak-and-dagger environment, full of spies and spooks, so no one seems too surprised. Winston Churchill once remarked: "In wartime, truth is so precarious that a bodyguard of lies should always attend her."

Remember Daniel Ellsberg? In 1971, he leaked the Pentagon Papers to the media, exposing the same credibility gap between what the public was being told and the reality on the ground in Vietnam. There is a history of leakers, suggesting that some consider nefarious deceptions unacceptable.

So we welcome our four panelists, all of whom are with us remotely, via our new app Time-Zoom. Please note that they all join us in their personal and private capacity. From North America, we welcome George Washington. From Britain, we welcome Malcolm Muggeridge. From South Africa, we welcome Desmond Tutu. And from India, we welcome Mohandas Gandhi.

This is our illustrious panel for the first series, on macro issues. Each panelist may pose one question to any of the three challengers. We hope that their questions are probing and penetrating enough to reveal the truth about each episode's topic. We encourage both challengers and panelists to help us sharpen our truth-seeking skills. All of them must tell the truth.

Please give it up for our first guest panelist!

North America's Panelist: George Washington
In my era, we were brought up to tell the truth. It was not just a virtue; it was an imperative. So I would like to direct my question to the challenger on the right. Do you think that I did the right thing, as a boy, when my father confronted me about a cherished cherry tree? I answered him that, yes, I cannot tell a lie, I did chop it down with my little hatchet.

Challenger on the Right
You did the right thing. However, you had not done things right! You should not have cut down that cherry tree without permission. But you didn't turn it into a blame game to try to exonerate yourself. You told the truth.

When I was growing up, this was the story that we associated with your name. It taught us honesty and integrity. But in today's world, all we hear is that it was environmentally unfriendly of you to cut down a tree. You were not thinking of food security by cutting down a cherry tree, which is why, when you grew up, you became an insensitive slave owner. I regard this new take on your legacy to be a slanderous insult. It is revisionist. It is defamatory to speak of America's first president like that, sir.

To be honest, I think that those who talk like that are suffering from the "woke mind virus." They don't speak the truth; they twist everything to fit their narrative. Ideologies are not the place to look for truth. You need to study facts. Historical facts, scientific facts, medical facts, and so on. They are the starting point, as opposed to starting with a "spin" and trying to rationalize the facts to fit your vantage point—or just ignoring them.

You could have started making excuses or laying the blame on someone else or even pleading ignorance that you didn't realize that it was a cherished tree. Maybe it was in the way, or you mistook it for a weed or an alien invasive species? But no, you respected your father's authority, and you fessed up. Good form, sir!

Going from specific to general, I believe that denying the authority of our Creator is leading to the death of truth. We need to obey revealed truth, and where we fail, we need to confess and try again. A father is proud of his children's honesty and integrity.

Britain's Guest Panelist: Malcolm Muggeridge
Picking up on the previous challenger's answer, let me address my question to the challenger on the left. One of the most cowardly things that ordinary people do is to ignore the facts. So do you think that the extraordinary lengths that the deep state went to in order to suppress the emerging story of the discovery of Hunter Biden's laptop were in order? Or was it basically a cover-up, in the weeks running up to the 2020 elections?

Challenger on the Left
That story simply had to be discredited. The impact that it otherwise could have had on the election outcome was too big a risk. Winning is everything.

There was a history of news stories about alleged Russian disinformation efforts intended to undermine Donald Trump. A first allegation of Russian collusion, which was later proved to be a fairy tale, had been used to impeach him. So that pointed to the way forward, to a familiar narrative. High-profile intelligence leaders were invited to sign an open letter stating that the Hunter Biden laptop story had all the features of another Russian disinformation effort. It was not genuine; it was expedient. It may have been CIA-induced. On Donald Trump's first day back in office, he signed an executive order rescinding the security clearance of all 51 of the signatories of that infamous letter.

Some years later, the same media platforms that helped suppress that story in 2020 concluded that it actually was the real deal. Sometimes it is hard to discern the truth. The public tends to believe what is in print, simply because it is in print. Obviously, news services can lean on their laurels, knowing people will believe what they print. And worse yet, politicians, parties, and their king-makers can coerce the media to emphasize a certain narrative.

Election campaigns do not wait—they cannot wait—for the judiciary or special investigations. Those processes take forever. Truth is sometimes sacrificed for expediency. Once a winner is declared and validated, there is no going back. Some things are just more important than getting down to the truth.

Years later, it has come to light that law enforcement already knew about the Biden family's wheeling and dealing and had already opened a docket before the emergence of the "laptop from hell." They probably knew that the truth would come out in due course. It always does, by its very nature. But they could suppress it long enough to win the election. Cover-ups have a way of causing way more problems than the wee crimes being covered up.

South Africa's Guest Panelist: Desmond Tutu

I did not like the tone of that last reply, so I direct my question to the challenger in the middle. First, please fill me in on terminology. What are "truth bombs"? And then, is there a difference between deception and pretending? In other words, is it sometimes OK, even playful, to bend the truth a bit, without breaking it?

Challenger in the Middle

Your question about truth bombs is pertinent. Because in a world full of propaganda, telling the truth can be quite explosive at times. For example, when whistleblowers come forward unexpectedly, especially if they bring evidence with them to corroborate their eyewitness accounts, it can blow apart the prevailing narrative. That's what truth bombs do.

Take the open letter already mentioned by my co-challenger on the left, for example. It was at work in the background in 2020 to get buy-in from the media that would discredit the Hunter Biden laptop story. But in 2023, a whistleblower came forward with that open letter just as the truth about that story was being revealed. Suddenly, we got a credible explanation—who drafted the letter, what his reward was, and who refused to sign the letter, seeing it for what it was. Exposing that the open letter was really an intel decoy was an example of a truth bomb.

The term *truth bomb* seems a little violent, but that whistleblower had to go into hiding, under protection, because his or her life was in danger. The stakes were very high because that investigation could have implicated the sitting president. The validity of the 2020 election was in question. The media now says that Hunter Biden's attorneys are getting very aggressive as well, intimidating the whistleblowers who came forward. Some voices are saying that the Attorney General at times acted like the president's own defense attorney!

Truth does not exist in a vacuum somewhere "out there." It is right here in real life, where bribery and corruption are rampant. The police and some judges are for sale. In the USA, judges are elected, so the partisan divide is creeping into the judiciary. In South Africa, a few truth bombs were dropped during the Zondo Commission. What about Babita Deokaran, who blew the whistle on corruption related to COVID-19 spending in South Africa? She was killed in cold blood. The ex-CEO of Eskom went into hiding for naming names connected to the corruption that plagues the power utility. At first, he was treated like a pariah by politicians in the executive branch. But his appearances before a parliamentary committee were quite illuminating, and some voices started asking why the police and politicians had ignored his warnings. The status quo obviously does not like it when truth bombs go off in their vicinity.

Is there any wiggle room? Can we just "pretend" without lying outright? In the fantasy world of children, there is room for that. It's not lying; it's creative imagination. The problem is that some of these pretenders never grow up. They keep up the charade, even in real adult life. They loot and steal under the cover of deception, as if life were just one big Monopoly game.

People speak of the Trump Derangement Syndrome, whereby some people got so militant that they would say anything or do anything to insult him, without thinking. They are diehards. They called their opponents MAGA extremists. It is a bit hard to square this with election results. In 2020, he got 72 million votes—the one that he lost! That was more votes than he got in 2016, when he won! In 2024, that rose to over 77 million votes. Are there that many extremists? This is irrational and dangerous. They are inciting.

Speaking from the middle, I worry that the "woke mind virus" is so rampant that even centrists like me are now seen as alt-right. That gives some idea of the distortions caused by the huge polarization in today's world. My view is that there are not two truths or more. There is but one. The key is to take time to listen and assess before judging or deciding how to vote. I worry that in South Africa, sir, people vote on automatic pilot, not because they have been diligently searching for the truth. So they keep riding in the same car, just changing the driver once in a while.

India's Guest Panelist: Mohandas Gandhi
India has become the world's biggest democracy. Its huge population magnifies the need for a coherent and consistent answer to what truth is. As democracies grow, they become more diverse in terms of demography, language, and religion. India is no exception. I was fortunate to study in Britain and to work for a period in South Africa before returning home to India. So it is that

coherence comes to my mind. You cannot have one truth in India, another in Britain, and another in South Africa. Or we will never have a global village. Nor is truth decided by majority vote. "Even if you are a minority of one, the truth is the truth." So I want to hear from the challenger on the left again. Is there such a thing as a universal truth?

Challenger on the Left

The world is too diverse for there to be only one truth. Even one country can have different truths. For Indigenous people in North America or Africa, their truth can be very different from the truth of the settlers. Some truths are the same everywhere, like $2 + 2 = 4$. Those are deductive. But inductive truths are based on experience, that is, on history, and that differs from one place to another. Each constituency has its history. Rural truth may be different from urban truth. India still has a strong caste system, which does not exist in Canada, for example. Even in Canada, Quebec has a special status, so its understanding of truth may differ from Anglophone provinces. Quebec uses Napoleonic law, whereas the other provinces use common law, based on historical cases, not on a systematized code.

When it comes right down to it, your truth can be different from mine. You may be religious and opposed to same-sex marriage or abortion. At the same time, I am more tolerant, pro-choice, and pro-trans because my truth is different from yours.

The British did a huge disservice to India at the time of Partition. They separated Muslims from Hindus, creating East and West Pakistan, now Bangladesh and Pakistan, respectively. They separated monotheists from polytheists. Why did they polarize people in this way, instead of leaving them homogenized?

To sum up, I do not believe that there is a universal truth, except in some spheres like mathematics. When Muslims invaded and occupied the Iberian peninsula, now Spain, they brought Arabic numerals with them. These proved much more useful—and enduring—than clumsy Roman numerals. So even though the Moors and Arabs were eventually pushed back to Africa, Europeans kept the Arabic numerals, which we still use. Sometimes truth can be traded or exported like this.

Those who support globalization do not have to agree that there is only one God or only one truth. Not everyone can believe that one historical person will return to judge every one of us. We should try to coexist—sharia law for some, Napoleonic law for others, and common law for others. For measuring distance, miles are OK in the USA, while kilometers are used in Canada. You can drive on the left side of the road in Britain, South Africa, and India, and on the right side in Europe and North America. This is not incoherent. It is just situational.

There are not two destinations for us, in some kind of grand Partition. There is only one destination for all—and it is right here on earth.

When most European countries used the prevalent WHO recommendations during the COVID-19 pandemic, Sweden did not. It did not require masking or vaccines, and there was no lockdown. Yet there is no difference in terms of the statistics for infection, mortality, or even surplus deaths. For each, their own. Two strategies ended up with precisely the same results.

Moderator

Thank you to the guest panelists and the articulate challengers. Now, will the real Truth about truth-telling please stand out?

CENSORSHIP

Moderator

Good day and welcome to another episode of *Telling the Truth*. We regard truth-telling as a virtue and deception as a vice.

This episode on censorship is vital. One of the precepts of democracy is freedom of speech, yet we are seeing more and more countries adopt legislation about hate speech. There has to be a red line. We also hear some voices talking about the right to information. But at the same time, one cannot forget the right to privacy. The paparazzi are notorious for invading the space of the rich and famous. The pushback comes when those suffering from "indecent exposure" sue for damages.

Censorship is now as familiar as having your Facebook post nixed by fact-checkers. This can be vexing, as people talk of the "establishment media," meaning that they are effectively spreading government propaganda and distorting the truth. For example, Canada has banned certain news outlets from the cable networks.

Tucker Carlson concluded that news networks, by their very nature, do not want the truth to be spoken or seen. They want the advertising revenues that come with high ratings, so they would rather broadcast banter about basically irrelevant topics than delve into really weighty matters. Thus, Tucker moved into a new mode, speaking from a platform that is not partisan. Ironically, the legacy media is so dominated by the left that any nonpartisan platform is perceived as alt-right.

Elbert Hubbard wrote: "Those who are able to see beyond the shadows and lies of their culture will never be understood, let alone believed by the masses."

We once again welcome our four global and historical panelists, all of whom are with us remotely, via our new app Time-Zoom. Please note that they always join us in their personal and private capacity. The panel is composed of people of huge influence—from North America, George Washington; from Britain, Malcolm Muggeridge; from South Africa, Desmond Tutu; and from India, we welcome Mohandas Gandhi.

This is our panel on macro issues like censorship throughout the first series. Please give it up for our illustrious panel!

Each panelist may pose one question to any one of the three challengers. We hope that the questions get down to where the rubber meets the road. We are seeking the truth about censorship, but more than that, we are looking for lessons about how to find the truth, generically. Lack of this useful life-skill can lead to the death of truth. For this episode, we ask Malcolm Muggeridge to start the process of uncovering the truth.

Britain's Guest Panelist: Malcolm Muggeridge
As a journalist, editor, and author, this topic is close to my heart. I believe the media's job is to track down the truth like bloodhounds track down a possum. So to the challenger on the left, I ask you to explain why the media pegged anyone who called COVID-19 "the Chinese virus" a racist? It was clear to a British think tank as early as February 2020 that principled Chinese doctors had tried to send out alerts and warnings about an unknown virus on the loose as early as November and December of 2019. Why were those voices silenced? Why was this narrative suppressed? Why were those demonized who have suspected all along that its origins were most probably from human error in a lab in Wuhan? A lab that had been illegally awarded gain-of-function funding from the USA. One would only expect a despotic regime like China to keep the truth under wraps to protect itself. But why did the democratic left politicize this, thereby letting China off the hook?

Challenger on the Left
These questions amount to 20/20 hindsight. Obviously, we were more worried about containing the pandemic than anything else at the time. It was unfortunate that the pandemic coincided with a crucial election in the USA. There is no question that the two got entangled.

People said to "follow the science." Well, as time marched on, the cases against masking and vaccines piled up. I have never met anyone who thinks that the lockdowns helped the economy—they were definitely detrimental. But at the time, government intervention was largely seen as well-intentioned, not as overreach.

While vaccines have certainly had negative side effects, they have probably saved lives and may have slowed the spread of the COVID-19 virus. The jury is still out on that, but at least some people still see value in the vaccines.

I think that the question of COVID-19 origins got buried in pandemic priorities. It was left simmering on the back burner. This was done by demonizing anyone who called it "the Chinese virus" as racist. But now that the pandemic is in the rearview mirror, and more facts are known, even the FBI says that there is about a 95 percent probability that the virus was man-made in a lab ... which then lost control of its hygiene. That triggered the catastrophe, and the fire burned out of control, metaphorically speaking. Firefighters prioritize saving lives and extinguishing the fire. They only investigate how the fire started after it has been put out.

The extent to which key people were actively sidestepping the question because they had vested interests in keeping it quiet is now being explored. Some left-of-center voices, like Robert F. Kennedy Jr., chided the official line as propaganda. He has been a vaccine sceptic, so this has not only come from the alt-right.

China's cozy relationship with Joe Biden when he was Obama's vice president is coming to light now through evidence contained in Hunter Biden's laptop and the emergence of some photos of Biden with Chinese people he claimed he had never met. Furthermore, some whistleblowers have dropped a few related truth bombs as well. Perhaps there were vested interests at play? Even in Canada, Chinese interference in its elections has been uncovered, causing some heads to roll. The existence of Chinese police stations in the USA raises eyebrows. Not to mention its weather balloons floating over America. The buying up of land by the Chinese has been banned in some states now. So all the Chinese saber-rattling about Taiwan can be seen as a decoy to scare investigators off the scent of the origins of the virus.

In my opinion, history will remember COVID-19 as "the Chinese virus" just as we still remember an earlier pandemic as "the Spanish flu," even though it did not originate in Spain. Censorship may work for a while, in the short term, but in the long run, the truth will out.

South Africa's Guest Panelist: Desmond Tutu
During the "lost decade" in South Africa under Jacob Zuma, he was able to capture the state, but not the media. State capture is an extreme form of

"weaponization," as our American friends would say. The media and the fifth estate remained free and played a huge role in exposing and turning around state capture.

Early in that lost decade, I invited the Dalai Lama to my eightieth birthday party. But the government would not issue him a visa because of its allegiance to China, especially as fellow members of BRICS. So I know what top-down interference feels like.

It makes me wonder: Why doesn't the government tell us the truth about UFOs? Governments have been collecting data about this, but it remains a closely guarded secret. One ex-Cabinet Minister in Canada spoke out after he retired, saying that there was intel about this, and that there had been encounters. But the government does not want to share what it knows with us. Isn't this a kind of censorship? Don't we have the right to know? I am addressing my question to the challenger on the right.

Challenger on the Right
I am a great believer in the saying that if you kill free speech, everything else goes. Yes, hiding intel about UFOs from us is a form of censorship. But if you get too noisy about it, you may be silenced. Like your friend, the Dalai Lama, not getting his visa to attend your birthday party.

Censorship is bigger than just fact-checkers blocking your posts on Facebook. Now we hear that the government has had some level of control or influence over social media sites like Twitter and Facebook as well. This was first revealed by the "Twitter files" after Elon Musk took it over. Even the journalists whom he gave access to expose these cases were blocked. Only after Donald Trump's reelection, the fact-checkers were dismissed by Facebook, and admissions were made about the intensity of Democratic Party interference.

Tucker Carlson has gone so far as to lament that news networks spend little or no time talking about important issues. They jam programming with unimportant topics, which is a soft form of censorship. So instead of just accepting an offer from another network after his sacking by Fox News, he decided to forget networks and move to a new medium—the public forum. We don't just need to look at the content, although there are issues there; we need to look at the process. That is the pathway to truth.

On the morning that Fox News fired Tucker Carlson, he had interviewed the police chief at the Capitol building on January 6, 2021. His name is Steven Sund, and his perspective is baffling. Without going into the content and what it implies, that interview was not aired—not until months later, when Tucker Carlson invited him to repeat the interview on his new X channel. The public has a right to know, and there are clearly efforts in the mainstream media to block the truth from getting out. They prefer the death of truth to being outfoxed, pun intended.

Father Desmond, your question could point to the selective topics chosen by news networks. They have a lot of power. Or it could be that they are intentionally lying by omission. Not lying by commission, by broadcasting lies, but just by playing a ball-possession strategy. As your Anglican prayer book says, it is a sin to do things that we ought not to have done, as well as not to do things that we ought to have done. You don't want people to end up saying, "We were lied to." But silence about any issue that affects the public is also a sin.

India's Guest Panelist: Mohandas Gandhi
Is there no place for censorship at all? The Defiance Campaign that I organized in India was nonviolent but very visible in the media, including in the British media. It caused a significant shift in public opinion. I am sure that some efforts were made to minimize media coverage in Britain of what was happening in India. But truth always has a way of leaking out. We all know that the media can mislead people as well. It can become a propaganda tool in the hands of dictators. What about age-based censorship? You can impose a minimum age for movie viewers or a call for parental guidance. On cell phones, you can set "parental consent" to protect children. To the middle challenger, I ask: Can't censorship sometimes protect people?

Challenger in the Middle
Yes, it can be useful. Free speech is a good thing, but it needs boundaries. For example, we have to limit hate speech. Xenophobic or racial outbursts are just unacceptable. Using the word *nigger* in the USA or *kaffir* in South Africa are out of bounds. In the arena of politics, red lines should also be marked for debate. For example, the New York City judge hearing the case brought against Donald Trump by Stormy Daniels banned Trump from commenting on this court case on Truth Social, his social media platform. Yes, he is limiting free speech, but as another election cycle was looming, the judge did not want disproportionate political pressure brought onto the judiciary by the leading contender for one party's nomination. Not to mention the campaign itself, which might be concurrent with the court case, so it was somehow ironic when the sentencing was an unconditional discharge on all 34 counts. The "convicted felon" is free to go—and to appeal.

There has to be some level of anti-disinformation. "Fake news" is out there. In principle, the government is supposed to be the referee. But too often, we find it out there on the playing field.

Some people like the Wikileaks gang believe that keeping intelligence secrets from the public is actually one form of spreading fake news. Interestingly, these reviled whistleblowers arise at periodic military moments. Many people see their leaks as betrayal, not as championing the First Amendment. Military commanders always have to assess the damage, on the front lines of battle, of their intelligence leaks.

One problem is coherence. In both India and South Africa, the treatments of choice for COVID-19 were ivermectin and hydroxychloroquine. These same drugs were scoffed at in Britain and North America. Scientists did studies in the Global South that proved their efficacy. In the north, scientists laughed at these meds, saying, "Well, at least they won't get worms or malaria."

Censorship ran both ways in the same pandemic! While masking had little effect as a preventative measure, it did diminish people's oxygen intake and has had terrible environmental side effects. We will be cleaning up masks from parks, rivers, and oceans for decades to come. One thing they did do was to make the government authority very visible. Fact-checkers censored anti-maskers; they were refused entry to shops and public transport and tormented by members of their own families. At the same time, the "control experiment" in Sweden suggests that none of these extreme measures made any significant difference at the end of the day. Social distancing and contact-tracing were enough.

My point is that while censorship can be vilified when it becomes regrettably excessive, it does serve some purpose.

North America's Guest Panelist: George Washington
I led the American Revolution in 1776. I served as the first president starting in 1789. Between these two dates, there was a transitional period that involved negotiating terms with the British, creating boundaries, and drafting the first ten constitutional amendments, comprising our Bill of Rights. The First Amendment, along with nine others, was adopted in 1791, during my presidency. So I am a great believer in freedom of speech. Our revolution could not have been possible without it. So, I am not impressed with what the challenger in the middle has to say.

I address my question to the challenger on the right. Here it is: Are there any exceptions? Is freedom of speech for all people regardless of their age, gender, color, or creed?

Challenger on the Right

Yes, sir. No exceptions. Otherwise, we end up living in a nanny state. The right to freedom of expression still applies to liars and perverts. They have a right to speak out.

However, this should happen in an open forum. If they speak from a leftist platform about pro-choice, or from an alt-right platform about the right to bear arms, they are not seeking truth. They are lobbying. They are biased. It is propaganda. We need to be able to converse with one another like adults and to stop yelling at those who disagree with us and riding our hobbyhorses.

That's what has happened to the news networks. If you are really seeking the truth, these days you have to consult both Breitbart and CNN, Townhall and the *New York Times*, Conservative Brief and *The Atlantic*. You have to weigh up the balance of probabilities, like a judge listening to two sides of a case story. After some time, you develop tools for your truth toolkit. You look for hard facts. You listen to eyewitnesses more than op-ed comments. You shed your skepticism for whistleblowers and give their truth bombs due consideration. You check if one platform is incoherent—not agreeing with itself. In other words, you have to hone your process skills as much as internalize the content.

If Mother Eve had taken more time to think through what the tempter was telling her, she might have seen that she was being hoodwinked. After a while, you develop this dialectical ingenuity. You scan the legacy media, then check out a few alt-right sites, and you find a via media—a middle of the road, a diplomacy par excellence. No platform has a monopoly on truth. They are all but versions of it.

The post-election ratings in 2025 make it clear that no one has cornered the market on truth. It exists in its own right. Relativism can bend it, but it won't break. It is resistant and will endure. Yes, it wanders a bit like the magnetic north pole, over time. But the light shines in the darkness, and the darkness has never put it out.

We need more truth seekers and fewer cheerleaders for a partisan political persuasion. If you are bullied, maligned, and intimidated, you are not engaging truth-seekers—you are encountering ideology peddlers. T. S. Eliot wrote: "Most of the trouble in the world is caused by people wanting to be important." Everyone wants to be right. The reductio ad absurdum of this approach leads to the death of truth.

Truth doesn't mind being questioned. A lie does. Speaking about censorship and propaganda, Tucker Carlson opined in a speech: "No one is punished for lying; people are only punished for telling the truth." There's another tip on how to tell the truth from a lie. Transparency is a key to unlock the truth. Don't let it die in the dark. Let it out into the light.

Moderator

Thank you to our guest panelists and the articulate challengers. Now, will the real Truth about censorship please stand out?

RIOTS

Moderator

Here we are with episode three of *Telling the Truth*. Our topic is riots.

According to the World Economic Forum, one of the three biggest problems in today's world is polarization. This is evident to anyone who thinks globally. Some would say that the WEF's ambition of globalism is failing. It is giving rise to a new isolationism and "cold war." This starts with culture wars and is moving onto the battlefield. Russia does not want Western decadence on its doorstep. Ugandan and Nigerian church leaders have disaffiliated from the Anglican Archbishop of Canterbury, saying he is apostate. Some sports heroes missed international competitions because they refused to be vaccinated for COVID-19.

Wherever you go, there are riots. The BLM riots in America in 2020 caused havoc far and wide across North America and beyond. The blowout in South Africa in mid-2021, following Jacob Zuma's incarceration, was widely regarded as an insurrection. In France, people have taken to the streets for different reasons. The yellow jackets were mostly nonviolent, but other outbreaks have involved massive looting and burning. And then came pro-Palestinian riots and campouts far and wide. The global intifada.

Was the fire in Notre Dame Cathedral arson? Was the fire in South Africa's House of Parliament arson? Was the January 6 march on the Capitol building in Washington a riot or an insurrection? One party thinks that it was treason, but it is accused of playing a blame game to weaken its opponent's chance at staging a comeback. How can we get to the truth behind all the polemics?

We welcome back our panel on macro issues, composed of four panelists representing North America, Britain, South Africa, and India. These are major English-speaking markets where we hope that our new version of *To Tell the Truth* is well received.

Our three challengers only appear as silhouettes, but they are ready to speak about riots. Together, here as a team—moderator, panelists, and challengers—we are trying to get to the truth because we all share the belief that the truth will set us free. To paraphrase the familiar dictum, "No justice, no peace," I say: "No truth, no freedom."

So it is Desmond Tutu's turn to start. What say you, Archbishop emeritus?

South Africa's Guest Panelist: Desmond Tutu

Thank you, esteemed moderator. I chaired the Truth and Reconciliation Commission in South Africa. The logic was simple: national reconciliation could only take place if we could first extract the truth from evidence, witnesses, and due process. Then, in principle, amnesty would be offered in exchange for honesty. So I salute your effort to seek out the truth. It is commendable.

Elections in South Africa take place every five years. In the USA, they are every four years. These two different cycles only connect every twenty years. So it is a useful exercise, especially for first-time voters, to rejig *To Tell the Truth* in a way that allows for some convergence. More people voted in elections worldwide in 2024 than in any previous year in history. Elections are a good time to reflect on what is true and what isn't. And to heed our warning about the death of truth.

I direct my question to the challenger in the middle. When is a protest no longer legitimate? When do protesters take it too far and step out of democratic bounds?

Challenger in the Middle

This is an important question. In general, I think the answer is simple—violence is undemocratic. But that means that you have to define violence. As you well know, South Africa has a culture of "service delivery protests." These can and do get violent, or at least dangerous, at times, but not always. Sometimes the mob gets out of control and burns vehicles or a school or a public library. Such action cannot be condoned as a legitimate protest. Sure, it is very graphic on the news, but that is short-lived.

Of course, the police are outnumbered, but they are also trained and equipped. It was a sad day in Ficksburg in 2014 when law enforcement overreacted and shot an activist and organizer of the protest march, Andries Tatane. God rest his soul. Police overreach is not uncommon in South Africa.

One thing protesters often do in South Africa is carry stones or rocks out onto the streets. This interrupts the flow of police vehicles used for crowd control. For a few moments, the people govern, taking back ownership of the streets. This is not violent, although it may be dangerous to anyone driving.

Another instance of police overreach was when George Floyd died. This violent act of policing, an ironic term that is very well-known in South Africa, triggered months of unrest. Rioting spread from city to city across the USA with the theme "I can't breathe." But only after it had blown sky high in Minneapolis. This raises another concern about legitimacy. On both sides of the spectrum, some people know how to stir things up and how to incite violence. Some say that such agents infiltrated the "mother of all BLM riots" in Minneapolis. They came in from other states and cities for that purpose. Then they helped to spread the protests to other cities and other countries. This is not a spontaneous protest; it is rabble-rousing. It loses its legitimacy.

On the other hand, most of the people protesting were not rioting, and the people's right to express their frustration and anger is entirely democratic. In the USA, it is a First Amendment right. The BLM riots in other countries, when they spread that far, were probably more legitimate and peaceful. This reflects that there was a genuine surge of protest that erupted in the wake of George Floyd's death. But that attracted an undemocratic element, which piggybacked on legitimate protest.

I cannot finish answering you, Father Desmond, without mentioning the legendary massacre at Sharpeville in 1960. It was South Africa's version of America's Boston Tea Party. Violence is not a legitimate response on the part of law enforcement, either, when they shoot live rounds into a crowd. That is totally undemocratic and way out of bounds. To shoot dozens of youths in cold blood shed more infamy on the oppressors and their regime than it did on the protesters and their aspirations. Suddenly, the police became the villains, and the rioters took the high moral ground. They became heroes. That was not a civilized way to contain a protest.

India's Guest Panelist: Mohandas Gandhi

Fascinating! I could not agree more that violence is never justified or right on either side. In fact, nonviolence is the strongest weapon we have ever had to protest. Even the term *freedom fighter* is an oxymoron to me. You can stand up peaceably to oppression, as we stood up to the British military in India. The media recorded man after man standing up to the arrogant British soldiers, only to be whacked down until the nonviolent wounded protesters were piling up sky high. This had a deeply troubling effect on the British public, seeing photos of it in the newspapers. The back-pressure rose to the point that they could see that the end of colonialism was inevitable. For perpetuating their rule in India was being done in a way that was inconsistent with their values. Public opinion turned against the British military when it was exposed for beating up peaceful protesters.

If we follow "an eye for an eye and a tooth for a tooth," then the whole world will end up blind and toothless!

So let me direct my question about riots to the challenger on the right: Is it necessary for those advocating a cause to train cadres to infiltrate crowds and turn them into mobs? Can this reality be justified?

Challenger on the Right
Let me use the January 6, 2021, riot in the Capitol building in Washington as a case study. Two accounts of what happened that day exist, but ultimately, there can only be one truth.

One version of events is that it was basically entrapment. The shakers and movers intentionally did not beef up security, even when Capitol police chief Steven Sund begged for backup. They even deployed dozens of "agents"— infiltrators, rabble-rousers, agitators, provocateurs, instigators—to work the crowds into a frenzy that was meant to bring their opponents into disrepute. These are simply referred to as FBI "assets." This is a confirmed fact.

It is said that a mob has the IQ of the dumbest person in it. Otherwise known as "dumbing down." When a "crowd" or a "march" becomes a "mob," then there is trouble. This is how the religious leaders who hated Jesus managed to turn public opinion against him. Only days before, he had entered Jerusalem riding on a donkey, greeted with acclaim and adulation. This clearly disturbed the religious elite, who knew that at festivals like Passover, the city would be teeming with pilgrims. This worried the Roman security forces as well, in terms of crowd control. They had dealt with insurrections before. The most recent had been led by Barabbas, who was behind bars.

The religious elite knew how to work the crowds. They spread rumors and gossip. They warned people of the consequences if Jesus was not brought to his knees. So there is nothing new about working the crowds. But it can be taken too far. The Jewish council, the Sanhedrin, met at night, which contravened its own rules. It did not have the power to approve the death penalty; only the Roman procurator could do that. So they took Jesus to see Pontius Pilate, inflating the allegations of heresy to treason against Rome. Pilate washed his hands in a bowl, publicly symbolizing that he was not convinced of these charges. But the religious elite had the mob in a frenzy. To calm things down, Pilate asked them who they wanted as a gesture of Roman solidarity— Barabbas or Jesus? Once again, the instigators agitated, and the people called for Barabbas. Pilate had little wiggle-room left. His wife, Claudia, was in the background, warning him about her dreams the night before. So he asked the mob what to do with Jesus. Their manipulated response was "Crucify him!"

My only purpose in retelling this familiar story is to concur with you, sir. Mob manipulation is a reality. Walkie-talkies, smartphones, and social media make this maneuvering more effective than ever. So people who came to attend a legitimate protest march on January 6, 2021, ended up being portrayed as "insurrectionists." There may have been alt-right agitators there as well. But we now know there were FBI "assets" deployed with a sinister mission. Why?

Those who wonder about the historicity of these events should bear in mind how the J6 Committee rigged its composition, tampered with its witnesses, and then shredded all its paper trail, which was an illegal act of violence. Needless to say, the Roman and Jewish leaders wanted to erase what they did, and it was only the Christian community that recorded the truth. This explains a lot.

The other narrative is that it was truly an insurrection. This was concluded by the Bent Congressional investigation, which covered its tracks due to the loss of control of Congress. Beware of investigators who cause all their backup records to disappear! So in pursuit of the real truth, a second investigation was launched after Congress changed hands from one party to another. Ostensibly, the conclusions of the first committee were based on thirty thousand hours of videotapes taken by security cameras throughout the Capitol building. When these tapes passed into the hands of the opposite party after they took over Congress, some inaccuracies were reported—starting with the fact that there were really forty thousand hours of tapes, much more than originally stated. The Speaker of the House allowed access to these tapes to Tucker Carlson, who cherry-picked some footage to show on his popular news hour. This was shocking because the videos that he chose to broadcast contained a totally different version of the truth. It looked more like tourism, people walking around gawking at all the patrimony, and the security cameras captured no visible signs of insurrection in those clips.

This starts to make it look like there can be two truths. But I think that there are learning points here—that infiltrators and rabble-rousers can only influence some people in their immediate vicinity. This crowd was way too big. Maybe at certain moments or in certain "hot spots," the temperature rose to the boiling point? But on the whole, overall, the protest was just a rebuke. Voters genuinely believed that victory had been hijacked. They believed that flawed election results could be turned over by due process. So they went out to protest, to send a strong message of disapproval. As George Carlin once wrote: "Never underestimate the power of stupid people in large groups."

Activists organizing protest marches should go around emphasizing the need for nonviolence among the protestors. I believe that I am preaching to the converted in answering your question this way, sir. You saw many riots during the Quit India Campaign, and later during the preparations for Partition. I'm sure you are aware that mobs can be incited. I also think that you know this has been going on forever, and there is a high probability that by ignoring Steven Sund's pleas to beef up security and by deploying FBI "assets" to stir it up, the stage was set to frame the opposition and bring them into disrepute. They were seen in a bad light. But it was a setup. The fact that Tucker Carlson's original interview with the Capitol police chief was never aired makes it even more suspicious. Often, the cover-up is worse than the crime.

Is there a way to sift the chaff from the grain? To let the honest protesters off with presidential pardons, while keeping those who damaged the Capitol in jail? Or is that favoritism? Was there any legitimacy to the police shooting Ashli Babbitt?

North America's Guest Panelist: George Washington
This reminds me so much of the Boston Tea Party! That was a legitimate British legislation allowed one concessionist to sell tea cheaper than merchants . Taxpayers in Boston strongly opposed this as imposed control, even tyranny. public protest in December 1773, staged by the Sons of Liberty in Massachusetts. In response, some of them dressed up as indigenous people and destroyed an entire shipment of tea being imported by the East India Company.

The demonstrators boarded the ships and threw the chests of tea into Boston Harbor. The British government considered this protest an act of treason and responded harshly. This escalated into the American Revolution. But there was already a strong resistance movement throughout the British colonies in America. They took exception to being taxed by a parliament they did not elect. They wanted their affairs to be governed only by their own elected representatives and not by a faraway parliament in which they had no voice.

Let me ask the challenger on the left: Are you using riots in a similar way to the Sons of Liberty? Are you once again playing a game of treason and insurrection?

Challenger on the Left
This has long been debated on the left. Idealists like Karl Marx believed that revolution would happen spontaneously. At the same time, pragmatists like Vladimir Lenin did not want to leave anything to chance or wait around for the optimal conditions to arrive. Leninism was brutal and certainly deployed mob instigators in the Bolshevik Revolution. One such 1920s leader in communist Russia was Vyacheslav Molotov. He is remembered by the ubiquitous tool for mob protest that emerged around this time—the Molotov cocktail.

The blend of these two views came to be known as Marxism-Leninism" and it moved beyond the expectation of spontaneous revolution to a more pragmatic approach: inducing revolution. Yes, this "inducing" often involved violence, not unlike the Boston Tea Party, which triggered the American Revolution.

In the French Revolution, instigators were used to sway the mobs. The term *mob mentality* arose from this historic event. The population was rising, and urbanization was creating high-density areas. Demagogues giving speeches is one highly visible way of revving up emotions. On the other hand, there is nothing wrong with oratory per se. Dr. Martin Luther King's "I Have a Dream" speech is a good example of nonviolent oratory. But from the French Revolution on, inducing revolution was recognized as another strategy, and mobs could be infiltrated by agents trained to fire them up, including FBI "assets."

This has adapted to media and social media. The news media have moved into the new era of infotainment. News is no longer a five-minute broadcast on the hour, every hour. Whole channels and networks are now dedicated to 24/7 news. The mix of news and comment has been diluted to the point that it is now prone to propagandists. No longer will a newspaper openly endorse a certain candidate in one particular election, explaining why in its editorial pages. News channels have become ideological. The *New York Times*, *The Atlantic*, the *Washington Post*, and CNN are now outlets of left-leaning propaganda. They are no longer the mainline media; they lean left. They peddle Democratic Party policies.

This explains why Elon Musk bought Twitter and turned it into a free-speech platform instead—now called X. He may buy a news network next. The leftist bias of the moderators was evident during the debate between Donald Trump and Kamala Harris.

Furthermore, the left has been successful in cornering platforms on social media. After Elon Musk took over Twitter, he was able to expose the extent to which the government had infiltrated and captured that platform. The left is clearly out to capture platforms to help popularize its progressive agenda. It has come to light that the day the Hunter Biden laptop story broke, the FBI told Twitter that it was real. They already knew about the Biden family's indiscretions. But they did not share that same intel with Facebook. Silence becomes a spin doctor, just like keeping the discovery of Biden's collection of classified documents from public view until after the runoff Senate election in Georgia between Warnock and Walker. That race was so close that it could easily have gone the other way if the truth had not been smothered. The excuse was that they didn't want to trigger more unrest.

There is a fine line between treason and insurrection on the one hand, and democratic due process on the other. Have we crossed that line? I will be the first to admit that the BLM riots in 2020 were very useful to our cause. George Floyd is one of our folk heroes. Not because he wasn't a criminal, but because his death illuminated that violence is so often used against us. So we responded with marching, looting, and burning. Empathy for our cause was based on the logic that law enforcement is equally violent. Truth can be bent without being broken.

We are now being accused of weaponizing some state agencies. This sounds a bit like treason and insurrection, doesn't it? The left has been accused of having a two-tier justice system—one that selectively favors one political party over another. That could be the cause of our undoing. That is, if the people still want to govern. It seems that American voters have seen through the gambit of a "vanguard party" in the grand Marxist tradition and decided to reject the left and welcome back the alt-right. Could the same be on the horizon for Germany, France, and Britain?

Britain's Guest Panelist: Malcolm Muggeridge
My, my. Challenger on the left, thank you for being so frank. I liked your answer. So I am going to continue the dialogue with you.

I worked in the media for many decades. I was cynical and tried to send up any person or policy I was writing about. I was the editor of *Punch*, and that magazine's name says it all. Only later in my life did I come full circle to rediscover faith. It was quite unexpected, and it burned all the cynicism out of me. So I want you to answer a fundamental question, as I see it. I am not asking who has the answer, who has the truth. I am rather asking you to say more about finding the truth. In a world of propaganda, how can we tell the difference between good riots and bad riots? When should we march? When should we stay home?

Challenger on the Left
As you know, there are leftists and then there are leftists …. In your time, there were the Soviets and also the Euro-communists. A few decades earlier, Tommy Douglas was the premier of Saskatchewan in Canada. He ran the first democratic socialist party in North America, starting in 1944. Its policies set the gold standard for public policy in Canada. It was called the CCF. That really stood for Co-operative Commonwealth Federation because it promoted co-op models, from agriculture to banking. Thus, its critics dubbed the CCF: "Communize Canada through Fear." Tommy Douglas responded that it rather stood for "Children Come First".

His brand of socialism was compared to the concurrent rise of the National Socialists in Germany, i.e., Nazis, and to the Soviet version of communism.

But he stood his ground, and since then, democratic socialism has become a global force.

As a teenager, Tommy Douglas watched a union march in downtown Winnipeg. The police opened fire using live rounds. Two protesters died. Later in life, he became a Baptist minister. Workers at a mine in his area were engaged in a strike. He went to help them with food and blankets, and once again observed police brutality. Three miners were killed. Soon after this, he left the Christian ministry and joined the CCF. He wanted to speak truth to power.

As a pastor, he knew the truth. Once in power, he became very influential. Many Canadians consider him to be the greatest compatriot ever. He found violence abhorrent. Yet I admit that other leftists see violence and armed struggle as inevitable. They think that the end justifies the means. So some can and do protest and march peacefully, in the footsteps of Martin Luther King. Others, I admit, loot and burn. We do not see eye to eye on this, even though we agree that socialism has more to offer people than capitalism.

If you march, keep it nonviolent and peaceful. If you debate, don't yell—let's stick to adult conversation and mutual respect. If you are a public speaker, take the high road like Nelson Mandela and MLK. If you are an activist or a labor organizer, cajole people to act peacefully. South African toyi-toying is OK, but burning police vans and looting shops is a no-no. It brings legitimate protest into disrepute.

The yellow jacket marches in France gained a lot of momentum, whereas the violence of the riots in the wake of Nahel Merzouk's shooting did more harm than good to the cause they tried to champion. You can be a radical dissenter without being a revolutionary. One is true to form; the other is an impostor. This in itself has a lot to say about the nature of truth.

Speaking of France, the solidarity of "I am Charlie" after the attack on *Charlie Hebdo* magazine is another honorable way to rebuke violence. When Hitler invaded Norway, he ordered all Jews to wear black armbands. The next morning, the King of Norway was observed riding his horse wearing a black armband. Silent solidarity and in-your-face mutuality are both effective ways to protest.

Moderator
Thank you to our guest panelists and the articulate challengers. Now, will the real Truth about riots please stand out?

GOVERNMENT OVERREACH

Moderator

Here we are with episode four of *Telling the Truth*. Our topic today is government overreach. We all remember Ronald Reagan saying that the nine most terrifying words in the English language are: "I'm from the government and I'm here to help you." Many countries are moving toward a Nanny State with cradle-to-grave protection for citizens. This means big government.

And now we don't just have municipal, provincial and national levels of government, but we have regional (e.g., European Union) and multilateral as well (i.e., United Nations). This means that tax rates are rising.

One wry observer expressed it this way: "Of course you're allowed to ask questions. Here is the list of approved questions .... You're absolutely free to research and investigate for yourself. Here are the approved sources .... We're not trying to stifle thought! We want you to learn everything you can as you reach the approved conclusions." So if the president goes senile and is secretly replaced by his support team with an autopen, or a candidate is chosen without primaries, who are we to question it? What about the recent prorogation of Canadian parliament followed by a new minority government going to work without bringing down a budget? These all seem like government overreach.

Our macroseries panel is still with us. It is the Indian panelist's turn to lead the questioning. Out of this exchange, we hope that we not only unpack the topic but also learn how to tell the truth from a lie. Without this ability, we are doomed to live in a post-truth world. Thank you for joining us on Time-Zoom, Mr. Gandhi. Go ahead!

India's Guest Panelist: Mohandas Gandhi

I am pleased to be part of this monumental exercise, Moderator. Those of us who struggled against colonialism in the Quit India Movement know only too well about government overreach, as you call it today. We never used that phrase, but we didn't like rulers being imposed on us. We wanted to elect our leaders. We had a right to self-determination, but even Partition was forced on us. I believed that both Hindus and Muslims were Indians, so I opposed Partition. It was a two-state solution. But it went ahead.

I called people to "do or die." This was a clarion call to civil disobedience. I never promoted violence. We should be ready to die for our cause, but we should never kill for it.

So my question is this: When does the government cross a red line today? By what criteria do you know when there is overreach? I would like to hear from the challenger on the right because, in principle, the left embraces big government, while the right disapproves of it.

Challenger on the Right

Your people were so courageous when they faced British brutality. This is what eventually turned public opinion around in Britain—watching news clips of ordinary Indians dressed in white being beaten and knocked down by the military of the British Raj. This was grossly unjust, even according to British values, but it was also unsustainable. The numbers were on your side, sir, not on the side of the imperialists. In a word, it was bullying. Look for signs of repression to know when overreach has risen to undemocratic proportions.

Also, imperialism meant that colonies in that empire were ruled by decree, not by an elected parliament. Sure, some local consultative mechanisms were put in place, but these were toothless. The power was in the imperial chain of command.

This kind of thing reached legendary proportions in South Africa during apartheid. Voting was limited to the white minority. The black majority was sequestered into homelands. They were *given* self-rule in those Bantustans. Self-rule was not self-determination. What blacks wanted was an integrated state with free and fair elections—one parliament for all. Not to be ruled by decree, backed up by military force from another continent. Or in the case of South Africa, by Afrikaner brutality.

Speaking of South Africa, we recently lived through a decade under Jacob Zuma when "state capture" corrupted democracy. Zuma and his cronies deployed so many sycophants in key state institutions and enterprises that he became a functional despot. It was called despotic democracy—an ironic term. Opposition parties and civil society worked tirelessly to expose and reverse this capture of the state. But it left a legacy. Zuma should still be in jail for what he did, but his cronies are embedded in the ruling party. In true Marxist fashion, the ruling party in South Africa is more powerful than its government. It is a vanguard party. So Zuma got early parole, which was challenged in the courts by the opposition. Ultimately, the Constitutional Court ruled that the steps taken to grant him early parole were unlawful, so he should go back to jail. The next day, he got on a plane to Russia, ostensibly for health reasons.

While he was convalescing in Russia, President Ramaphosa visited Moscow, ostensibly on a peacemaking effort to stop the war in Ukraine. It seems that there may have been some internal peacemaking going on out of sight, as well. Soon after, Jacob Zuma returned to South Africa and was jailed for two hours! That same day, the president announced a blanket pardon that freed over nine thousand prisoners serving time for nonviolent crimes. It was a clever way of letting Jacob Zuma off the hook, indirectly, for he was one of them. What lengths the elite comrades will go to help one another!

In the USA, they use a different term for state capture: "weaponization" of state agencies by the government. This is obviously overreach. When the Department of Justice, prosecutors, the Federal Bureau of Investigation, and the police show favoritism, these agencies have been weaponized. That is government overreach par excellence. Political opponents become targets of retributive litigation. Those are the shenanigans of a banana republic. It's pure chicanery. Meanwhile, the same favoritism protects the guilty elite.

I know that opposing unjust, top-down authoritarianism is in your bones, sir. That is why you are called "Mahatma."

North America's Guest Panelist: George Washington
At the root of the American Revolution was an abiding disgust with government overreach. Britain's colonies in America were overtaxed, and a parliament imposed that taxation on another continent. This got out of control.

So we revolted. We didn't agonize; we organized! So I have a question for the challenger on the left. Some of the heaviest tax burdens anywhere are in socialist countries. Because that system believes in a planned economy. Thus, the government has a much larger role to play than in a free market economy. Here's my question—isn't that just institutionalizing government overreach?

Challenger on the Left
Certainly, we believe in state intervention in the economy. For example, we prefer a state bank to the multitude of credit unions that you find in a free market economy. I can see why you regard this as government overreach, coming from your background of throwing off the burden of colonial taxes imposed on you by essentially a foreign government.

But the point of socialism is not that we overreach, but that we enlarge the boundaries. We adopt policies that make the space that the government reaches into much larger. This is a social contract, not an imposition.

A classic example is Medicare, which was first piloted in the province of Saskatchewan in Canada in 1962. Doctors left the province in droves, convinced that it would perpetually undermine the quality of medical care. But instead, it has become the model for health care across Canada. State health care is almost synonymous now with being a Canadian. And if you go to other countries like Britain and Sweden, you find similar health-care systems. This means that the boundaries have been enlarged, not that the government

111

is overreaching. How sustainable this is, we are still debating many decades later.

However, we do still hear complaints about "judicial overreach," where a court may make a very heavy ruling. We also hear of police brutality—another touchstone of government overreach. Both of these can and do happen in the enlarged space of socialist settings, assuming that the socialist state is democratic. Where socialism is despotic, you are entering Nazi territory. The price you pay for enlarged social benefits is the loss of your civil liberties. Totalitarian socialist states are reputed for their secret police and even reeducation camps.

As a leftist, I am ashamed of the way that the Chinese Communist Party has treated the Tibetans and Uighurs. Socialism can be totalitarian, but it can also be democratic.

Britain's Guest Panelist: Malcolm Muggeridge
One of my favorite proverbs is from India: "A village is fit to live in only when there is a moneylender from whom to borrow at need, a physician to treat an illness, a priest to minister to the soul, and a stream that does not dry up in summer." So putting aside the debate over state banks versus credit unions, about Medicare over a privatized health-care system, and state service provision of water, roads, and security, I think there is also a spiritual aspect to this topic.

Let me pose my question to the challenger in the middle. Aside from our physical and economic realities, is the state meddling in church affairs? Or worse yet, is the state in favor of secularization and intentionally diminishing the role of religion?

Challenger in the Middle
There is plenty of evidence in North America that left-leaning regimes are against religion—for example, the way the FBI, weaponized by the Biden administration, went after Roman Catholics. RCs are traditionally pro-life, and suddenly this meant that they were "a basket of deplorables."

In Britain, the Church of England, which is a state church, has basically adopted the politically correct stance on same-sex marriage. This has caused its African bishops in Uganda and Nigeria, where there are far more Anglicans now than the dwindling attendance in Britain, to challenge the authority of the archbishop of Canterbury. They call his views unbiblical and even heretical. This could be leading toward a definitive schism, like the one unfolding in the United Methodist Church in the USA. About a quarter of all UMC congregations, almost 7,000 in all congregations have disaffiliated with the UMC, although not all individuals in those congregations wanted to disaffiliate. A new denomination has been formed called the Global Methodist Church, and its theology would line up, more or less, with the African Anglicans.

Ironically, Eastern Orthodox churches remain opposed to same-sex marriage, especially the Russian Orthodox Church, which regards it as anathema. Vladimir Putin, a staunch Russian Orthodox himself, gets his spiritual spark from the primate of that state church. There is a new "axis" of Russian Orthodoxy, Islam in the Middle East, and African Christians from Uganda to Nigeria that do not want WEF globalism or the United Nations, which worships human rights, to challenge their respective spiritualities. It is dividing the UN, which is no longer "united" at this deep level.

The Church of England originated as a via media between the radical Protestant reformers and the Roman Catholic Church. It prides itself on not being extremist at either pole, but not being irrelevant either. King Henry VIII nationalized the church. His daughter Queen Elizabeth I worked hard at keeping the Church of England from backsliding into Catholicism or sliding down the slippery slope into "Nonconformist" theology. She had to condemn her sister, Mary Queen of Scots, to death for refusing to recant Catholicism. That left Mary's son James I to succeed Elizabeth and to carry on the via media. He did this brilliantly in many ways. One strategy was organizing a single "authorized" translation of the Bible into English—the King James Version. His teams of translators included Nonconformist and Catholic scholars. He wanted one Bible for all. This was a huge effort on the part of the state to both keep up with the times, the Protestant Reformation, and yet not to lose the spiritual anchor going back to Roman times.

Unfortunately, the combined force of the United Nations, WEF-induced globalism, and left-leaning regimes has abandoned this wisdom of a via media. It has become a juggernaut, causing polarization and a backlash. Many are the people and nations who oppose the death of truth as we know it.

Perhaps the influence of Marxism is just too strong. Marx did not believe in God, and as a system, it is atheistic. Marx called religion "the opiate of the people." It is much harder to find common ground between atheists and monotheists than it was between radical reformers and Roman Catholics. At least they both believed in God! But there was still huge acrimony that had to be overcome. At this point in history, supernational authorities like the UN and WEF have already taken sides in the culture wars, with no monarchs left to champion a via media.

In North America, we are noticing today that Christians and church leaders are marginalized on school councils because left-leaning secular leaders despise them. And Muslim parents are joining Christian parents in speaking out against radical change! At least Muslims and Christians share a belief in God, and neither wants to see boys competing in girls' sports, males entering female washrooms, school curriculum content that offends both religions, and an imposed change of pronouns, inter alia.

Post-COVID church attendance has not rebounded to pre-COVID levels. Some still worship online. Others have fallen away. One can only wonder if this was an intentional strategy of the government's overreach inherent in mask mandates, lockdowns, and obligatory vaccination. The jury is still out on this, but possibly the WHO-led strategies were designed to diminish the influence of churches, which, on the whole, have been pro-life, skeptical about same-sex marriage, and generally supportive of populist political figures. When we see manipulation of the media, interference in social media, and weaponization of state agencies, it is not unthinkable that one of the purposes of COVID-induced government overreach was to weaken the church and to sideline those who opposed the left's sense of direction toward globalization.

While declining church attendance is happening mostly in the Western democracies, the church is growing fast in Africa and Latin America. In China, both Muslims and Christians are getting squeezed, now that the CCP has tamed Tibetan Buddhists. So it varies, but on the whole, the ideological left has been harder on religion and the church than the populist right has been.

The death of truth will shake civilizations. From the oracle of Delphi to Moses finding a burning bush that did not consume itself, the West has accepted revealed truth first as polytheists and later as monotheists. Out of Arabia has come Islam, also promoting revealed truth both in the East and the West. In the East, the polytheist Hindus also believe in revealed truth. We need to stand on guard. We need to get back to scripture reading, worship, prayer, and meditation. Revealed truth should be cherished.

South Africa's Guest Panelist: Desmond Tutu
Let me explore this topic a bit further. We are not here to blame the left or the right. We are here to seek the truth—and more especially, to recognize the truth in a world full of deception and propaganda. Deception is nothing new; it goes all the way back to the garden of Eden, when the father of lies seduced Mother Eve.

But when Lucifer fell out of heaven, I have heard that 30 percent of the angels fell with him. It was a collective force, so there are plenty of arch-demons and demons on the loose, along with evil spirits and unclean spirits and all. Ultimately, they are our enemy—more so than any particular religion or ideology.

So I want to pose a sharp question again to the challenger on the left. Is it true that leftists are on the attack against Christianity in particular, Christianity being the biggest world religion of all? Do we have to abandon faith and our love of God and his son, Jesus, to lean left?

Challenger on the Left

Father Desmond, you know that the truth is otherwise. Think of the greatest leaders of the African National Congress in South Africa—John Dube, Albert Luthuli, and Nelson Mandela. Of these, some were men of the cloth and others were avid churchgoers. What would South Africa be if it were not for Christian missionaries like Dr. Johannes van der Kemp, Janet Burnside-Soga, and Trevor Huddleston? I lament that of late, we have voted some rascals into leadership, who have brought our ruling party, once our liberation movement, into disrepute. They belong in the dustbin of history.

There are different degrees of socialism. The far left is atheistic and radical and will accept violence as a means to an end. The near left has religious motives for reform—I have mentioned Tommy Douglas, a Baptist minister in Canada who formed the first democratic socialist government in North America. Another man of the cloth was the Reverend Martin Luther King. He espoused and practiced nonviolence, but he wanted racial justice.

I am a leftist, but I also believe in God. I go to church. I love to praise and worship—not at home, online, but in the company of the saints. There is no substitute for worship in a sanctuary. It is the Bible that has taught me about justice and truth. Justice is the pathway to peace. Truth is the pathway to freedom. You can only find repression where there are deception and lies. Shine light into such settings, and it germinates the seeds of freedom. True freedom cannot exist in the dark, without transparency. Anyone who tells you that is deceiving you.

That is why I have problems with liberation theology, which tolerates violence.

You did it the right way, padre! You left the teaching profession when the government overreach imposed that all schools should operate in Afrikaans. You went into the ministry. You taught nonviolence. You were courageous. When asked about sanctions in a TV interview in Denmark, you spoke the truth. They would help, you said. Upon your return, the repressive, racist regime demanded that you recant your radical views. You refused. Your dear wife, Leah, said she would rather see you happy on Robben Island than miserable in your SACC office in Braamfontein. So you hung tough. They backed off. Truth is a very powerful force, and they knew that you spoke it. Putting you in jail would only have caused sanctions to be imposed sooner.

You set up the Institute for Contextual Theology, which produced the Kairos Document, which pulled the theological rug out from under apartheid. That led to apartheid being declared a heresy at the World Council of Churches conference in Ottawa in 1986. The Dutch Reformed Church had to repent, and Afrikaners were confronted at this deep spiritual level. At that moment, the truth came out of the shadows into the light, and the darkness of deception started to fade away.

Winston Churchill once said, "Three things cannot be long hidden—the sun, the moon, and the truth."

You brought out the truth, and that paved the way to freedom. We do not need to abandon faith and truth to lean left. But the challenge remains—not all leftists believe in God, and some follow extremist ideologies that are incompatible with other, more moderate socialist views—my views.

Carl Sagan made a pertinent observation: "One of the saddest lessons of history is this: If we've been bamboozled long enough, we tend to reject any evidence of the bamboozle. We're no longer interested in finding out the truth. The bamboozle has captured us. It's simply too painful to acknowledge, even to ourselves, that we've been taken. Once you give a charlatan power over you, you almost never get it back."

I salute you, Archbishop emeritus, for always seeking the truth and for never getting bamboozled.

Moderator
Once again, we want to thank our guest panelists and articulate challengers not just for their probing questions about this topic but also for their roles over the past four episodes. Next week, we move into a new series on political issues, with a whole new panel. Now, will the real Truth about government overreach please stand out?

14

POLITICAL ISSUES

ELECTION SWINDLES

Moderator

HELLO, AND WELCOME to the fifth episode of *Telling the Truth*. We are starting a new series this week on political issues. We have invited a new panel of four from the same settings: North America, Britain, South Africa, and India. The combined population of these places comes to over two billion people, roughly a quarter of humanity. Of course, each country has various cultures and languages, but the common denominator is that English is the lingua franca for them all.

Let's welcome our new panelists. Once again, they are engaging with us over the amazing new app, Time-Zoom. From North America is Abraham Lincoln, from Britain is Margaret Thatcher, from South Africa is Nelson Mandela, and from India is Jawaharlal Nehru. It's a pleasure to welcome you all! Each of you has a wealth of political acumen to probe into the five topics in this series. And as always, we welcome our three challengers.

Our topic today is election swindles. Democracy comes in many shapes and sizes. But wherever you go, best practice calls for free and fair elections. In settings where there is only one candidate on the ballot, despotism is wearing a mask.

Some classic episodes of swindled elections come to mind. Jonas Savimbi was sure that the 1992 elections in Angola were rigged. Lists of polling stations were given to the international election observers. When the results started to come in, even before the polls closed, twice as many polling stations in Huila province were heard from as appeared on the lists. This kind of thing always raises questions about accuracy and whether election results are valid.

Morgan Tsvangirai was swindled in the 2008 presidential elections in Zimbabwe. Mugabe must have realized late in the game that Tsvangirai could win. For during that election campaign, a Chinese ship was docked in Durban harbor. It contained a boatload of arms and munitions for Robert Mugabe. That's what tyrants do to stay in power. The Anglican bishop of Durban hastened to court and obtained an injunction to prevent the ship from unloading.

In solidarity, union workers in the port downed tools and refused to unload it. Mugabe's rescue strategy was blocked.

Eventually, the ship left Durban and sailed around the Cape to the port of Luanda in Angola, where President Dos Santos owed Mugabe a debt of gratitude for helping to finally hunt down Jonas Savimbi in 2002, ten years after the swindled elections of 1992, a decade of all-out war. In the battle of Huambo alone, probably fifty thousand lives were lost. In the subsequent battle of Cuito, perhaps another thirty thousand lives were lost. Dos Santos had oil revenues to keep his despotic democracy going. But Mugabe's economy was floundering. He could ill afford this donation of munitions to his socialist ally.

So much international pressure against Robert Mugabe arose from this that he ended up appointing Tsvangirai, the leader of the opposition, as his prime minister in a unity government! How's that for backpedaling?

George W. Bush did not win the popular vote in 2000, but he won the election due to the Electoral College system used in the USA. This happened again in 2016 when Donald Trump squeaked through, without winning the popular vote. Contested elections are happening all over the world, all the time. The losers inevitably feel swindled.

Sometimes, this is due to procedural flaws in vote-counting. But more often, it concerns "undue influence" of indirect and harder-to-pin-down forces. Kari Lake battled for years in the Arizona courts, contending that there were technical flaws in the vote-counting system. But the quest for truth goes deeper than that. It involves subjects like media interference, targeted censorship, and even brainwashing. As the saying goes, it gets complicated.

This is our first episode with our panel of four on political issues. They each pose probing questions to our three challengers. Together, we consider what is true election interference and hone our ability to sniff out the truth. It's North America's turn to start the questioning, so over to you, Mr. Lincoln.

North American Guest Panelist: Abraham Lincoln
Watching current affairs, I wonder at times whether the truth is hidden or whether people are hiding from the truth. There are more information and communication tools now than ever before, so hiding the truth should be getting harder and harder. But at the same time, the polarization of opinion seems to me to be a result of people hiding their heads in the sand. They don't want to know that their party lost an election. They don't want to know that the deficit will be a burden to their grandchildren. They seem to ignore reality. Mark Twain wrote: "It's easier to fool people than to convince them that they have been fooled."

So I ask the challenger in the middle: Why do people cling to their opinions and preferences, even when it seems irrational?

Challenger in the Middle
Thanks for asking. Let me share something that happened in 2016. The Denver *Guardian* ran a satirical article reporting the late Pope Francis had endorsed Donald Trump for the presidential election. Guess what? More than one million people believed it and shared this article on social media. It was humorously preposterous, but they wanted to believe it.

Speaking of which, Facebook has untold numbers of fake accounts held by fake organizations. These are there to mislead people, like with the Russian interference scandal. Fake social media and fake news can have a significant impact on voters.

If truth is getting alignment between belief and reality, then we do need some fact-checking. The problem is that fact-checkers become gatekeepers for a certain version of the truth. The COVID-19 crisis comes to mind. The anti-maskers and vaccine denialists are just as adamant today as they always were. Similarly, those who complied with government overreach throughout the crisis do not really want to read the science anymore. Plenty of scientific evidence has come to the fore that suggests that measures like masking and vaccines may have done more harm than good. Not to mention the "control experiment" in Sweden. People on both sides are dug in.

That same kind of obstinacy applies to election results. There are "denialists" who simply reject the outcome. They refuse to concede, and they call for endless recounts. But in a world where we are knee-deep in deception, it is good to be cautious and not to cave in without doing some calculations. Transparency is a virtue.

Many people found it hard to believe that Joe Biden could garner fifteen million more votes than Barack Obama. Never mind the win-lose vote count; they just found that to be disproportionate. Meanwhile, Trump felt swindled because he won more votes in 2020 than in 2016 but still lost the election. This was also perplexing.

In real life, no one likes to get swindled. It sucks when you get taken in by fraud.

One example of the close margins was the runoff election between Raphael Warnock and Herschel Walker in 2022. There were other candidates in the midterm elections, so neither of these two won an outright majority. Georgia's rules called for a runoff. It was to be run a month later, in early December. Only four months earlier, in August, the FBI had raided Donald Trump's residence with a search warrant and seized some classified documents that he held there. This brought his name—and his party—into disrepute only three months before the midterms. Was it election interference? It must have affected voters in Georgia to some degree. It certainly didn't help Herschel Walker.

Walker lost the runoff by a whisker. Donald Trump had endorsed him. Then a month later in January, news broke that President Joe Biden had kept classified documents that were spread out in several locations accessible to the public. Investigators had discovered this several weeks before the midterms— almost two months before the runoff in Georgia. But it was kept from the eyes of voters both for the midterms and for the subsequent runoff in Georgia. Walker was tainted by his association with Donald Trump, who was under investigation related to keeping classified documents after completing his term as president. Warnock should have been tainted too, but the truth was kept under wraps to protect him. To some people's way of thinking, this was swindling. The truth was kept in the dark. No truth, no freedom.

Britain's Guest Panelist: Margaret Thatcher
This line of questioning helps us understand the word *swindling*. It is different from the word *rigged*, which is more mechanical, whereas swindling has a broader semantic range.

As Dos Santos, Mugabe, and Biden were all left-leaning, let me pursue this with the challenger on the right. Sir, do you think that election results can also be tampered with—not by rigging per se, but by broader and deeper interference? And if this is true, how can voters be dislodged from their abiding loyalties, turf out the swindlers, and vote in some honest lawmakers and leaders?

Challenger on the Right
I have thought a lot about this topic. Let me tell you the parable of a Canadian football game. Canadian football tends to throw the ball rather than run it on the ground because it only has three downs, not four like American football.

One game took place on a very windy day. The teams were evenly matched, and not even the bookies could predict a winner. When they tossed the coin, the home team chose to play into the wind during the first half. They would keep this natural advantage for the second half. Every pass they made in the first half was into a gale-force wind. This shortened the passes and sometimes the ball hung up in the air for so long, chafing against the wind, that the runner would pass the practiced point of contact before the ball descended. When the away team took possession, its passes sailed like frisbees. Their receivers ran flat out, arms outstretched, and managed to catch the ball with their fingertips with tacklers a step behind them. It did not go well for the home team.

Then came halftime and a pause. Inexplicably, and unpredicted by the meteorologists, the wind switched from an offshore breeze to an onshore breeze, and it blew hard.

The home team arrived back on the field ready for a better second half. They expected the wind to be on their side, a huge advantage in the last half of the game. But alas, they were once again playing into the wind. They couldn't believe it. It was unprecedented. It was demoralizing. Their passing game never came right, and they lost the game in front of their home fans. They felt swindled.

I think you get the allegory. It is not always the fumbles and turnovers on the field of play that determine the direction that a game goes. There are bigger factors—the fans, the weather, injuries, and so on. You can play hard and expect to win, or at least to have a good shot at winning, free and fair elections. But sometimes you feel swindled because no matter how well you perform, there are bigger forces at play.

Incumbents always tend to have an advantage in elections. They tend to have better leverage with electoral commissions and voting mechanisms. That is where gerrymandering comes in—while in power, they can change boundaries in ways that give their party an advantage at the next election.

South Africa's Guest Panelist: Nelson Mandela
Martin Luther King Jr. stated that while he happened to be working against black oppression by whites, he would equally work against white oppression by blacks, if it ever came to that. I concur with his view of equality.

But in South Africa, we know that votes are bought with gifts of money. We know that dead people vote and that some people vote more than once, at different polling stations. Our rules are quite strict. Only South African citizens can vote—that seems right to me. However, in American elections, even illegal immigrants have been allowed to vote in some states.

Let me ask the challenger on the left: Do you have a problem with collusion between social media platforms that all lean in the direction of the same party, like a row of palm trees in the wind? If the tech barons are left-leaning and they collaborate, does that not tamper with elections?

Challenger on the Left
Well, I think that—like the question of violent protest—there are differences on the left between democratic socialists and Marxist-Leninists in this respect. Some want to play fair on a level playing field. But extremists feel that the end

justifies the means, so they may cheat or deceive in the belief that winning is everything.

I have been told that in some cultures, stealing is not regarded as a vice—if you can get away with it. Whistleblowers won't report you; that would be disloyal to the culture. It's called "snitching." This is why whistleblowers tend to be pariahs. The truth is, however, that crimes should be reported if you know about them. But that is predicated on a value system that holds honesty up as a virtue. If you belong to a culture where stealing is a virtue, like it was for Robin Hood, then if you can swindle elections and get away with it, you may be applauded. That seems to have happened among the tech barons.

You see, corruption needs to bounce back and forth between the public and private sectors to remain hidden. Civil servants need corrupt counterparts in the private sector whom they can award tender contracts to. Then those "tenderpreneurs" pay kickbacks to the government officials. In the private sector, corrupt businesspeople can hide in the underbrush, so to speak. They can create shell companies to handle payments flowing back to their counterparts in the public sector. This makes it hard to keep track of the subterfuge, but as Deep Throat kept saying during the Watergate scandal, "Follow the money."

This seems to be why the tech barons followed the FBI's advice on curtailing content. It wasn't money; it was misinformation. But the result was to influence voters. Thomas Paine said, "He who dares not offend cannot be honest."

Then along came Elon Musk, offering to buy Twitter. He almost backed out when he sniffed dishonesty—an inflated number of accounts—but he persisted, and soon after taking it over, the truth came out. The Twitter Files showed only the tip of the iceberg. There had been collusion, and it amounted to election interference.

Madiba, thinking back to the latter years of apartheid, under pressure to hold free and fair elections, the racist regime introduced what they called a "tricameral parliament." It was composed of a house for whites, a house for blacks, and a house for coloreds and Indians. Some politicians and voters played along with this charade; to stay in power, parties will undergo all sorts of contortions. They weren't just tampering with elections—they were tampering with democracy!

Ironically, we hear from both the extreme left and from the alt-right that democracy is in danger. It's a load of gaslighting, because they are blaming their opponents for exactly what they are doing! They both do it. And in doing so, they exacerbate the polarization. When you hear either side saying that they worry about democracy's future, beware. They are just trying to distract you from what they are doing themselves.

India's Guest Panelist: Jawaharlal Nehru
I want to return to the mention of gerrymandering. This is when a party in power changes or adjusts the borders of voting districts to improve its chances of winning.

Because political parties on both sides do this when they are in power, let me ask the challenger in the middle about it. Isn't it a form of swindling?

Challenger in the Middle
It happens in all democracies, no matter who is in power. It is a semilegal form of manipulating election outcomes. You may have heard of a recent example in the USA, in the state of Alabama. This example has the additional dimension of racism because it is not so much about keeping one party in power as about diminishing the impact of the black vote. Some call it racial gerrymandering.

While 25 percent of Alabama's population is black, six out of its seven congressional districts are largely white. This is disproportionate, but it shows that planners can distort borders to favor a particular group. This tends to corrupt the democratic principle that "the people shall govern." It is more a case of those in power perpetuating their hegemony.

Moderator
It's time again to thank our four guest panelists and three articulate challengers, who have given us a lot to consider. Now, will the real Truth about election swindles please stand out?

THE SEPARATION OF POWERS

Moderator
Here we are again with episode six of *Telling the Truth*.

Our four panelists are with us through the new app Time-Zoom. Welcome to them all from America, Britain, South Africa, and India.

Of course, our three challengers are on the left, in the middle, and on the right, facing the panel. Our stage lighting is such that the panelists only see three silhouettes. These challengers may be no-name brands, but they are very well informed and articulate.

This week's topic is the separation of powers, which is mission-critical to democracy. Normally, we speak of three branches of government—the legislature, the executive branch, and the judiciary. Of course, different countries have different variations contained in their respective constitutions, but democratic principles remain much the same.

At times, the lines between these three branches can get blurred. That is undemocratic and a violation of this sacred principle. So let's start this series by inviting Britain's guest panelist to start the questioning. Ladies first!

Britain's Guest Panelist: Margaret Thatcher
Thank you. I want to begin by asking the challenger on the left: If socialism is undemocratic, that is, despotic, then how can it strive for the classless ideal? Won't there always be an elite, and will that not fuel class discontent?

Challenger on the Left
Yes, you are right. In fact, you are far right, pun intended! Because at both ends of the spectrum, elites emerge. On the far right, we have dictators running totalitarian regimes where civil liberties are suspended and ordinary people live in fear and trepidation. Ironically, the same thing has happened historically on the left, when an elite, sometimes referred to as a "vanguard," is convinced that it knows better than anyone how to govern. So in fact, the people do not govern; they are governed harshly because there are no checks and balances.

This happened in the "lost decade" in South Africa when Jacob Zuma and his cronies became an untouchable elite. In fact, when former liberation movements graduate into a democratic environment, they often lose their way. It is a hard transition to make. In Marxist theory, the party is more important than the state. This vanguard party tends to dominate the executive branch, which sidelines the oversight role of parliament. The legislature becomes just a rubber stamp of what the despots are doing. And the judiciary sometimes cowers or is crippled by appointments to key positions that render it toothless. However, in some cases, a courageous judiciary—perhaps the Supreme Court—can stand up to a tyrant. Especially if a free press champions authentic democratic principles.

When Jacob Zuma was finally elected president, it was an unexpected comeback. A few years before, he had been relieved of his duties as deputy president by then-President Thabo Mbeki, only to defend himself in court successfully. But there was still a lingering corruption scandal around an arms deal from the time when Nelson Mandela was president that would just not go away. After Jacob Zuma got his revenge on Thabo Mbeki, a caretaker president was installed pending the next election. Then Jacob Zuma was elected president. But many felt that he was tainted and that he would try to stave off impending litigation with a power grab. That is precisely what happened.

A senior judge in the Western Cape province named John Hlophe spoke to some other judges who were handling that corruption case. He tried to influence them to back off or to go soft on Jacob Zuma, which created a backlash. The two judges he had spoken to in 2008 were scandalized. They reported it to then-Chief Justice Pius Langa. For fourteen years, their complaint wound its way through the corridors and committees of the judiciary until President Ramaphosa finally suspended it in 2022. Hlophe had crossed a red line.

Much of this period is what is now called the "lost decade." Jacob Zuma and his cronies tried to make it impossible for Zuma to be nailed for the arms deal corruption. Amazingly, Zuma's Stalingrad strategy delayed that case ad infinitum, earning him the nickname "the Artful Dodger."

Jacob Zuma's short stint in jail was not for that corruption. That case is still pending. In fact, it was for contempt of court because he refused to attend the hearings of the Zondo Commission into State Capture. This was a special investigation that had been set up because Jacob Zuma had so weakened the judiciary during his tenure. He closed the Scorpions (the anticorruption unit of the police) and appointed a sycophant at the National Prosecuting Authority, and judges like Hlophe were actively lobbying for him. Meanwhile, a Dominican priest filed a complaint with the Public Protector—an ombudswoman. She recommended that a commission be set up. Judge Raymond Zondo was chosen to lead that commission. Jacob Zuma defiantly refused to give evidence to Zondo, so he was sentenced to jail time for contempt.

Then, soon after the commission filed its final report, Judge Zondo was chosen to be the new Chief Justice. There was some hope that he would be able to enforce the recommendations made by his commission. However, litigating is different from investigating, and the NPA, even under new leadership, is having difficulty prosecuting perpetrators. Judge Zondo did expose them, but putting them on trial for crimes and misdemeanors entails a higher threshold. It requires proof beyond a reasonable doubt, not just the balance of probability.

In my view, socialism can be democratic. However, some on the far left will bend or break the rule of law to get their way. We agree to disagree about that.

If Jacob Zuma and his cronies were not held accountable, they would have demolished all the checks and balances, and then a ruling class would have emerged. This is what happened in the Soviet republics, where all people were considered equal—it's just that some were more equal than others! It's a kind of oligarchy.

During the reign of Leonid Brezhnev, one lane on the Moscow freeways was kept open just for him so that he did not have to waste time in traffic; he loved fast cars! All other comrades and compatriots had to share the remaining lanes. This is symbolic of how socialism functions when it is undemocratic. And yes, that fueled discontent. Big time. There was no freedom of expression, at least not until Gorbachev opened a pressure relief valve called glasnost ("openness"). That opened a Pandora's box. Soon, there came perestroika ("restructuring"). And before very long, the Berlin Wall came down and the Second World faded away. That's why, for many decades now, we have only had the First World and the Third World. Although some pundits think that the Second World just ran and hid under the green movement, to emerge in its new incarnation under wokeism.

South Africa's Guest Panelist: Nelson Mandela
Comrade, you are well informed. I am so disappointed to see how things have gone in the Rainbow Nation of late. We not only had economic classes—subsistence farmers, urban laborers, a middle class that included the Boers, that is "farmers" in Afrikaans, and a small but vastly wealthy upper class, but also, we were divided by ethnic demarcations into ethnic homelands called Bantustans. The whole system was totally undemocratic, disruptive, and self-alienating. It will take time for the lessons of democracy to sink in and take hold.

Ms. Thatcher addressed her question to the left, so I address mine to the challenger on the right. Is there not meant to be a separation of powers between the three distinct levels of government? Namely, national or federal, provincial or state, and municipal or local government. Ms. Thatcher's government, for example, had an ongoing struggle with local councils, especially when Labour dominated them. Are such checks and balances enough? Are there additional ways to add value to democracy's balancing act?

Challenger on the Right
Safeguards vary from one country to another. In a federal system, there is more devolution of power to the states. Whereas in a highly centralized republic, the states have to fall in line with national policy. In Canada, provinces have some very large portfolios, like education and health. This gives them some sense of autonomy. At the same time, the federal government handles defense and foreign affairs with some exceptions. For example, the province of Quebec has a "General Delegation" in Paris, and France has a Consulate-General in Quebec.

The USA has fifty states, India has twenty-eight provinces and eight territories, Canada has ten provinces plus three territories, and South Africa has nine provinces. Britain has united four nations into one kingdom.

India's most populous state is Uttar Pradesh, with 241 million people, compared to the whole republic of South Africa, which has 63 million. The most populous state in the USA is California, with 39 million. This is more people than the twenty-one least populous states combined, and on a par with the whole of Canada.

I am saying this to point out that not all provinces or territories can offer much counterbalance to the central government. The variance is too great. But at least some heavyweight states like California, Texas, Florida, and Pennsylvania can meaningfully resist centralized rule.

I would say that a bigger destabilizer is the "two centers of power" phenomenon that comes with a vanguard party. This is Marxist doctrine, but for thirty years in the free and democratic South Africa, there has been a tug-of-war between the State President in the Union Buildings and the Secretary General of the ruling party in Luthuli House. The problem this creates is not a lack of checks and balances. The problem is, rather, who's in charge? In other countries, once a government is formed post-elections, then parties shrink into the background to deal with membership issues, strategic planning, and future elections. But in South Africa, the government is destabilized on a daily basis by this "two-centered power" structure, especially because the party handles cadre deployment.

Remember, South African elections count proportional representation, so the electoral commission allocates a certain number of seats to each party. Then, the party gets to decide, from its lists of cadres, who will be appointed to sit in parliament. MPs are not elected from a local constituency. They do not represent a "riding" per se but a party. And the party can discipline them if they step out of line.

The legislature, with its oversight role, and the judiciary, with its blindfold, provide more stabilizing checks and balances than the multitiered levels of government.

The American judiciary is spread over 94 districts, so these are smaller than the fifty states. But they are clustered in 13 regional circuits, some of which embrace all or parts of more than one state. Activist judges have been trying to balance the president's executive orders by issuing "universal injunctions" that make them apply countrywide which is far beyond their limited jurisdiction. This is creating similar headaches to those our esteemed panelist Maggie Thatcher had with Labour-dominated local councils.

India's Guest Panelist: Jawaharlal Nehru
We should not forget that among all the checks and balances is the party system itself. I was a member of the India National Congress, but today, India is ruled by another party—the Bharatiya Janata Party (BJP), a Hindu nationalist

party. I was the first prime minister of India, and my daughter Indira became our first woman prime minister.

Parties have a way of allowing voters to replace tired and corrupt governments with other options. Unless, of course, you are in a one-party state, the model which promotes the vanguard party. It takes a long time for governments that arise from liberation movements to be discarded. During those long decades, other mechanisms provide the checks and balances.

I would like to ask the challenger in the middle—what about telling the truth? How can you distinguish between politicians who are liars and those whose integrity is still intact? When has a whole party gone so rotten that it must be discarded? Can we recover the spiritual high ground in politics? Mahatma Gandhi would start fasting when there was too much violence, out of his disapproval. He would get thin. He refused to eat until the violence subsided. His spirituality was mixed with his leadership. But these days, when you have liars, cheaters, and looters in power, they seem to get away with it. How can they be exposed, discarded, and replaced with honest and inspiring leaders?

Challenger in the Middle
Gandhi was one of a kind. Common people so revered him. And so religious.

I like the connection that this program, *Telling the Truth*, is making between truth and freedom. It is hard for me to imagine a context of freedom disconnected from spirituality, or worse yet, where you could deceive or harm people with impunity. People talk of an island where the rich and famous could fly to, just to play dirty. They could pleasure themselves in any way they wanted, outside the bounds of morality and law. If this sounds to you like paradise, you have a problem. But it was still a billion-dollar business. That seems to impress people more than the depravity of it. Until the truth slipped out about Jeffrey Epstein. Truth has died with him in a way. But truth somehow has a way of slipping out, sooner or later. Deception should not be used to protect the image of leaders. If they lack integrity, the people have a right to know.

It is OK for a spiritual leader to advise his followers to render to Caesar what belongs to Caesar, and to God what belongs to God. Pay your taxes, don't dodge the draft, and report crime when you are aware of it. That's good citizenship. But political and military leaders need more than just their face imprinted on coins. That actually sounds a bit narcissistic. They need to be humble, transparent, and accountable. Those are virtues that enter the spiritual realm and guarantee truth. That's the right stuff that good leaders are made of.

There is generally a huge gap in today's world between integrity and practice. Politics is a dirty game, and the best cadres seek out other vocations where they can succeed without getting contaminated in the public sphere. What I am really saying is that moral and spiritual forces are needed as checks and balances too. Without the "plumb line" that they provide, politics gets messier and messier.

The gatekeepers of truth, after all, have never been business tycoons or populist demagogues. Philosophers, prophets, and poets opine about the death of truth. But the others may not miss it too much, for it can get very inconvenient.

North America's Guest Panelist: Abraham Lincoln
Amen! I recently read about the Global Freedom Status, an instrument used to compare countries. Out of 100, Britain scores 93. They score better than the USA, which is at 83. South Africa is next at 79. And India scores only 66.

It amazes me that Britain, which denied its colonies the freedom they longed for, is now ahead of these three former colonies! There has been a turnaround. I would like to ask the challenger in the middle if he might compare these four nations by the separation of powers, and by the extent to which they champion the truth.

Challenger in the Middle
Well, I daresay that Britain has been at it a bit longer than the others. So its quality of life is benefiting from the long brewing period of democracy. No discussion of checks and balances would be complete without mention of the free press and the "fifth estate." Freedom of expression is the baseline of electioneering and debate. Britain is very good at this, in a generally nonviolent way. Its people are now very tolerant.

Britain's high score must also reflect its societal civility. It has fought hard for a pluralistic society with space for many divergent views. In contrast, India is ruled by a Hindu nationalist party and tends to pressure the media and civil society organizations to toe the line.

The church is usually considered to be separate from government, and thus it can speak with influence on public policy and debate. Ironically, in Britain, the Church of England is a state church, although that is not true of the Roman Catholic or the Nonconformist churches. The state church thus tends to validate government views, but opposition can still come from the wider spectrum of denominations.

The Church of England naturally spread to the former colonies, and now we have the phenomenon of African Anglicans outnumbering the dwindling attendance in Britain. And the African bishops have rebuked the Archbishop of Canterbury for condoning public policies that do not align with what the Bible says. This reminds me of what Aleksandr Solzhenitsyn once wrote: "The simple step of the courageous individual is not to take part in the lie."

The term "fifth estate" is used to describe any outliers beyond the usual checks and balances. Certainly, social media fits into this bandwidth. So does music when it is politicized. Two names that come to mind are Pete Seeger and Bob Dylan. Songs like "If I Had a Hammer" and "Blowin' in the Wind" were very influential. The Irish band U2 took the fifth estate about as high as ever. Bono is a huge influencer. The First Amendment guarantees freedom of expression, and whether you agree or not, some voices are tweaking the consciences of voters. A recent example is the hit "Rich Men North of Richmond" by American country-folk singer Oliver Anthony.

Social media is part of the "fifth estate," yet we now know that Facebook reduced its posts about COVID-19 by half when pressured directly by the White House. So not all platforms can provide honest checks and balances. They can be intimidated.

My last point in answering your question is about the alt-right media. It became very shrill in Britain in the run-up to Brexit and has risen to a new level of influence in America as well. In Canada there are new platforms like Rebel News and The Epoch Times. I read this as the truth slipping out, as it is prone to do. A lie doesn't become truth, wrong doesn't become right, and evil doesn't become good just because the majority accepts it.

A good citation is the news story about the discovery of Hunter Biden's laptop. Remembering the Watergate scandal, you would have thought that the *Washington Post* and *New York Times* should have jumped onto this story. Instead, they smothered it. What we now know is that the FBI was already aware of and investigating Biden family improprieties before the story ever broke. But it was not what the deep state wanted the public to hear. So the mainline media just sat on it. Several years later, they sheepishly admitted that the laptop is a legitimate source of evidence in this case. This is tantamount to confessing that they print propaganda. The journalist who broke that scoop was exonerated.

The 2024 Special Counsel's report on how Hunter Biden enriched himself by peddling his father's name when he was Obama's VP is another example of the truth slipping out, eventually. But by then, his father had given him a presidential pardon. The fact that his impunity was sealed did not stop the truth from slipping out. It always does, sooner or later.

There has been a split in the media. I would say that only certain newspapers and internet platforms are now in the "inner circle" of genuinely impartial checks and balances, along with the churches and, in some countries, the nobility. In other words, among those who would normally speak out first. Regrettably, this inner circle has been very much tamed. One can now access media services such as Ground News, which, on a story-by-story basis, tracks where coverage is mostly coming from—left, center, or right-leaning sources. Sadly, this is determined to some extent by which newspapers and media services are deemed to belong to each category. To an alt-right die-hard, the BBC looks rather leftist. To a flaming Marxist, CNN might be seen as centrist, not leftist. This is an example of truth being somewhat situational. It is important, as in *Telling the Truth*, to listen to all sides before coming to an informed opinion.

And just because churches agree with a political party does not mean that they do not have their very own reasons for the views that they hold dear. Too often, the church is accused of partisanship when in truth, it has its theologies that explain its beliefs, convictions, and views.

In India, this means that the media is war-crazy. It is Hindu nationalist to the point of backing war with Pakistan. That is, unless you dare to critique the Modi regime!

According to *Time* magazine, "Independent journalism is being made a de facto crime in what is supposed to be the world's biggest democracy." In fact, from 2010 to 2020, some 150 journalists were arrested in India. Freedom of expression in the world's largest democracy has dropped on all the charts.

The alt-right media in Britain and America started as part of the fifth estate, not of the press. These voices were outliers, but they have now gained so much ground in terms of their critiques and general influence that they are starting to eclipse the legacy media. Just look at the ratings! They refused to be silent and complicit. That is precisely why then-Speaker of the House Kevin McCarthy turned over the January 6 tapes to Tucker Carlson when he was still at Fox News. His report was opposed to coverage offered by the tamed mainstream media. Many believe that those once independent and reliable news services have now become propaganda outlets for the deep state. It was a reporter at Breitbart News who broke the story about Hunter Biden's laptop. But she was thrown under the bus by the establishment. Only years later was she able to hold her head high and say, "I told you so." She was right, pun intended!

There is a lesson in this about the very nature of truth. Thomas Sowell put it this way: "When you want to help people, you tell them the truth. When you want to help yourself, you tell them what they want to hear." When journalism stoops this low, it is not worth very much. Evidence has come to light that Facebook capitulated to censorship pressure deriving from the White House. There go the checks and balances! This is much like what happened with the Twitter Files.

When Twitter froze out Donald Trump before its takeover by Elon Musk, Trump launched his own social media platform. It is called Truth Social, a direct critique of the manipulation of both the press and the fifth estate. Placing "Truth" in his new platform's name indirectly said something pointed about Twitter. This debate rages on into 2025 with Governor Gavin Newsom saying, in the public spat over the Los Angeles fires, that Donald Trump's "wild-eyed fantasies" are "damaging" the notion of truth. Debates like this make it all the more important to seek out the truth about truth!

In South Africa, there is still a small window of journalism speaking truth to power. The Daily Maverick and BizNews come to mind for their fierce criticism of anyone who deserves it.

Moderator

It's time to thank our four guest panelists for their probing questions. And to salute our three articulate challengers, who have explained so much to us. Now, will the real Truth about the separation of powers please stand out?

CULTURE WARS

Moderator

Here we are again with episode seven of *Telling the Truth*. Our topic today is culture wars. Culture is a human construct. Probably its main feature is language. People grow up loving their homeland, their language, and their culture—that is, their folklore, music, dress, food, and history.

In each of the four Anglophone settings that are represented on our panel, there are many cultures. In addition to many aboriginal cultures in North America, there are several settler traditions—for example, French in Quebec, German in Pennsylvania, and Spanish in New Mexico. English is now the main language, but large enclaves speak Spanish and French as well. The presence of African Americans must also be noted. These are sometimes called "subcultures."

In Britain, English has become predominant, but Gaelic dialects are still spoken in Scotland, Wales, Cornwall, and Ireland. In South Africa, there are eleven national languages—English and Afrikaans, as well as nine Bantu languages. For some unknown reason, the Indigenous languages of the San and the Khoi have not been officialized. In India, the official language is Hindi, but it is only one of 22 Indigenous languages. English is used as a lingua franca across India.

So our panelists and challengers are no strangers to cultural issues—cross-cultural, intercultural, and transcultural. There has also been a massive influx of religion. Christianity invaded South Africa and India, and eastern religions have spread into South Africa, Britain, and North America.

Our panelists probe the meaning of the term "culture wars" as it pertains to us today. It is South Africa's turn to start the questioning; go ahead, Mr. Mandela.

South Africa's Guest Panelist: Nelson Mandela
One of the first things I realized when I got out of prison was that the world had moved on during the twenty-seven years I was incarcerated. At first, I was busy trying to track the changes in South Africa. Then, a year later, J. D. Hunter published a book called *Culture Wars*. I thought it would help me better understand how the wide world had changed while I was locked away, for I was no longer just a South African politician. I had become a global icon.

Let me ask the challenger in the middle to try to define the term *culture war* and comment on whether it is still relevant.

Challenger in the Middle
Politico recently interviewed J. D. Hunter. He said originally, the term *culture war* was about secularization. Its objections were tied to and justified by theologies. Then he went on to say that this is no longer the case: "You rarely see people on the right rooting their positions within a biblical theology or ecclesiastical tradition. It is a position that is mainly rooted in fear of extinction."

I am reminded of Voltaire saying, "There is no God, but don't tell that to my servant, lest he murder me at night." Somehow people connect theology and morality with behavior and conduct. They worry about such fundamental changes.

There is a perennial connection between reform and revolts. The morning star of the Protestant Reformation was John Wycliffe. He led the Lollards. They pressed for reforms, but their exuberance brought about the Peasants' Revolt. It was led by John Ball, who preached Lollardy. This then caused a conservative backlash. The establishment had tolerated the Lollards because they respected royalty. They wanted change, but a popular revolt was too much. The small level of protection that the Lollards had enjoyed suddenly evaporated.

A similar thing happened in Germany when Martin Luther had been preaching reform for less than ten years. The sense of exuberance led to a peasant uprising led by Hans Müller, who was even supported by some nobles and radical theologians. One hundred thousand lives were lost as the establishment cracked down on this revolt, which Martin Luther himself actually opposed.

My point is that sometimes, when reform gains momentum, revolt is not far behind. Culture wars today involve some deep concerns, such as abortion, same-sex marriage, critical race theory, and gender modification. J. D. Hunter is right in a way—these combined reforms have triggered an exuberance that has destabilized Western civilization as we once knew it. When one man in Canada is mailing sachets of legal poison to people contemplating suicide all over the world, this has reached the proportions of revolt. So there has been a rising backlash, deriving from the polarization that pressing for these reforms has caused. When protests get violent, the same escalation can be noted. That overexuberance is unlawful and immoral.

India's Guest Panelist: Jawaharlal Nehru

New worldviews like Marxism rejected the very existence of God and the supernatural. They have become secular religions, otherwise known as ideologies. But culture war is very much like religious intolerance. This is what led to Partition—the belief that Hindus and Muslims could never peacefully occupy the same space. So they were separated by the colonial regime before independence was granted to India, Pakistan, and what is now Bangladesh.

It seems that support for deep cultural reforms is usually labeled a left-leaning agenda, while those trying to conserve the status quo are the alt-right. So I would like to pose my question to the challenger on the left. Do you now see that too much polarization and rapid change can historically lead to a backlash? How do you assess the risks in this respect?

Challenger on the Left

We thought we outnumbered our opponents. We assumed that time was on our side. For example, there was a growing awareness that the history of America did not begin in 1776 with the American Revolution but much earlier. In 1619, the first shipment of African slaves arrived from present-day Angola in Virginia. The Atlantic slave trade had started long before that, with deliveries to other ports in the Caribbean and Latin America, but this was its first landing in North America. So we started to rewrite history.

This renewed the civil rights movement of the 1950s and 1960s. Its new name is Black Lives Matter, and George Floyd's death gave new impetus to reform. Critical race theory (CRT) also emerged. It is an interdisciplinary academic field devoted to analyzing how laws, social and political movements, and media shape and are shaped by social conceptions of race and ethnicity.

Similarly, the rainbow symbol, which was once a biblical symbol, was co-opted by gays and lesbians who have a new label—LGBTQIA+. This aspect of reform, on the basis of rights, came to be very open and accepted in the West. It expanded to include gender modification as well. "Trans" activists have been very proactive as the movement for change gained momentum. The English word *gay* has been totally redefined, and the term *drag race* has taken on a whole new meaning!

We want to put a stop to the adoption of Indigenous children by white Christian families because they will be "groomed" into assimilation. We would rather they be brought up by families from the Indigenous peoples of America.

And of course, abortion on demand is now regarded by many as a human right in spite of setbacks caused by the overruling of *Roe v. Wade*.

My risk assessment changed with Donald Trump's reelection. We seemed to be on a roll, but now that impetus is shaky. Was it an illusion? We may have to eat some humble pie. Partition is not an option, as our great divide is mainly rural/urban. So those who oppose the reforms refuse to grin and bear it. There is a strong pushback. How strong and enduring that backlash will be remains to be seen.

North America's Guest Panelist: Abraham Lincoln
The abolition movement was very strong in my time. Christians led it, and books like *Uncle Tom's Cabin* put that reform agenda into every believer's language. The consequent polarization led to a civil war. My question accepts the assumption that Partition is not an option. A one-size-fits-all solution must be found.

To the challenger on the right, I ask—can another civil war be averted?

Challenger on the Right
Well, in a way, a proxy war is being fought in Ukraine. The loss of life has been horrendous. Some say it is just a territorial border dispute, but I see it as a proxy war. That is the only explanation I can come up with for the huge inputs that NATO has poured into it on Ukraine's side, and China and Iran on Russia's side. The West is trying to subdue those who have vociferously opposed its "woke" agenda. Asia (led by Russia), the Middle East, and Africa largely oppose it. They see it as Western decadence. That new "axis" explains the rapid expansion of BRICS and why it wants to challenge the predominance of the US dollar. The backlash that wokeism has invited should not be underestimated. Russia is partly European and partly Asian; it straddles the two continents.

When it says it does not want NATO on its doorstep, it is not just talking about ballistic missiles. It wants to keep decadence at bay.

Aside from this external front at the frontier where Europe meets Asia, there is rising internal back-pressure within America to roll back the reforms. For fifty years, conservatives railed against the *Roe v. Wade* court decision, and the pro-life agenda seemed to get a boost against the pro-choice camp when the Supreme Court overruled it. Donald Trump's reelection signals a sea change.

The rapid rise to the top of the charts of Jason Aldean's song "Try That in a Small Town" showed that many people still hold traditional beliefs and values.

My view is that Western thought has been upended by two secular religions, humanism and Marxism, causing much upheaval in both society and the church. Remember that the Moors and Arabs joined forces to invade Europe, namely the Iberian Peninsula. There, they reigned for 781 years until they were pushed back to North Africa in 1492. Just months before, Columbus sailed across the ocean blue, starting a new era.

When first invaded, the Europeans pulled back, far north into the mountains. They regrouped and formed alliances, for there was not one Spain as we know it today. Groups like the Catalonians, the Basques, and the Portuguese kept fighting back. Eventually, they got some help from Charlemagne in what is now France and started to squeeze the invaders out. They simply did not regard their Christian religion and culture as compatible with what the invaders brought. There were periods of peaceful coexistence, but on the whole, the Europeans wanted the Iberian peninsula back. And this eventually happened. In Spanish, it is called the "Reconquista Crista."

Having said this, I acknowledge that the Moors and Arabs contributed a lot to European life. In monetary terms, gold from West Africa poured in. This buoyed up an economy ravaged by the black plague. In academic terms, Europe made the switch from clumsy Roman numerals to Arabic numerals, and other gains. In many ways, Europe benefited from the invasion. But in the end, it was rebuffed. That is what I expect to happen to Western civilization. I think that there has been a burst of reforms that has almost overpowered the status quo. But the pendulum is swinging back again, because the change agenda reached revolt proportions. Pushback may take some time, but the fact that Partition is not an option means the resistance is not going to surrender.

I don't think there will be another civil war. I think Western civilization is too deeply embedded to be dislodged. For one thing, we can count on external solidarity, and we can just keep up the resistance until we do prevail. And don't forget—we do believe that God is on our side. Why would he champion people who don't even believe that he is there? But the engagement will be in open lawfare, not in warfare. It will be at the bar, not on the battlefield. This is playing out with all the restraining orders issued by judges to contain the president's decrees. The media has been largely captured along with education, universities, and the "weaponized" state agencies, but Christian values will prevail in the end. They have a coherence and cohesiveness that wokeism lacks. The weak underbelly of the al-Andalus was that it had divided loyalties—Arab and Moor. A house that is divided against itself cannot stand. The incoherence of woke reform and revolt will render it a spent force. There are clearly extremists and moderates on the left.

Britain's Guest Panelist: Margaret Thatcher
Yes, I am encouraged to hear these sentiments. I would like to prod the challenger on the right to keep talking more about the positive ways that the resistance can disrupt the invasion of reform and revolt.

Can you think of other examples of this in our four respective countries?

Challenger on the Right
In Britain, you can see that the disproportionate influence of the nobility has remained. This took a lot of time, as it had deep roots in feudalism. But at the same time, you still have a gentry and a House of Lords. The monarchy is largely symbolic at this stage, unlike the only remaining executive monarchy in today's world, in Eswatini. During your thirty years without a monarch, under Cromwell, there was a huge longing for the monarchy's return. In a way, this is what the West has recently experienced, a radical period, but one that can't last.

Brexit is another example. Although Britain never gave up the pound sterling for the euro, it did join the European Union. Sort of. But then its conserving instinct kicked in, and it backed out. Labour is trying to reconnect UK to the EU somehow, but the new Reform Party is likely to prevail.

In South Africa, resistance shook off apartheid. It was an institutionalized form of racism that had already existed under colonialism. Amazingly, civil war was averted. There was certainly a risk that it would come to that, and that whites would be pushed into the sea. I think that blacks and whites were able to find one another in the end because of their common commitment to Christianity. Every parish of the Reformed Church, even though it espoused the heresy of apartheid, had both a pastor and a missionary. The pastor ministered to the white settlers. The missionary ministered to the black farm workers. They would visit a farm together, so the pastor could visit the Boer family inside the farmhouse, while the missionary convened the blacks out back and ministered to them. This ironically came to teach blacks the Christian message of equality and liberation. But at the same time, both blacks and whites shared a common belief in God, morality, and decency. So in the end, they were able to make the turn without crashing.

But now blacks dominate whites, who still have a lot to offer. Resistance to this supremacy could bring back a spirit of nonracialism. After all, 88 percent of citizens identify as Christians. Affirmative action in favor of the majority has never been helpful. It causes awful distortions, which some call "economic genocide."

In India, the caste system has been entrenched for centuries. Democracy has helped to soften social apartheid, and Christian missionary work has helped as well, especially among the lower castes. Much of the lowest caste has experienced Christian conversion. I don't say "revival" because it was not previously Christian. Whereas Hinduism has condoned the caste system fatalistically, Christianity confronted it. Regress in this respect could bring about the death of truth.

In North America, there are significant numbers of African Americans and a rising immigration of Latinos. These are both major subcultures. African Americans compose 14 percent of the population, and Latinos compose 19.5 percent. That totals 33.5 percent or one out of three. Many of the millions of illegal immigrants in the USA today are Latinos, causing this enclave to double in size.

In Canada, the French-speaking population in Quebec accounts for about 20 percent of the national population. The challenge is how to conserve these enclaves on an equal footing, allowing them due rights and privileges for their language and culture without going overboard. A recent Supreme Court decision in the USA is most helpful in keeping affirmative action from disadvantaging the majority. The Declaration of Independence must be taken at its word—that all are created equal.

Just remember what C. S. Lewis said: "When the whole world is running towards a cliff, he who is running in the opposite direction appears to have lost his mind." If you feel discouraged or isolated, never, never give up. Lots of people get seduced by secular religions, and we need to engage them with the truth whenever we can. The light shines in the darkness, and the darkness has never extinguished it.

To sum up, the death of truth is a risk, but not yet a reality.

Moderator

Once again, thanks to our four guest panelists for their probing questions as we seek the truth and to our three articulate challengers, whose answers give us lots to think about. Now, will the real Truth about culture wars please stand out?

REVISIONISM

Moderator

Welcome to episode eight of *Telling the Truth*. We are back with a new topic: revisionism. This term means reexamining and revising history as it has been known, and refers to the reinterpretation of a historical event, theory, or narrative, often challenging established or orthodox views.

Perhaps revisionism is a superficial sign of a deeper reality. Predominant views have been replaced. So we need to revisit some of our folklore. In America, in the wake of George Floyd's death, during the BLM riots, more than a hundred statues were pulled down. Several of these were monuments to General Robert E. Lee or Confederate soldiers. But this was a monumental shift—pun intended.

The statue of cleric and educator Egerton Ryerson was torn down in Toronto. In Britain, the statue of slave trader Edward Colston was torn down in Bristol. In Cape Town, the statue of tycoon Cecil Rhodes was torn down.

India was far ahead of the times in this respect. In the 1960s, it had already torn down twenty-two statues of British heroes at various locations. In 2018, it tore down the statue of Vladimir Lenin in Tripura state. In 2021, the statue of spiritual leader Sai Baba, who had combined both Muslim and Hindu principles in his teachings, was torn down in Delhi. In 2022, the statue of Jesus was torn down in Gokunte village of Karnataka.

Statue-toppling is nothing new. The statue of Saddam Hussein was torn down in Baghdad, and the statue of Lenin in Berlin. These statues are not just religious. They are military, cultural, and political. But when they are raised on a pedestal, they are milestones along the road of human history. Revisionism starts when they are taken down.

Today, our panelist from India will start the questioning. Go ahead, Mr. Nehru.

India's Guest Panelist: Jawaharlal Nehru

I know of twenty statues of myself, including mere busts, around India. I dread the day that radicals start to pull them down. On more than one occasion, radicals have disfigured my statues, but so far, none have been torn down.

I am aware of about ten statues of my co-panelist Nelson Mandela, including one at the Union Buildings and another in London. However, I have only managed a bust in London.

As for my co-panelist, Baroness Thatcher, I know of a statue erected in her hometown and one in St. Peter's Hill Green in London. Both have been vandalized more than once.

By comparison, there are at least 191 statues of our co-panelist Abraham Lincoln across his homeland, including at the Lincoln Memorial in Washington and Mount Rushmore. That exceeds even the number for George Washington, which stands at 171. But then, number 1 was a slave-owner.

Can I ask the challenger in the middle: What do you make of this comparison? By their very nature, statues are meant to endure. But some don't. Or do they just fade away into the sands of time, like the statue of Ozymandias?

Challenger in the Middle
First, I wonder if there is an emerging standardization of measurement, for I have read that there are twenty-seven statues of Jesus worldwide that are over twenty-two meters tall. Like the archetypical one in Rio de Janeiro—Christ the Redeemer—at forty meters tall, it is almost half the height of the Statue of Liberty in New York, at ninety-three meters tall.

By comparison, the Sphinx of Egypt is twenty meters tall, and the four faces carved into Mount Rushmore are eighteen meters tall.

The Motherland Calls statue in Volgograd is eighty-five meters tall, almost as tall as the Statue of Liberty. It was unveiled in 1967 during the Soviet era, when that city was called Stalingrad.

There are a dozen Buddha statues in Asia over eighty-five meters high. The most recent was built in Henan, China, and is the biggest-ever Buddha statue. The Spring Temple Buddha stands 153 meters, compared to the Statue of Liberty's ninety-three meters. It was completed in 2008.

Then Narendra Modi announced the building of a statue of Indian statesman Vallabhbhai Patel, which was completed in 2018. At 182 meters, it is now the tallest monument in the world. It is standing in the Narmada valley in Gujarat. It is called the Statue of Unity.

I have been rambling to try to answer your question. You must be aware, even proud, that the tallest statue of them all is in India! And it is one of your colleagues at the time of independence. This is not a religious figure like the Buddha or Jesus. Nor is it a symbol like Lady Liberty or the winged Motherland. Somehow, those figures seem to be less susceptible to statue-toppling than those real-life figures.

An earthquake toppled the Colossus of Rhodes, which stood thirty-six meters high and was one of the seven wonders of the ancient world.

Statues are important reminders of people, events, and beliefs. So statue-topping is certainly significant in understanding revisionism.

North America's Guest Panelist: Abraham Lincoln
I am humbled by the reminder of how many statues have been erected in my honor. I especially love the Lincoln Memorial in Washington. The statue is only six meters tall, but I am sitting. Don't they get tired of standing after a few centuries pass? Best of all is the setting, the building, the pillars, the landscaping, and so forth.

Still, I am remembered for freedom—for freeing the slaves. George Washington is also associated with freedom from colonial rule.

I wonder if people understand the deep connection between truth and freedom. There were decades of debate during the abolitionist movement, as there were in the run-up to our Revolutionary War. But until we could see the truth clearly from this firestorm of debate, we could not take decisive action.

"Then you will know the truth, and the truth shall set you free." No truth, no freedom.

Can I ask the challenger on the left—aren't you judging what happened long ago by today's standards? If your activist agenda is divisive, is it true? Can't your left-leaning inclinations find rapprochement with your co-heirs to the republic on the right?

Challenger on the Left
We, too, have debated issues ad nauseam. Our focus on the left is no longer truth but power. We have to look to the future, not to the past. Conserving, by its very nature, looks backward. Progressives look ahead.

This mantra goes by different names—the Great Reset, globalization, the new normal, etc. We believed that change was unstoppable. Religion is our main opponent—Orthodox Christianity in Russia, Islam in the Middle East, Buddhism in Asia, and evangelical Christianity in Africa and Latin America. Roman Catholics are divided everywhere—some are for us and some against us. Even the late pope seemed to warm up to our radical point of view. But it appears that the pendulum may be swinging back to the right. The new Pope is American and well aware that our fortunes are changing.

Wherever we go, we try to do a power census to keep ahead of the game. We are not inclined to debate at this stage. Just power silence works best. Look ahead, not back. Smother the talk, and focus on the walk. This might explain why Kamala Harris gave so few interviews during her election campaign. She got overconfident, to be sure, beguiled by the polls and predictions of the legacy media.

Democratic inconveniences are constraining the problem for us. Sometimes the journey to our destination gets interrupted by our opponents. The Supreme Court has a nasty way of disrupting our plans. They overturned *Roe v. Wade*, which legitimized our efforts for fifty years in the pro-choice camp. Now they have ruled in favor of the irrelevant Declaration of Independence, that all are created equal. This disrupts affirmative action. So we wanted to populate the Supreme Court with left-leaning judges. However, the timelines to do so are too long. We are impatient. We were going to introduce legislation to enlarge the Supreme Court so that we could speed it up. But then we lost control of Congress at the midterms. More delays. More frustrations. More fight-back. The endgame is that our opponents took control of the legislature, both the House and the Senate, as well as the executive branch. Will we ever recover as a party and as a movement broadly called woke? Rapprochement may be inevitable.

In Britain, the pro-Scotland movement has lost some impetus. Labour won the most recent election, but its government is sinking slowly. The roots of liberalism in Britain run very deep, so swing voters don't see socialism as the only option to the Tories, who have behaved badly. It is starting to look like Nigel Farage and his Reform Party may be on the up and up. It was reported that Reform now has a bigger membership than the Conservatives, so Labour is not expected to land a second consecutive term.

In South Africa, the left-leaning ruling party is slowly sinking into oblivion. Waste, corruption, and patronage are rife. Efforts to clean it up are not very convincing. Basically, the party has brought its concept of a "broad church" into a full-fledged Government of National Unity. In 2024, voters opted for a coalition of parties, not trusting any one party to form a government. This GNU joins left-leaning parties with former opposition parties that lean to the right. Strange bedfellows. It is too early to see what effect the incompatibility will have on effectiveness. No one can see where this is going. Can rapprochement work better than a vanguard party?

In India, Modi is hanging tough. He has ruled for almost a decade, and his Hindu-nationalist stance is not unlike the "Make America Great Again" message in his context. India looks inward, but it has had major conflicts brewing with Pakistan to the west and China to the north. Nationalism has a way of doing that historically, although the disputed border with China may be cooling off a bit.

We had so little esteem for the past that we didn't want to cooperate with those who did. We just wanted to get on with it. Power was the focus, not truth. It cost us dearly. Warnings about the death of truth didn't worry us—we did not plan to attend its funeral. But this has led to one setback after another. We need to take another look at rapprochement because the alt-right is just not going away.

Britain's Guest Panelist: Margaret Thatcher
I never liked the left's bravado. My government broke Labour. We broke the unions. We stayed in power so long that the opposition party had to come back to the near left. That is where your extremism has taken you, again.

It occurs to me that the left is nothing more than a coalition of the wounded—pro-choice activists whose world was turned upside down by the overturning of *Roe v. Wade*; activists who want to decriminalize prostitution and allow men who identify as women into women's washrooms and sports; environmentalists whose predictions are repeatedly inaccurate; gender modification activists who want access to children; and disproportionately small groups of gays and lesbians who want democracy to put minority rights ahead of majority rule.

So I direct my question to the challenger on the right. What are you doing to compensate for this attack on truth itself? Can you stop or slow down this slide into an abyss of deception? Are you raising awareness about this slump?

Challenger on the Right
Thanks for asking, baroness. Yes, we are proactively gearing up a response that will make you proud.

One nation—Sweden—has recently signaled a public warning to other nations to regard the World Economic Forum's globalist agenda as dangerous. Sweden was the only country not to follow the World Health Organization's COVID-19 protocols, and it fared no worse than other nations. It was a kind of "control experiment," and now it has seen the light, shining in the darkness.

In North America, a number of things come to mind. Thousands of church congregations are disaffiliating with their mother denominations where liberal theology does not line up with Bible teaching. Pro-life activists are succeeding in a number of states to roll back abortion on demand, in diverse legislations. Congress has begun to really squeeze in its pursuit of "weaponization" of law enforcement, which arose under a presidency of dark pretenses. Favoritism has certainly been exposed, especially as a way of perpetuating one party in power and disadvantaging the opposition. One movie succeeded brilliantly in exposing the horrors of human/child trafficking. This horror sped up with the unrestricted open border policy, which has since been brought under control. In Canada, in the wake of the statue of Egerton Ryerson, a Methodist minister, being torn down, and the college named in his honor being renamed, a Friends of Egerton Ryerson foundation has emerged. Governors like Ron DeSantis in Florida have taken on woke companies like Disney and openly questioned and debated with opponents like Governor Gavin Newsom. Leaders on the right recognize the dangers of the wars in Ukraine and the Middle East ballooning into World War III. After Fox News parted ways with Tucker Carlson, it was surprised to find that public opinion went out the door with him. His career is thriving, and his legacy at Fox explains why its ratings remain high. He has become a larger-than-life icon and remains a leading influencer.

In 2025, Team Trump is consolidating along the lines of the Monroe Doctrine of old. This could trigger a golden age, with a ripple effect felt around the world.

In South Africa, the James Michener narrative about Indigenous people has been challenged. His narrative was that when the Portuguese, Dutch, and British arrived by sea at the Cape, there were only Hottentots. He wrote that blacks entered the space that we now call South Africa either simultaneously with whites, or even after them. The fact is, whites focused on the west coast, by sea, and blacks entered overland from the east and central Africa. The timing has been corrected by research. Not changed by revisionism, but by academic research. Blacks have been in the eastern region of South Africa much longer, but they are not the aboriginals. Those are the Khoi and the San, now called Khoisan, who retreated to the drier west as the Bantus migrated south. Thus, it is true that the white settlers encountered and mistreated the Khoisan, whom they called "Hottentots" or Bushmen.

I am mentioning this to you to note a huge difference between research and revisionism. I am talking about getting to the truth. Georg Cantor once warned about resisting research: "A false conclusion once arrived at and widely accepted is not easily dislodged, and the less it is understood, the more tenaciously it is held." The effect this has on truth can be deadly.

While this is a valid warning, we can also be encouraged. For views that are grounded in real truth will be hard to budge. We have not seen the death of truth yet, but where we used to be only ankle-deep in deception, we are now knee-deep in it. So we have to keep putting points up on the board.

South Africa's Guest Panelist: Nelson Mandela
After a lot of reflection, I believe that we made a huge mistake by not including an aboriginal language along with the nine Bantu languages in our elev-

en national languages. I am aware that although the remnant of Indigenous peoples in North America is now low in population, they have extensive land claims. Both whites and blacks have acted to the detriment of our First Nations.

I attended mission schools and then went to a Christian university. It did not all go well for me, but on the whole, I felt that schools like these have done more good than harm. So I have been disturbed by reading that the residential schools for Indian children in North America have been accused of "cultural genocide." Those are strong words, especially if they were receiving a free education from the state.

Let me ask the challenger in the middle. Was that really a genocide? All the missionaries that I knew, like the late, great Trevor Huddleston, were terrific. How could it be that mission schools became death traps? Not just for assimilation into Western culture, but also leading to fields of unmarked graves where Indian children were buried. This does not add up—is it more revisionism?

Challenger in the Middle
It could go either way, because we just don't know. At the moment, there are only allegations and insinuations. There is no hard evidence that children are buried in fields near the residential schools. And if their remains are interred, if it was indeed a result of foul play, this could be another chapter in the revisionist playbook.

In mid-2023, excavations took place in a Catholic church facility in Manitoba, the former site of the Pine Creek residential school. No human remains were found, so the allegations of malevolence remain unproven.

Unfortunately, the accused are guilty until proven innocent. That has been the odd reality under the Liberal Canadian government, supported by the socialist NDP.

You know, the left-leaning press is quick to dismiss reasonable conjecture as "conspiracy theories." It's a knee-jerk response to any narrative that does not fit into their framework. It's an easy way to deflect the truth. This is taking us down the road to the death of truth.

Here are ten so-called conspiracy theories: 1. The COVID-19 virus originated in a lab in Wuhan due to human error. 2. Anthony Fauci was funding gain-of-function research in China because he thought it could not be traced. 3. COVID-19 vaccines are harmful. 4. Masking restricts oxygen intake. 5. Hunter Biden was so high that he left his laptop in a repair shop and forgot about it. 6. Hunter Biden was not entitled to earn what Burisma was paying him to sit on its board because he doesn't speak Ukrainian. 7. Joe Biden's vice-presidential influence was up for sale. 8. Joe Biden was not vastly more popular than Barack Obama, so he could not win 15 million more votes. 9. American law enforcement is weaponized by not being distant enough from the executive branch; there is a double standard in the Department of Justice—a two-tier justice system. 10. The trucker convoy that converged on Ottawa was a legitimate form of public protest.

Each one was labeled a conspiracy theory. But most, if not all, are true.

Mr. Mandela, you were regarded as a rabble-rouser and a criminal. But you managed to reverse the engines so that the treason trials actually put apartheid on trial. You were able to turn the conspiracy theory that you were a violent and dangerous outlaw into the reality that you were the people's choice to lead reform.

You have a good nose for the truth. If revisionism teaches anything about telling the truth, it is what Bertolt Brecht said: "Who does not know the truth, is simply a fool; yet who knows the truth and calls it a lie, is a criminal."

Mr. Mandela, you were incarcerated unjustly. It was political persecution. Eventually, the truth came out—you were innocent and apartheid was guilty. Now, instead of law enforcement detaining and punishing the innocent, we have an equally abhorrent reality—law enforcement protecting liars and criminals from prosecution and punishment. Pick the country—it happens everywhere.

Watch this space! Truth will make a comeback. For example, some American troops were penalized because they refused to take the COVID-19 "jabs." They deserve to get their back pay as the whole truth comes to light.

Moderator

It's time again to thank our four guest panelists and to salute our three challengers for shining light on the pathway to truth. Now, will the real Truth about the revisionism please stand out?

UKRAINE'S FUTURE

Moderator

Here we are again with episode nine of *Telling the Truth*. We are in our second series, on politics. Our illustrious panel is joining us via the amazing and useful new app Time-Zoom. Our topic is Ukraine's future. How does truth shape the way forward?

There has been a bloody war in the east of Ukraine. At first, Russia invaded and then annexed Crimea in 2014. It is a peninsula on the north shore of the Black Sea. The east shore of the Black Sea is considered by many to be in Asia. Then, in early 2022, Russia invaded the eastern side of Ukraine, crossing the border from Russia. In this geographical space, the majority of citizens are Russian-speaking and feel that Ukrainians, who dominate the central and western parts of the country, have discriminated against them. This had been the complaint of Russians living in Crimea as well.

Russia had been adamant for some time that it did not approve of Ukraine joining NATO, the North Atlantic Treaty Organization. But NATO countries championed a democratic government in Kyiv, Ukraine's capital. There was a turnover in February 2014 when the successor to the Orange Revolution was turfed out. Relations with Russia deteriorated after it invaded Crimea a month later. At the elections in 2019, a new president was elected—a comedian who said Ukraine was part of Europe. No, really, that's no joke!

Russia disapproved of increasing support from the West and steps taken by Kyiv to join NATO. Of course, there are deep ethnic roots that go far back. Once upon a time, Kyiv was the capital of the Rus culture. But then it was decimated by Genghis Khan. When Rus culture revived, its resurgence was around Moscow, not Kyiv. So these nations are cousins, and Russia was always frank and open about its disapproval of Ukraine joining NATO. Just as the USA objected when Russia started to set up strategic missiles in Cuba, in its backyard, Russia objected to the prospect of NATO arriving on its doorstep.

On the other hand, invasion is a no-no in terms of United Nations protocols. This was aggression, but when Crimea was annexed, that was not met by force. In the USA, Obama was replaced by Trump, who got on quite well with Putin of Russia. So there was a pause. But by the time Russia invaded in 2022, Biden had replaced Trump. NATO rallied to support Ukraine, without putting boots on the ground. But it has provided huge military and logistics support to Ukraine's military. In all these zigs and zags, one senses that there are strong doses of deception. Who is actually telling the truth? Or must we just fatalistically accept the decay of truth?

Today, it is our North American panelist's turn to pose the leading question about this vexing topic. What say you, Mr. Lincoln?

North America's Guest Panelist: Abraham Lincoln
War is a terrible thing and should always be the last resort. I very reluctantly declared war on the Confederacy. And I never expected it to get as messy as it did. Even a commander finds it hard to steer through all the surprises and ambiguities.

So let me pose a question to the challenger on the left. I thought that the rednecks started wars on the right. Iraq and Afghanistan, for example. How is it that globalists support a war, when the mantra of regionalization is to prevent war? Why did Joe Biden back this war, when Barack Obama did not respond to the invasion of Crimea?

Challenger on the Left

Crimea was invaded in March 2014. Obama had been reelected for his second term in 2012, and there was a sense that it would take time, more time than he had left, to build up the Ukrainian military to take on a superpower like Russia on the battlefield. Goliath had just stolen some property from David.

Russia must have been prepared to move into Crimea only weeks after a change of government in Kyiv. This was stealth. It shows that Russia's moves are strategic, and that where there are Russian speakers, it senses an ethnic duty to defend them from discrimination. Russia is very determined to have a "Slavic space" between Europe and Asia. To Putin, Europeans are decadent and have lost touch with their past. They have secularized and gone astray. They need a rebuke.

Perhaps Putin sensed that Biden was weak. His withdrawal from Afghanistan a year before was chaotic, and the USA military lost a lot of munitions and equipment, not to mention its reputation. Germany, like Japan, is still reluctant to get involved in military engagement. Trump had been busy "making America great again," and he had been cajoling NATO members to lean less on the USA. The European Union does not have its own military, but it can and has offered massive economic relief to Ukraine.

Also, Biden may have seen this coming. There is a sense of inevitability about this war. Because as Obama's vice president, he had directly engaged Ukraine and some other countries in that region, like Romania. So he must have heard the drums of war beating. Or was he blinded by his wheeling and dealing behind the scenes?

As far as we know, Biden never approved American boots on the ground, but incidents like blowing up the Nord Stream pipeline were suspected to be American-led. Some voices are saying that, like Vietnam, the American public is being kept in the dark about the deployment of American troops. In wartime, it is very hard to get accurate intel. That is precisely why WikiLeaks exists. Its founder, Julian Assange, argues that "regardless of the outcome, the truth is always the best place to start" and without it, "we have nothing." He holds a very high view of truth, almost idealistically so. But it landed him in jail.

At the same time, people who couldn't care less about the death of truth are prospering.

Britain's Guest Panelist: Margaret Thatcher
I am a bit more cynical about the timing. No one knows better than I how helpful a clean military victory can be to a leader's career. Yes, it was probably too late in Obama's second term to go to war. But Russia invaded Ukraine again only a year into Joe Biden's first term. What better leverage than a military victory to win himself a second term? My quick victory in the Falklands worked magic for me and for Thatcherism to take hold. And like Ukraine, the Falklands had been invaded. We had to defend against aggression.

May I ask the defender on the right, Donald Trump campaigned on ending the war, and he was elected. Will his peacemaking efforts work?

Challenger on the Right
It was easier said than done. He did not say how, but I think he and Putin had got along very well, so I think he did hope for an immediate ceasefire, with talks. In point of fact, the talks at the end of World War II were held in Crimea—at Yalta! That's where Roosevelt, Churchill, and Stalin worked out their final agreement and divided the spoils, so to speak. I think that Trump really wanted to host such an event, like Bill Clinton hosting the Oslo Accords between Yitzhak Rabin and Yasser Arafat.

Trump has said repeatedly that his main reason for wanting to end the war is the horrific loss of life. I think that whistleblower Jack Texeira has already brought some discrepancies to light between fact and propaganda. The high-water mark for loss of life on the battlefield was in December 2024, when Russia lost two thousand soldiers in one day. Trump has said repeatedly that five thousand people are dying every week, including civilians. How long Russia's military-industrial complex can keep up the supply of munitions and equipment to the front lines is unclear, especially as this conflict has depleted its Soviet-era war machinery, all the more so after a drone swarm knocked out a third of its bombers in one overnight strike.

Putin has repeatedly stated that he is open to talks. But so far, there have been no talks—just "talks about talks." Chinese leader Xi Jinping had a peace plan, but his future within China seems to be changing. A delegation of African leaders, led by South Africa's Cyril Ramaphosa, also tried to get some peace talks going. Blessed are the peacemakers, including Turkey's Tayyip Erdoğan. Ukrainian leader Volodymyr Zelenskyy says he is ready for peace talks. He seems to have come to terms with the fact that Russia basically outguns Ukraine.

One problem is the long delivery timelines for the weapons pledged to Ukraine by its NATO allies. Not only are there long supply chains, but training is required. For example, it takes time to train pilots how to fly the bigger, faster jets. So, Zelenskyy was reluctant at first to attend peace talks. He wanted to get his long-awaited counteroffensives underway so that he could bargain from a stronger position. He even invaded Russia in 2024! But this conflict has basically become a war of attrition. Probably an unwinnable war at the end of the day?

It gets embarrassing and seems futile at times. Like when a Russian missile hits an arsenal of imported weapons deep inside Ukraine, packed and waiting for the latest military offensive to get going. Alas. Russia has also taken some sporadic hits in Crimea and on the Black Sea, and drone swarms attacked four of its air bases in one strike.

To answer your question, Donald Trump's good rapport with Putin seems to have dissipated, and other NATO countries are beefing up their military budgets.

Another one of his concerns could be the grain deliveries from Ukraine, which exports huge quantities to Africa. Disrupting the grain trade can cause hunger and affect food prices. This war has caused Russia to become a client state of China, but the future of Xi Jinping seems uncertain.

This war has highlighted a question of priorities. Is any territorial gain worth the loss of one million lives? By focusing on that issue, Donald Trump has struggled to convince either side to give it up.

South Africa's Guest Panelist: Nelson Mandela
The jingle "No justice, no peace" is better known than our theme here, "No truth, no freedom." I think that both of these will be necessary to end this war.

Putin started the invasion with a floundering rush toward Kyiv. He may have been looking for a "quick fix" like my copanelist's ten-week campaign in the Falklands. She wasted no time in achieving victory, but that eluded Putin.

Let me ask the challenger in the middle—can this war be won on the battlefield? Or is it becoming an unwinnable war that may end in a stalemate like Korea? Or will Russia fight on until Ukraine surrenders?

Challenger in the Middle
America is in another hemisphere, far away. What the war may have accomplished is diminishing Russia to the point that any risk of expansionism will be held in check. At the same time, Russia's show of force has weakened the spread of globalism. Some critics call it a mere "border dispute," but it has served a purpose in strategic terms. Russia has paid a huge price for

its adventurism. Meanwhile, the conservatives in the West have switched modes from runaway "manifest destiny" to an isolationism called "America first."

NATO's answer kept coming back: defend democracy. And yet Ukraine is suspending elections because of the war, and its record on civil liberties is not good. It has been particularly hard on the church and the clergy. There is a proxy clash between the Ukrainian Orthodox church and the Russian Orthodox church. Crime and corruption are rife in Ukraine. This seems to have dirtied the Biden family in an unfortunate way, one that could put the American effort there in a very bad light. That is still under investigation. Was this war the biggest "GoFundMe" project ever?

Winning seems elusive to both sides. A via media might be found to create some "territories" or "autonomous republics" that allow for majority rule within those spaces; that might be the pathway to justice and a true sense of freedom, if that is predicated on truth. For they are neither wholly Russian nor Ukrainian, they are mixed. This could also be a way for Russia to "save face" by backing down, without a return to the prewar status quo. These areas may provide a buffer zone. They would assure that NATO is not right on Russia's doorstep, even if Ukraine can join, which is not a sure thing. In size, they would be comparable to the Baltic states, and ethnically, they would remain Slavic. Look at old Yugoslavia and how the map changed after the war there. Conflict brings about changes such as these, and could that be a way forward?

Not everyone may ratify this. By 2023, Kosovo was recognized by only 101 out of 193 United Nations member states, 22 out of 27 European Union member states, 27 out of 31 NATO member states, and 33 out of 57 Organization of Islamic Cooperation member states. But this is still better than an ongoing war.

What does total defeat accomplish? There is no point in humiliating and weakening Russia too much. It has already been diminished and pushed into the arms of the Chinese (pun intended). Its expansionist ambitions have been rejoined. The key is to handle aggression in a way that does not provoke a nuclear strike and the danger of triggering World War III. God forbid.

India's Guest Panelist: Jawaharlal Nehru
For me it is déjà vu. I think the Cuban Missile Crisis distracted the world media from what happened along the China-India border in 1962. We called it a war, although formal relations were never broken off on either side. In this mountainous terrain, with the chaos of Partition first and then China swallowing up Tibet on our northern border, there were border areas that were still not

151

settled when the British left. Bureaucrats redrew the lines more than once, trying to find solutions suitable to both sides. But there were also border skirmishes, and the lines that exist today were not drawn up in meetings. They are the legacy of a border war.

I was the prime minister of India, and Mao Zedong was the chairman of China. We were called the two Asian giants. The USA was adamantly opposed to communism, so we were able to source bigger and better weapons from them.

To the challenger in the middle, I ask—is there no place for another Non-Aligned Movement in the new Cold War that is emerging? It is no longer a cold war between capitalism and communism. It seems to be between globalism and the vestiges of nationalism—Hindu nationalism in India, MAGA in the USA, etc. The word *polarization* is used more now than the term *cold war*, because this great divide occurs inside nations, too, not so much between blocs. Is there a space in the middle?

Challenger in the Middle

I think that the African delegation of peacemakers led by Cyril Ramaphosa saw itself in this light. They are nonbelligerents in the Ukraine war, and they desperately need an uninterrupted flow of grain exported by Ukraine. Unfortunately, China is backing Russia, and NATO involves much of Europe and America. Some Muslim states like Iran are sending weapons to support Russia, and North Korea has deployed troops there. So I think Africa is as neutral as you can get. India has tried its best not to take sides, but it is not on the best of terms with China. Its relations with Russia are intact, not too strained by the war.

South Africa belongs to BRICS (Brazil, Russia, India, China, South Africa). This became very awkward in 2023 when it was South Africa's turn to host the biennial summit of BRICS. Normally, Putin would attend. But the ICC (International Criminal Court) had issued an arrest warrant against him. This was for the forced removal of orphans and children from the occupied areas of eastern Ukraine, back into Mother Russia. This qualifies as genocide in international law. And South Africa is a member of the ICC. Worse yet, there were some suspected exports of South African arms and munitions to Russia, which South Africa has vociferously denied. Nevertheless, African leaders rose to the occasion and tried to arrange peace talks based on neutrality.

Putin did not attend the BRICS summit, but China's Xi and India's Modi did rock up. There was a significant enlargement of BRICS membership, including countries like Ethiopia and Iran. So it combines nonbelligerent countries with others that support Russia. This bloc is occupying the space that the old Non-Aligned Movement used to. Nations that oppose NATO (like China and Iran) are being joined by those that guard their neutrality. This is a gentle rebuke to NATO.

This polarization is not unlike what happened in England after the Protestant Reformation. There were originally two camps—the Roman Catholics and the Nonconformists. But when King Henry VIII nationalized the church, he broke from Rome while preserving many of its rites and rituals in Church of England worship. The look and feel of Anglican worship is still very Roman, compared to the radical Nonconformists, who sidelined the sacraments and put a pulpit in place of the altar. The Bible became central.

Henry's daughter, Elizabeth I, did her best to keep this via media going. She even had to condemn her sister, Mary Queen of Scots, to death when she would not recant Catholicism. The risk was too great that the Church of England would backslide. So Mary's son James was raised and taught by Nonconformists in his homeland of Scotland, while he awaited the end of Elizabeth's reign. In a sense, he was nonaligned.

When he was crowned King of England and Scotland, the cross of St. George (+) and the cross of St. Andrew (x) were combined to make a new flag—the British ensign. This was very symbolic of how James I set about to secure the via media. He recognized that there were as many Bible translations as there were church denominations. So he recruited scholars and formed them into teams to adopt a "one-size-fits-all" Bible translation. It is still called the King James version or the Authorized version. To his credit, there was a good mix of scholarship from right across the spectrum. The monarch ordered them to work together, and the result was remarkable. The same Bible was now esteemed in all churches. He had found a way to unite a nation without closing down churches at either extreme.

Mr. Nehru, when Mao Zedong went to war with you, he stated bluntly that his ambition was to ruin you. It was vindictive, even though you were both statesmen who had spent long hours talking together in previous years. In the disputed border areas, not one country or the other conquered them. They were and are still divided. There have been tensions and skirmishes since, but the "battlefield borders" have held.

In the absence of a Non-Aligned Movement to keep nations from enlisting in nuclear war or even a World War III scenario (God forbid) and without an executive monarch strong enough to impose a via media, I think that the "battlefield borders" may end up determining the end of this war, like they did in the Sino-Indian war and Korea. The African initiative was too weak, and the stronger BRICS is not impartial.

Often, the truth can be found in history. If we don't study it, we are doomed to repeat it. So truth-seekers should read about the past and look for guidance there.

If we only look ahead through the windshield without ever checking our rearview mirrors, we could induce the death of truth.

Moderator
The time has come again to thank our four lucid guest panelists and salute our three challengers for the insights they have shared as we seek the truth. Now, will the real Truth about Ukraine's future please stand out?

15

LEGAL ISSUES

SELECTIVE LAW ENFORCEMENT

Moderator

HELLO AND WELCOME once again to our third series of *Telling the Truth*. This new series looks at topics in the field of law. We hope that you will find our quest for truth stimulating and utterly devoid of falsehood, hypocrisy, guile, or manipulation. We are here to expose fake news, fact-check, cross-examine, and listen to three witnesses. We welcome these spokespersons for the right, left, and middle—our challengers.

Today, we are also welcoming a new panel. As usual, they are joining us courtesy of the new app Time-Zoom. The global village is shrinking even more with this app, to include not only our contemporaries far and wide, but thought leaders of previous generations as well. Today we welcome John Diefenbaker from North America, Peter Benenson from Britain, Abraham Fischer from South Africa, and Indira Gandhi from India.

Welcome to everyone! Panelists are selected for their historic grasp of the big issues in each series. John was an eloquent criminal defense lawyer before entering politics and serving six years as Prime Minister of Canada. Peter was the attorney who founded Amnesty International. Bram was the Afrikaner who defended Nelson Mandela and his co-accused at the Rivonia trials. Indira studied history at Oxford. She is the daughter of Nehru and later became Prime Minister of India herself. There is little doubt that this panel champions the truth and can help us find it.

Our first topic in this series is selective law enforcement. In one word, this means favoritism.

We are seeing signs of this in the world today. Some citizens seem to be above the law. Others become targets of law enforcement, singled out for persecution. This raises questions about the distance between the executive branch of government and the judiciary. People are arrested first and then investigated later. Then the charges are withdrawn because the initial police brutality was not based on the truth. So the punishment comes first—detention and loss of reputation. Then the case comes before a judge, who dismisses it because there was never any truth to the charges.

Remember that charges have to be proved in a court. In civil cases, the balance of probabilities is enough. But in a criminal case, there is a much higher threshold—prosecutors must prove the charges beyond a reasonable doubt. If no bail is granted, the defendant can be detained for long periods pending investigation and trial. Prosecutors don't investigate—they only prosecute in the courts with evidence, testimony, and a good working knowledge of the law. The police do the investigation, and this can cause delays, which can be intentional. There are ways that the police can stretch the time pending a court appearance, either in jail or out on bail. This is abusive, but it happens all the time.

One old trick is when the police arrest someone on a Friday afternoon. Many lawyers knock off early to play golf and don't work on weekends. So even though the law says that everyone charged has a right to come before a judge within forty-eight hours, it won't happen if they give you a "weekend special." You won't get to court until Monday morning after being held for three nights. Four nights if it's a holiday weekend! This is a classic act of selective law enforcement. The police investigators know how to punish you as much as they can before you ever reach a courtroom. They can even arrange to harm you while you are in detention.

It is Britain's turn to launch the questioning in a new series, so please get us started, Advocate Benenson.

Britain's Guest Panelist: Peter Benenson
This is exactly what prompted me to launch Amnesty International! I was a practicing barrister. During a period of convalescence in Italy, in 1958, I converted to Catholicism. I sensed fire in the belly against injustices by the regime of the Portuguese dictator Salazar. People were going to prison for speaking out against his repression. They were being accused of subversion for critiquing his renaming of Portugal's colonies as its "overseas provinces." They didn't like the rising military intervention overseas and warned that it could not stem the tide of *uhuru* (freedom) and *amandla* (power).

This is why I absolutely hate the term "conspiracy theory." Salazar imprisoned people for speaking truth to power, not just whistleblowers but genuine political protesters. Salazar did not understand the term *loyal opposition*. Everything his critics said was shrugged off as a conspiracy theory.

Every narrative that goes against the prevailing regime's version of events becomes a lie—a "conspiracy theory"! Challenger on the right, please confirm if civil liberties are still an issue to the alt-right. Are we no wiser now to that conspiracy theory trap? Who are the spin doctors in today's world? How do we tell a spin doctor from a prophet?

Challenger on the Right
Thank you for asking. Yes, I can assure you that in democratic countries, there is now a high respect for peaceniks and dissidents—until they step out of bounds, that is, as Julian Assange did. He founded WikiLeaks in 2006, forty-four years after the meeting you convened to launch Amnesty International in 1962. Personal computers and the Internet appeared during this interval.

Of course, left-leaners might sympathize more with activists who have crossed red lines. Greenpeace has acquired a solid reputation for stepping out of bounds. But that does not mean the alt-right is against whistleblowers. In fact, they are quick to tap what whistleblowers can tell, to poke holes in the Big Lie. The people who get mad at you for telling the truth are the people who are living a lie.

There are two sides to the coin—the censor and the spin doctor. The desire to censor people comes from an inability either to counter their ideas or to defend one's own. It's easier to silence them with fact-checkers and gag orders. Sometimes they disrupt access to social media and even throw journalists into jail. But the role of propaganda is there too. Flood the media and social media platforms with disinformation—lean hard on the tech barons and insist that they manipulate their algorithms according to your narrative.

Yes, you can bet that the military junta in Myanmar regards Aung San Suu Kyi as a conspiracy theorist. Vladimir Putin regarded Alexei Navalny as a conspiracy theorist, God rest his soul. Alexander Lukashenko regards exiled Belarusian opposition leader Sviatlana Tsikhanouskaya as a conspiracy theorist. She is lucky enough to have been convicted in absentia, whereas the opposition leader in Myanmar was held under house arrest. In Russia, Navalny was also incarcerated, where he died. I think you will agree with me that the real spin doctors are not Aung San Suu Kyi, Alexei Navalny, and Sviatlana Tsikhanouskaya.

Beware of people who speak of conspiracy theories. They are more than likely gaslighting!

I think people have been too quick to criticize religion and to run to secular alternatives. They might call me a conspiracy theorist for saying so, but the deepest roots of both liberalism and socialism are in Christianity. Liberals believe in the free and sacred nature of each individual. That can be traced back to the Christian belief in free and eternal individual souls.

Humanists borrowed that conviction and made it a new starting point—that the unique nature of *Homo sapiens* is the most important thing in the world. They replaced the concept of God-given truth with a new meaning. The supreme good is the good of the human species. That is their truth.

Further to the left, socialist humanism is also borrowed from Christianity. Socialists have a different starting point—that all humans are created equal. This can be traced back to the monotheist conviction that all souls are equal before God. So, for socialists, "humanity" is paramount, not humans. Collective solutions are better than the individualistic approach, which can be divisive. This is their truth.

The reason that Nazis are really left-leaning, contrary to popular disinformation, is that they agree that "humanity" is the starting point, not the individual. However, the National Socialists blended this with a doctrine of evolution—the survival of the fittest. In their view, the human race is always mutating and has been evolving all along. That is where the notion of an Aryan superrace came from. Social Darwinism suggests that evolution has its winners and its losers. So, while *sapiens* is our core identity, we all have about 4 percent genetic content from Neanderthals. This lingers long after that species went extinct. The Nazis wanted to reign for a thousand years, to dominate the subhumans.

Who are the real prophets that guide us? Well, in the book of Genesis, Joseph was sold by his older brothers into slavery in Egypt. But his predictions came true. The prophet Jeremiah was thrown down a well by an angry king who didn't like his "conspiracy theories"! Nevertheless, they came true. John the Baptist was beheaded for speaking truth to power. But he rightly predicted who the messiah was. And Jesus was crucified, ostensibly for sorcery. But what he said was true—not one stone of the temple was left standing. This conspiracy theory prediction came to pass about forty years after his victory over death. This view of revealed truth remains with many of us. For "we beheld his glory, ... full of grace and truth" (John 1:14 KJV).

South Africa's Guest Panelist: Bram Fischer
I am a communist. After the Rivonia trials, I was even arrested and tried because of my political persuasion. But I am also a lawyer, and as such, I believe in the rule of law. I do not like to see bribery of the police or, worse yet, of judges, but it happens in South Africa. Magistrates are for sale, and some people think that bribes are cheaper than speeding tickets, so they pay off the police in cash, thereby corrupting due process.

So I am disturbed by a prison inmate getting parole early, when that parole is judged by the Constitutional Court to have been done unlawfully. I am speaking of Jacob Zuma, who was jailed for contempt of court. While he and I do see eye-to-eye politically, I am also a ward of the court. I bow every time I enter a courtroom, and I turn and bow again every time I leave it. I am programmed to respect the law, especially the "bench." So how can I abide such disrespect? We have to play by the rules because if the rules are suspended, then it becomes a free-for-all. Anarchy.

Let me ask the challenger on the left, my comrade—are we not all equal before the law? Can you lump a crime like contempt of court in with other political charges, such as those that were faced by the treason defendants? In a free and democratic South Africa, why is there still this kind of selective law enforcement? Isn't it an abuse of the judiciary?

Challenger on the Left

First, I need to remind you of what I have said before: there are different shades of red on the left. It starts with pink on the near left and runs to crimson on the far left. I have also indicated that although I am left-leaning, I do believe in democracy, and that includes the rule of law. To some people, the phrase *democratic revolution* is an oxymoron. They fear that revolution is always violent and destructive, trying to tear down capitalism before building up socialism. But not all socialists see violence as the strategy of choice.

This gets us to a point about truth. If you say something often enough, people will believe it to be true. That is where the uncritical belief comes from that all left-leaners are violent. That is just not true. But most people don't really want the truth. They just want constant reassurance that what they believe is true. As a Jedi might say, tongue-in-cheek: "May the Farce be with you."

It's a downright lie that violence pervades pink as well as red. There are gradations, and some of us on the left are law-abiding. As for me, for example, I consider selective law enforcement to be a political and social cancer.

So to answer your question directly, cheating your way out of jail says a lot about you and also the prison system. Jacob Zuma was playing to the gallery. Because he served his country for decades in public office, he felt that this rap was "persecution." But that is politicizing a crime that he committed.

He is trying to do what the treason trialists did. With your help, Bram, they said they wanted to turn the whole thing around backward—to put apartheid on trial in front of the world media. They succeeded in exposing it for what it was—a political charade. They had clearly been singled out as a political threat to the racist regime. But Jacob Zuma is not succeeding in doing this.

And his "Stalingrad strategy" is also running out of steam, after seventeen years of zigging and zagging. The corruption trial will happen in due course, and that could get him another jail sentence. There is always talk of a presidential pardon. However, with periodic elections always on the horizon, that is fraught with risks for Zuma's successors. Eventually, the corruption case may finally get to trial, so Jacob Zuma still may be sent back to jail if he is convicted and sentenced again. But at his age, he won't languish there for long. His epitaph might be "He fought the law, and the law won."

India's Guest Panelist: Indira Gandhi

I am no stranger to the inherent risks of leadership in a democracy. My 1971 election was voided by the Allahabad High Court in 1975. By then, I had already ruled for four years. So we imposed a state of emergency, and I ruled by decree for another two years. I called an election in 1977 as a reality check, but public opinion had turned against me. The opposition alliance said it was the last chance voters would have to choose between dictatorship and democracy. Sound familiar? So I was defeated. But in 1980, I ran again and won another election, by a landslide. It seems to me that history repeats itself.

Sometimes the judiciary can be used to overturn elections. But sometimes it is too late—fait accompli—by the time the courts get around to deciding. Delays in the courts of India are legendary, and they are getting worse, not better. So as someone who has been elected, who has been convicted, who has ruled by decree, who has lost an election, and who has made a comeback, I want to ask a question to the challenger on the right.

What is the logic of "defund the police"? Is that any way to punish the boys in blue for selectively enforcing the law? Is the answer to that injustice really to diminish law enforcement? When I faced a situation of chaos and confusion, my damage control was to tighten up security, not to loosen it, without abandoning democracy altogether. Declaring a state of emergency is, in fact, a constitutional option. Defunding the police seems to be the wrong gesture.

Challenger on the Right

Defunding the police was certainly meant to take the claws and the teeth out of an animal that was seen to be selectively enforcing the law, in the wake of George Floyd's death. During the BLM riots of 2020, sometimes the police basically surrendered and opted instead to march side by side with the protesters. This put a good face on it. But that was a mask. It was tactical, not strategic.

The truth about the Capitol riot in 2021 is still being sought. One narrative is that senior Democrats resisted police requests to scale up the security precautions. Some read this as entrapment, but it does align with defund-the-police thinking. The Capitol police chief on January 6 was Steven Sund. He called repeatedly for backup as he watched the crowd turn into a mob. It was denied to him, a fact that was overlooked by the first investigation, which conveniently then destroyed all its records, an unlawful act of sabotage. Who are the criminals, one wonders? The so-called insurrectionists who stormed the Capitol? Or the politicians who blocked Steven Sund's pleas for backup and then shredded all the records of their committee?

You ask me about the logic of it. I can't answer that question because defunding the police is not rational. It is irrational. How do you explain anarchy? Wouldn't it make more sense to spend more, albeit in new ways, like psychological support for first responders?

Look at Portland, one of the fifty biggest cities in the USA. According to the IRS, the latest income tax returns (filed in 2020 and 2021) show that Multnomah County lost a net of 14,257 tax filers and their dependents. As a result, the county suffered a net income loss topping $1 billion for the first time. The IRS has been tracking moving data for a decade, and this has never happened before. People and businesses just left as a result of the breakdown in security. It was an exodus.

In June 2023, the *Wall Street Journal* reported that almost 3 percent of Portland's population decided to leave between 2020 and 2022. It cited the US Census for its calculations. "The drop of about 17,400 to 635,000 was the sixth largest decline among the 50 largest cities," the *WSJ* stated. It noted that local leaders are now desperate to keep people from moving out. Ms. Gandhi, I think you could teach them a thing or two about despotic democracy and cracking down. Without law and order, chaos ensues.

Some may say, "Oh, that's like the French Revolution," but it settled down after a while, and people got on fine without a monarchy. Except that not long after, an emperor called Napoleon arose, and democracy was scrapped, just like Julius Caesar crossing the Rubicon and defeating the Roman Senate. When you create a power vacuum, someone powerful will step into it. Defunding the police is part of the problem, not part of the solution.

In the two hundred years since Napoleon, the closest thing we have seen to him is Donald Trump.

North America's Guest Panelist: John Diefenbaker
I cut my teeth in politics as a newsboy, selling newspapers. This experience taught me how to monitor current events. Later, I studied law and became a criminal defense lawyer.

It seems to me that any country where the government goes after its political opponents by indicting them, thereby denying the electorate its right to vote for them or against them, is known as a banana republic.

Are we presumed guilty until proven innocent? I want to ask the challenger in the middle about "implicit bias." What is it? Can it be avoided or at least minimized? Is that getting down to where the rubber meets the road?

Challenger in the Middle

Implicit bias is something you have to work around. It happens everywhere, especially where juries are utilized in reaching verdicts. In North America, something like one out of ten people is black. It is the reverse in South Africa, where one out of ten people is white. There is a systemic bias in the courts of both countries. Let's say a young African American man is the defendant, and jury duty falls on ten people from his community. A majority of jury members will likely be white, bringing along their cultural baggage with inevitable prejudice, just because of the demography of his city. This essentially means that the defendant will not get a fair trial. Or so it will seem to him. But he cannot plead a mistrial because implicit bias is embedded in the system—que será será.

The reverse happens in South Africa. In South Africa, a young white couple was forced to stop by two other cars. One slowed down and stopped in front of them on the highway. The other car crowded them from behind so that they could not back up to go around the car in front. They feared it was a carjacking in progress, so the driver crashed back and forth into both cars until he found room to escape. Then he raced to the nearest police station. He was followed by the two cars. He ran into the police station and pleaded for protection. The black drivers of the other two cars chased him and started attacking him.

The bewildered black police officers stood by while two black men fought with one white man in the hall of their precinct. The police failed to intervene. The protagonists ended up in a wrestling match on the floor. The police did not try to break it up. The white man's wife had her cell phone with her, so she made a video of this fight with the police standing idly by. She sent this to the media, and it was on the national news that night. It got onto social media as well. The adverse publicity has ruined the young white man's career, making it hard for him to find work. This is the way implicit bias works under a black majority.

So I disagree that it is "just an American thing." It has to do with being outnumbered. Both Nelson Mandela and Martin Luther King said in speeches that while they had struggled against the oppression of blacks by whites, they would also oppose the domination of whites by blacks, if it should ever come to that.

Defunding the police has not brought about any improvement. Cities like New York, Chicago, and San Francisco are becoming hot spots of crime. The city center of San Francisco looks like a ghost town. Dozens of citizens are shot and murdered every weekend in Chicago. Youth sometimes occupy certain streets in outright lawlessness, and the police look the other way. Riots in New York are beyond the capacity of the NYPD. This is largely because of the irrational policy to defund the police.

Similarly, the murder rate in South Africa is horrifying. Corruption continues unabated because the police are soft on crime. In fact, various mafias are emerging, so organized crime is on the rise. These mafiosos bled the wealth out of Eskom, the country's power utility, on an ongoing basis, to the point that power cuts or "load shedding" became ubiquitous right across the country. Every citizen feels the negative impact of it while the mafias prosper. Afrikaners feel it disproportionately because when they raise concerns about genocide, the government just says that crime affects everyone.

Ironically, the very cities where crime runs out of control are where the prosecutors are on a witch hunt for ill-conceived political targets. Speaking of which, selectivity runs both ways—law enforcement has slow-walked investigations into relatives of those in power. Once charged, they are offered unusually lenient plea bargains even though protestors at the January 6 Capitol riot have been treated harshly, by comparison. Implicit bias makes it look like a two-tiered justice system where revenge and leniency are both handed out for political expediency.

Moderator

Oh wow! Our challengers have a way of making us dig deep in search of truth.

Thanks again to our four guest panelists for incisive cross-examination. Asking questions is one way to find the truth. Keep us digging until we hit the mother lode that we are all here looking for together! Now, will the real Truth about selective law enforcement please stand out?

POLITICAL CORRECTNESS

Moderator

Welcome once again to the eleventh episode of *Telling the Truth*. Our topic today is political correctness.

Some words are used so much that their meaning becomes ambiguous. For example, the word *appropriate* tends to be overused to the point that its meaning gets blurred. Then some words get black-listed. It may even get you into trouble for hate-speech to utter certain words like *nigger* in America and *kaffir* in South Africa.

Our four panelists will put this topic to the test. They have joined us via the new app Time-Zoom. They may address whichever of our three challenges they wish. As a team, we are all working together to be honest so as to illuminate the truth.

No one here is lying, not intentionally so. This is a safe space where differences of opinion are accepted as natural, as different trees in the forest. We are not all the same size or color, but we are all trees. Some offer a canopy of shade, others bear fruit, others generate lots of wood for fuel or lumber, and others fill in the underbrush for the safety of the animal kingdom. That's why God created vegetation on the third day and animals on the fifth day. The plant kingdom creates the conditions for the animal kingdom to prosper.

Here we welcome adult conversation without yelling, mocking, or bullying.

We despise lying of any kind because of our shared commitment to finding the truth. When people lie, it is deceitful, and that says something about them. When they lie in court or before congressional hearings, it is perjury. That is a crime. That's why witnesses are asked to take an oath before testifying. A distinction must be made between different perceptions and bearing false witness.

So we need to choose our words carefully, which leads to a debate over our language and how to use it in just and non-misleading ways.

It is South Africa's turn to start the questioning, so over to you, Advocate Fischer.

South Africa's Guest Panelist: Bram Fischer
It is uncommon, but not unheard of, for a tribal chief in Africa to be a woman. So we are better than the ancient Romans in this respect, but we still have a long way to go. Neither South Africa nor the USA has ever elected a woman to the highest office of president, but Britain and India have both done so.

As a communist, I am convinced that to win people over to a new way of thinking, you have to tweak the language. Otherwise, you are always playing defense, talking someone else's language. To play offense in the forum of ideas, you have to get people talking your language. Karl Marx did this with vocabulary like the *industrial proletariat*, the *petty bourgeoisie*, the *masses*, and so on. He could have just kept talking about the working class, the middle class, and progressives. But he put a new spin on it.

To my comrade on the left, may I ask whether the real problem is unlearning what we know already—that is, learning new vocabulary. Words represent ideas in our heads, and once an idea is loaded and locked in our brain, it comes with certain associated words. Isn't the whole point of political correctness to change the way people think, not just the way they talk?

Challenger on the Left

Exactly! Some of Africa's thought leaders speak of "colonization of the mind" being worse than colonization itself. Even when the external forms of it were dismantled, the deeper reality remained.

The Zulus' first name for whites was "magicians" (*abelumbi*) because King Shaka witnessed a white man killing a man without touching him (with a gun). As far as he knew, only a witch could kill someone without physical contact. It took generations for the "demystification of the gun" to take place. Only after that could the black majority rise against the white minority. And now gun control has become a huge problem. The murder rate in South Africa is horrendous.

Gun violence is a global human rights issue because guns threaten our most fundamental human right—the right to life. But again, the language of the gun lobby is most familiar. It is playing offense. "I am packing." "Concealed carry." "Vermont carry." The only answer that I have seen is a sign on the door of an NGO: "You are entering a gun-free zone." There are such places where guns must be surrendered, like inside churches and synagogues.

So there is more to PC language than just using words that won't offend people. It's a mind game. Changing *deaf* to *hearing impaired* is pretty tame. Whereas the change from AD to CE, for example, says something that may be offensive to some who believe in revealed truth. Those beliefs have come to be embedded in our language, so reframing history is redefining reality.

Calling a short person "vertically challenged" or a bald person "follically challenged" is almost silly. But changing *chairman* to *chairperson* is a gentle reminder of gender activism. Changing *prostitute* to *sex worker* is even stronger activism. It says something about swapping morality for human rights.

For our purposes here, the change from a "liar" to one who is "economical with the truth" is most relevant. That really softens what was once regarded as immoral, back in the days when we all memorized the Ten Commandments. Lying used to be antisocial, when there was a right and wrong, as opposed to the era of relativism, where there is some social space even for a liar. They serve a purpose in the ecology of humankind (not *mankind*).

For some on the far left, it may be convenient or even necessary to abandon God and morality. Voltaire has already been quoted. He famously said: "There is no God, but don't tell that to my servant, lest he murder me at night." To run any society, you will need a philosophy of truth. Beware a society in which truth is totally subjective. It might all boil down to who has the biggest guns.

In the motion picture *Oppenheimer*, the famous nuclear physicist succeeds in splitting the atom first, before Germany or Russia manages to do so. But he then ends up in a postwar crisis of conscience. For this, American Prometheus takes firepower from "the gods" and gives it to man. Earlier in life, he learns a language that does not seem relevant until he ages. Then it really changes him.

In the movie, this crisis of conscience comes out of nowhere. Except for some light foreshadowing—a few hints dropped here and there in on-screen conversations about World War II and the Holocaust, including discrimination against Jews in America. Deeper than the science, some beliefs and convictions were lurking. But there was a disconnect between that and his ambitions. Oppenheimer was Jewish and had German family connections. So the oppression of Jews in Germany, along with discrimination in America, symbolized this deeper level. The fact is, Oppenheimer was not a practicing Jew, having opted for secular humanism and rationalism. The movie is all but silent about this, so you wondered where he was coming from. But it grew from seeds planted in his mind earlier in his life.

The movie has a lot to say about truth, and it does not end until the truth comes out. The truth vindicates Oppenheimer after a flawed investigation and then a congressional hearing during the McCarthy firestorm. How was the truth arrived at? Evidence, cross-examination, rationality, and then a vote. A few words spoken along life's path germinated slowly.

This inner crisis led him to become an early proponent of nuclear disarmament. The motion picture's message is that only the truth can set you free. Without truth, there is no freedom.

Oddly enough, as a rationalist and a scientist, he rejected revealed truth. He substituted objective truth in its place and stuck to it. He was victimized by those who subscribed to subjective truth. The deeper we get into science and technology, the more we should worry about the death of truth as we have known it in the past. Oppenheimer had a brilliant mind, which is not true of everyone. He was a clear thinker, which not everyone is. In practical terms, can we afford to abandon revealed truth? It has served us well for millennia.

India's Guest Panelist: Indira Gandhi

I must start by saying that although English is an official language in India, it is not my native tongue. I speak several Asian languages, and in terms of European languages, I am more comfortable in French than in English. But I don't speak any ergative-absolutive languages, which can really muddle your mind. Tibetan and Basque languages are among these.

So learning vocabulary, or unlearning it in some cases, is relatively easy for me. Let me ask the challenger in the middle: can you give us examples of vocabulary changes? How can we be progressive without losing what we love most about our tongue?

Challenger in the Middle

English has evolved from the Old Saxon language. At one stage long ago, Old English and Old German were the same language. Then came Middle English, the language in which Chaucer wrote *The Canterbury Tales*. The next phase was Elizabethan English, famous for the dramas of Shakespeare. By the time King James I ordered that scholars from across the denominational spectrum prepare a single one-size-fits-all translation of the Bible, English had moved on again. But Shakespearean English was so cherished and esteemed that King James I ordained that his "Authorized version" should be in Elizabethan English, not even the English of his day. So, it not only sounds old-fashioned to us, but it also sounded old-fashioned when it was first published. This was a statement and a strategy. Also, King James recognized that literacy rates were generally low, especially among the common people. So the teams of translators were instructed to agree on phrasing that would sound best when read aloud. Reading from a digital tablet by scrolling down and listening to an audio-Bible were still a long way off. Most people would hear the English read by their clergyman, so the king wanted the best audible translation possible, in what was regarded as the best English ever, even though it was already seventy years out of date by the time it was completed.

Anyone who knows Elizabethan English will remember that its vocabulary still included *thee* and *thou*. "Unto thee, O Lord … Thou shalt not commit murder." In today's Portuguese language, there is some retention of *ti* and *tu*, especially in Portugal. "A ti, O Senhor … Não matarás."

What is interesting is that Portuguese is gradually dropping pronouns altogether. Even in English, you can drop the pronoun and say, more directly, Don't murder. Don't stay out too late. Don't get the wrong idea! In Elizabethan English, *you* denoted more than one person—the second-person plural. The second person singular was thou. What happened? Where did those pronouns go? Why was English streamlined and refined when Elizabethan English was proudly regarded as the high-water mark?

One explanation is that Queen Victoria disliked anything too personal or "familiar." So she prudishly discouraged the use of *thou* and *thee*. In terms of body language, she also discouraged handshakes. She preferred the very formal greeting, "How do you do?" Not to mention her dislike of kissing in public—and kissing on the lips, never! One kiss on each cheek was much too personal, and a third kiss was decadent.

My point is that English usage does evolve. So it is no surprise to see certain words being preferred and others being sidelined. But there is surely some level of politicization in this "live" etymology.

North America's Guest Panelist: John Diefenbaker

I know that history moves on. My family moved from Ontario to the Northwest Territories in 1903, only to find ourselves living in a new province called Saskatchewan starting in 1905. My province grew from 19,200 families in 1901 to 150,300 families only fifteen years later. This was a direct result of the emergence of Marquis wheat, which could be harvested within the short growing season on the prairies.

However, I am conservative to the core. I held my hat over my heart and hung my head low when the red ensign was replaced with a new Canadian flag. Likewise, I lament the changing semantic range of the word *gay*, which used to be straight vocabulary. The word *homosexual* works fine for me, with its counterpart *lesbian*.

I am not opposed to change for the better. I introduced a Bill of Rights to Canada, including for our Indigenous people. I eliminated racial discrimination from Canada's immigration policy, and my opposition to apartheid secured the departure of South Africa from the Commonwealth of Nations.

But really, do we need to revise our classics? And our pronouns? Please, can the challenger on the right speak to this ridiculous revisionism, for I suspect that you think more or less as I do on this topic. Why don't the 99 percent of us who aren't offended by everything quit catering to the one percent who are?

Challenger on the Right

Ridiculous is right! We are in good company, thinking this way. Film director Steven Spielberg agrees, and so does Piers Morgan. When Spielberg edited the motion picture *E.T. the Extraterrestrial* for its twentieth anniversary in 2002, he replaced guns in the hands of policemen with walkie-talkies. Another twenty years on, he stated that it was his mistake to do so, because *E.T.* was a film in its particular era. Following on this logic, he stated that changing the language in some of the classics of literature, which publishers have been doing of late, is a form of censorship.

Piers Morgan had an even stronger word for it. He called it cultural vandalism. He was commenting on Puffin's decision to edit phrases and words within Roald Dahl's children's books. This editing was done by Inclusive Minds ("passionate about inclusion, diversity, equality, and accessibility in children's literature"). They removed any language that they regarded as too strong, including a reference to one character's double chins. Dahl fans took exception to editors rewriting an author's manuscript without permission. Publishers have gone the way of universities and schools, so deep into wokeism that they are losing authenticity.

Peter Hitchens says that the past is being obliterated. James Bond is being cleaned up. Even Chaucer has been removed from curricula at some universities for the offense of relaying fourteenth-century attitudes toward women. Homer is steeped in toxic masculinity.

Do you remember John Lennon being asked at a news conference in the mid-1960s what he thought about women? He answered with a pun: "Women should be obscene and not heard." Everyone laughed because Beatlemania was raging. It would be edited out today. Comments like this must be contextualized.

They would really ruin some Monty Python skits. Setting red lines for new artwork is one thing, but redacting existing masterpieces is over the top.

Gender pronouns are the focus of redaction. Gender-neutral language is the goal. The moderate approach is to replace *he* and *she* with *they*. This works, but a more radical approach is to introduce a single personal pronoun that encompasses both genders. Some suggestions are "thon, hes, zhe, hu": Thon loves baseball ... Hes is going to the game ... Zhe has a front row seat ... Hu is on first.

It's really hard to find a balance between grammatical integrity and gender neutrality. Ultimately, the truth is not subject to opinion. You can call a fork a spoon all day long, but the soup will still run through it. So let's not let the one percent minority rule the 99 percent majority. That is undemocratic.

Britain's Guest Panelist: Peter Benenson
I am a lawyer, and we are trained to be very careful with words. The way people use words can also imply something unsaid. For example, when the Truth and Reconciliation Commission found, in its final report in 2015, that the Canadian residential schools system constituted "cultural genocide," it

conspicuously avoided saying that it was "genocide." The qualifier adjective says a lot. This was the TRC's term and is not a legal finding of genocide or even a statement that the legal definition, unqualified by "cultural," was met.

Shortly thereafter, the then–Chief Justice of Canada, Beverly McLaughlin, stated publicly the same thing—the system was "cultural genocide." This was a public statement by the Chief Justice, not in a court judgment. Her comment was not a legal conclusion. She, too, avoided saying that it was "genocide." There is simply no abiding definition of this term, as there is for *genocide*. The relevant definition would be the one included in the UN Convention on the Prevention of the Crime of Genocide, adopted in 1948. Beverly McLaughlin did not say that it was that. The use of words is very telling.

Political correctness wades into the area of hate speech. So, to the challenger on the left, can you convince us that political correctness is really correct? Or is it just more annoying, inconvenient overreach?

Challenger on the Left
Languages change. In the 1960s, a hip word was *groovy*. It came and went. A generation later, a favorite word was *grody*. It's gone out of use now; you no longer hear anyone saying, "Grody to the max and gag me with a spoon." Around this time, the word *awesome* gained popularity. It may prove to be more enduring.

So why not intervene in language to meet societal trends? Why not seek out gender-neutral pronouns to expose that the male advantage is embedded in language, which is part of culture? Is this not scientific?

In Western culture, there are many languages. Embedded in all of them is an advantage to the male gender. It's not just English that does this. But to promote awareness and change in the Anglophone world, intervention speeds up the process.

Now I have to be quite honest with you. Religion is very deep both in individual psyches and in culture. And since Rome unbanned the church and adopted monotheism to replace polytheism, which had been widely practiced up to the conversion of the emperor Constantine, some aspects of Roman culture became entangled with Christianity. I am not accusing Jesus of being a male chauvinist. He was not. That is clear from all accounts of his followers and of his encounters with women, like the lady at the well in Samaria. We have every reason to believe that the early Christian church held women in high esteem. They were integral to that movement, and this simply got corrupted when Rome and Christianity converged.

There were advantages to this merger, but there were setbacks as well. The role of women remained important, but not equal. Constantine's mother, Helena, was instrumental in his conversion, and his wives and family engaged in the rise of Christianity. But the radical views of Jesus on gender parity were lost. Can anyone name a Roman emperor who was a woman? Certainly, there were powerful wives like Fulvia, first wife of Mark Antony; his third wife, Cleopatra; and Livia Drusilla, wife of Caesar Augustus and the first Empress. But Roman law kept the levers of power for men only. Thus, the radical views of Jesus were left behind until the heyday of the suffragettes.

Unfortunately, this was cemented by orthodoxy until after the Protestant Reformation. Orthodoxy came out with its creeds, which had a Roman way of trying to standardize theology. This caused some major controversies, but the point that I am getting at is that the Council of Nicaea was held in AD 325, not long after Constantine's conversion in 312. As the content of the New Testament was written and circulated before that, there was no mention of the Trinity. This concept was first articulated by an African church leader called Tertullian. Certainly, the Holy Spirit was often mentioned in the documents but was neither transcendent like God the Father nor incarnate like God the Son. The Holy Spirit appeared as a dove descending on Jesus when he was baptized, as tongues of fire on the day of Pentecost, as a seal in the letter of St. Paul to Ephesus, as a cloud, and in other manifestations.

My point is that in Greek and Latin, all nouns belong to a gender. For example, "dove" in Greek is *peristerá* and in Latin *columba*. Both feminine genders. So it was that in documents and correspondence of the early church, the Holy Spirit (i.e., God) was sometimes referred to as "she." Pronouns have become so conspicuous these days!

This had to be addressed, and so one of the resolutions of the Council of Nicaea was that God should always be called "he." Alas. After the Protestant Reformation, there was a renaissance of early church theology, and views of women began to slowly radicalize. Of course, there were occasional exceptions like Joan of Arc, but on the whole, Catholic practice hardened its heart on this matter. No pope has agreed to ordain women, although in Protestant circles this is becoming more and more common. This is the legacy of the merger of Rome and Christianity.

I am not saying that God is a woman. That is different than saying the church lacks gender parity. But I am sadly aware that some may see the redaction of English in this respect as a rebellion against God. Of course, to my radical colleagues on the crimson far left—who already deny the existence of God—this is as it should be.

In closing, can I quote Tertullian on truth? He wrote, "The first reaction to truth is hatred." So I am not surprised when I hear conservatives say that they hate political correctness. Hopefully, they will get over it. If they find it annoying, they should pray the Serenity Prayer, for language is dynamic, not static. Sometimes it needs sharpening.

Moderator
Our time is up. It's time once again to thank our four guest panelists. And we thank our three articulate challengers, whose ramblings are very helpful. Now, will the real Truth about political correctness please stand out?

GENOCIDE

Moderator
Welcome to the twelfth episode of *Telling the Truth*. We are continuing our law series, and today's topic is genocide.

Our four panelists examine this topic closely. They join us via the useful new app Time-Zoom. They may address any of our three challengers.

As a team, we work together to illuminate the truth. We do not lie, but our views differ. We look for truth, topic by topic. Above all, we try to identify ways and means of finding the truth in a world full of debates and controversies.

Genocide is a heavy topic, perhaps the heaviest of all on our show, with the possible exception of assisted suicide, which we are leaving until the end, for our closing episode.

Genocide is also topical, for Vladimir Putin of Russia has been charged with genocide by the International Criminal Court. This is making his life even more complicated than usual, as he tries to prevent NATO from arriving on Russia's doorstep. The ICC has issued an arrest warrant for him. It is based on the removal of children from the areas of Ukraine occupied by Russia's 2022 invasion, ostensibly for their protection, to remove them from a war zone. More on that from our panelists and challengers later.

Furthermore, South Africa has charged leaders of Israel with genocide in Gaza, only to be confronted by the Afrikaners for "economic genocide" against the white minority.

It is India's turn to ask the opening question. Please go ahead, Ms. Gandhi.

India's Guest Panelist: Indira Gandhi
As the population of the world reaches eight billion, it seems that we have more outbreaks of these atrocities than ever before. As a historian, though,

I look back and wonder—was the Partition of India and Pakistan not ethnic cleansing?

Today, I am burdened by femicide in India. The way that the Meitei mob of men paraded two naked Kuki women is an example of tribal tensions that have simmered for years. The Kuki are predominantly Christian, and the Meitei are mainly Hindu. They dwell together in the province of Manipur, which is sandwiched between Bangladesh and Myanmar. The Meitei compose the majority in the province; the Kuki are one of several minorities. But the violence is not tribal or religious; it is gender-based. Prime Minister Narendra Modi said that this incident shamed India.

Can I ask the challenger in the middle why violence centers on gender when the two tribes are distinct and have different religions. The fault lines are deep, but one would think the cracking would come along ethnic or religious lines. Can you explain this hatred and violence against women?

Challenger in the Middle
Perhaps this is yet another symptom of the far left versus alt-right polarization.

I sense that wokeism is hard to define. The reason is that it has so many strands. Feminism is one of these strands, quite distinct from pro-choice, globalism, Marxism, LGBTQIA+ rights, gender modification (i.e., the "trans" agenda), and, above all, environmental activism. What these diverse agendas have in common is that they all push for change. Beyond that, each strand is on its own.

In the past decade, the dominant party in Indian politics has been Hindu-nationalist. Let's say that this is quite conserving, almost the polar opposite of woke thinking.

Possibly, men who are fatalistic about the caste system and accustomed to strict gender roles are antagonized by the massive change agenda. Perhaps they did not pray for enough "wisdom to know the difference" between accepting what they cannot change with serenity and changing what they can with courage. It is the opposite of courage for a man to strike a woman. That is cowardice.

When the British first colonized India, *suttee* was widely practiced. A man's widow was burned alive or immolated herself with him on his funeral pyre. That practice has been terminated, but the status of women remains a fundamental problem.

Violence begets violence. There is a vicious cycle of reprisals. This has happened between clans everywhere. Like the feuding clans of old in the USA. Like the raiding in Mongolia that caused Temüjin to lose his beloved Börte, only to go on the attack and win her back. That dynamic caused him to keep raiding and fighting until he had built the biggest empire in human history—the Yuan Empire of the Great Khan. I am not condoning violence, but some cultures do champion it.

Why has China moved Uighurs from their homes and placed them in concentration camps? They want to reeducate them, to avoid the emergence of hostile Muslim extremism right at the western end of China. And right in plain sight of Tibet, which capitulated without much armed resistance in the 1950s. Again, I am not justifying what they are doing, which is said to include sterilization. If so, that is genocide. I am only trying to stand in their shoes, to understand their point of view. That also sounds rather like ethnic cleansing to me. The British did the same to the Boers during the Anglo-Boer War, but that was in the context of formal hostilities. China is conducting this extermination in peacetime.

Speaking of extermination, was it not practiced in the USA against the Indigenous people of North America? It was never adopted as the official policy, but there was a huge gap between policy and practice. Variously, the official policies were called segregation, assimilation, and allotment. But annihilation was obviously on General Sherman's mind when he remarked that the more Indians he killed this year, the less he would have to kill next year.

Something similar to Manipur is happening in North America. Indigenous women are a special target. Their disappearances and murders are on the rise. Why do they use a health term to describe it ("epidemic")? Gender-based violence is taking on the proportions of a silent genocide. But this is a slow-onset disaster, not a fast-onset crisis like the Rwanda genocide. Again, there is no link to official policy, as there was in the case of the Armenian genocide and the Jewish Holocaust. But at the level of crime, it is happening, just as in Manipur.

The best medicine is to create open forums, safe spaces like *Telling the Truth*, where topics can be vetted and all rational sides can be heard in adult conversation.

North America's Guest Panelist: John Diefenbaker
Before entering politics, I was a criminal defense lawyer. So this topic really interests me. One thing about criminal law is that the truth threshold is very high. Prosecutors must prove beyond a reasonable doubt that the charges are true.

What exactly do we mean by "true"? Truth cannot admit even a shadow of doubt. Doubt has to be obliterated by evidence, witnesses giving testimony, the relevant opinion of experts, and a clear logical argument.

A criminal lawyer does not need to prove the defendant's innocence. He or she merely needs to raise enough doubt that the truth of the charges is clouded. Truth casts out uncertainty. If there is no doubt, there will be a conviction.

To the challenger on the left, do you sympathize with Putin? I wonder if you think that there is a safe defense strategy for the indicted. Or can the case against Putin hold water without leaking?

Challenger on the Left

First, I want to clarify something. I do lean left. But does Putin? Is he or Russia still communist? Or has he become a dictator? He is clearly unfriendly to NATO and Western culture, especially in its most recent manifestations. But is that because of the orthodoxy he learned in the KGB? Or does he hold to the doctrines of orthodox Christianity? Or because he is a Slavic nationalist who wants to ensure a perpetual space for his "Rus" culture? His close ties to the Russian Orthodox Church suggest that he is more an ethnic champion than a Marxist atheist.

Sorry, but I think there may be some guilt by association embedded in your question about me sympathizing with Putin. The fact is, I am a democratic socialist. I abhor totalitarian governance. The war in Ukraine is not communist aggression, per se, because I don't think Russia has regressed to soviet socialism. It is rather holding firm to its sense of national and global importance and resisting what it regards as decadence in the West. Russia wants to safeguard its hemisphere.

I believe that his defense, should he ever be captured and brought before the ICC, would be weak. Let's start with the definition of genocide in the UN Convention. It is very specific about the treatment of children: "(e) Forcibly transferring children of the group to another group." This follows after the phrase: "acts committed with intent to destroy, in whole or in part, a national, ethnical, racial or religious group." In other words, is Russia abducting children to force them to adopt its culture?

Putin's defense is likely that he did not intend to destroy the group that the children removed from Ukraine belonged to. In fact, he may argue that he intended to get them out of harm's way. He may point out that when parents from Ukraine came forward seeking their children, they were allowed to take their children back to Ukraine with them.

He may add that in the occupied areas, including Crimea, there has long been a Russian majority. And that Ukrainians had a habit of discriminating against Russians, who were a minority in the vast country, but a majority in the border areas now occupied by Russia. Thus, Putin was not just saving the children from the dangers of living in a combat zone, but in ethnic and religious terms as well.

He might even point to the removal of British children to the colonies during World War II. Or to the removal of Jewish children from Germany during World War II, lest they end up in dire straits like Anne Frank.

This defense will meet the force of truth. Russia annexed Crimea unlawfully. Russia invaded Ukraine. Russia waged war on Ukraine, and the children are basically prisoners of war. Children, Ukrainian citizens, even if they were ethnically Russian, were forcibly transferred to homes or institutions in Russia. There might be a caveat here—if the children were transferred to Russian-occupied Crimea, which is technically still part of Ukraine.

However, the prosecutors will have a tough job to convince the bench that Putin had the intent to destroy any ethnic group. Kyivan Rus culture has roots going back in history over a thousand years. It was basically part of the Byzantine Empire—the eastern empire, long after the primacy of Rome in the west had fallen away. That started when Constantine became emperor—he was from Dacia, not from Italy. That is on the western shores of the Black Sea. He abandoned polytheism and adopted monotheism, specifically Christianity, as the religion of the empire. So, while Christianity remained predominant in Western Europe long after the empire's capital shifted to the east, that was Roman Catholicism. Kyiv Rus culture was Eastern Orthodox, and its ethnic connections were Slavic. Constantine's capital was named after him until its name was changed later to Istanbul.

Then along came the Mongols. In AD 1240, Kyiv was decimated, and Slavic culture was fragmented. One site where it reemerged in later centuries was Moscow. So Putin would probably argue that Ukrainians are cousins to the Russians and Belarusians, if not siblings, and that removing children was to save the "Rus" ethnicity, not to harm it.

Eastern Europe remained part of the Mongol Empire for another 240 years after Genghis Khan conquered it. All I will say is that this Slavic space still has very strong ties to Asia, and there is a lingering resistance to being swallowed up by Europe and its decadent postmodern values and customs. Seen through Russian eyes, the West has become intoxicated with pleasure. This has eroded its foundational values like hard work, sacrifice, and frugality. People no longer even agree on what truth is! Russia would rather keep close ties to Asia than to Europe. The war has made it a client state of China.

I agree with the moderator that genocide is very topical in today's world, starting with the alleged abduction of children from Ukraine, but also on other continents.

Britain's Guest Panelist: Peter Beneson
As a human rights organization, Amnesty International is constantly on the lookout for genocide. It recently concluded that there is no evidence of it in Tigray, in the recent civil war in Ethiopia. But it has found evidence of Russian war crimes in Ukraine. Beyond the abduction of children, that is, in Russia's military actions.

It is very hard to take preventive steps against genocide. The Rwandan genocide comes to mind. The senior UN official, Romeo Dallaire, tried his best to sound a warning. He was a Canadian military deployee who felt that his warnings fell on deaf ears at the UN. We see genocide mostly in the aftermath. That is why the International Criminal Court was set up in 1998. However, although 123 countries have signed onto its charter (the Rome Statute), there are some major holdouts, notably the USA, Russia, India, and China. That gap could be its undoing.

Let me start by asking the challenger in the middle to make a distinction between genocide and crimes against humanity. Are they synonymous? And speaking of semantics, when some citizens kill others as occurred in Rwanda, is that tribalism? Racism? Genocide?

Challenger in the Middle
These two terms are distinct. Genocide has its definition, which my colleague just quoted. The term "crimes against humanity" is broader, encompassing a list of crimes, including but not limited to murder, extermination, enslavement, deportation, unjust imprisonment or deprivation, torture, sexual crimes—rape, sexual slavery, human trafficking, sterilization, inter alia—persecution, enforced disappearance, apartheid, and attacks on civilian populations. All are inhumane acts against humanity.

The ICC's remit is to enforce international law on four crimes. *Genocide* and *crimes against humanity* are the first two. Genocide intends to exterminate. Crimes against humanity are intended to inflict great suffering.

Then there are *war crimes* and *ethnic cleansing* as well. War crimes obviously cannot happen in peacetime. One example is the death squads of El Salvador. Which brings to mind another term, *assassination*, like the murder of archbishop Oscar Romero in El Salvador.

Patrice Lumumba's killing was an assassination by the Belgians, a murder. But that involved a racial dimension. As was the case with the assassination of Martin Luther King Jr., which occurred in peacetime.

Incidentally, the motel where MLK was assassinated has been turned into a Human Rights Museum in Memphis, Tennessee. And the one tooth that survived of Patrice Lumumba's gruesome murder has been returned from Belgium to the Congo for burial.

Ethnic cleansing is implicitly racial. But it may not involve killing; it may be forced relocation or sequestration. Resettlement of people can be legal if it is properly negotiated and they are compensated and supported—for example, if they live in a valley that will be flooded after a new dam is constructed. However, if they are simply forced to flee, urbanize, or cross a border to seek refuge, that is ethnic cleansing.

Your question about semantics included terms like tribalism and racism. Clearly, there is an overlap of terminology. In the case of the Armenian genocide, the Turks were Muslims trying to eradicate Christians. That is genocide, but how different are the Turks and Armenians racially? They are both Caucasians, but their languages have different roots. Whereas when the Egyptians of old enslaved the Jews, these were two different races. Egyptians were of black African descent, and Jews were from the Middle East. A distinction is sometimes made between the post-flood descendants of Shem (Semites) and the descendants of Ham (father of Cush), two of the sons of Noah. If they were distantly related, how different could they really be?

Soon after gaining power in Zimbabwe, Robert Mugabe tried to decimate his opponent's tribe in Matabeleland, a region in the south of that country, in 1982. That was tribalism. Both the majority Shona and the minority Ndebele are Bantu tribes. So the series of mass killings, the Gukurahundi, was not racism. But it was a genocide. It ended with the Unity Accord in 1987. Joshua Nkomo may have been able to mitigate the genocide, but it was fierce. The name derives from a Shona-language term which loosely translates: the early rain that washes away the chaff before the spring rains.

Whereas the Hutus and the Tutsis, in the Rwanda genocide of 1994, are different tribes from different races. The Hutus are Bantus, short and brown. The Tutsis are Nilotics—cousins to the Dinka and the Nuer of Sudan, the Ethiopians and Somalis of the Horn of Africa. They are tall and dark. The physical difference between the two is very clear. Thus, the Hutus spoke of the Tutsis as "cockroaches." This was incendiary hate speech. Incitement. That genocide was racist, but not all are.

South Africa's Guest Panelist: Bram Fischer
I would like to ask about two different related factors. Nowhere in all these conventions is "femicide" mentioned. It is possibly the greatest social evil in South Africa today. Where does it fit into the framework of crimes against humanity?

Also, thinking back to sanctions which were controversial but finally imposed on the racist apartheid regime, isn't there an international responsibility to protect? The ICC basically investigates cases forensically. But "an ounce of prevention is worth a pound of cure." So is there any way to enforce international justice before these horrible atrocities occur?

Let me give the challenger on the right an opportunity to speak.

Challenger on the Right
Thank you, esteemed advocate. On the term *femicide*, it is the killing of women or girls because they are female. Please note that the UN Convention on genocide reads: "intent to destroy, in whole or in part, a national, ethnical, racial or religious group, as such." So gender is never cited. However, when a man kills a woman because she is female, it is not just "misogyny"; it is a hate crime. This is the most extreme and detestable form of gender-based violence—GBV.

Biologically, it would be imprudent for men of any ethnicity to wipe out all the females. So perhaps it is more a form of "crimes against humanity" than of genocide per se. Or perhaps it is confronted more on a case-by-case, person-to-person basis. In some places, it has reached proportions that are on a par with genocide.

Like the term *cultural genocide*, which has been used to describe the system of residential schools in Canada, the term *femicide* cannot muster the legal definition of genocide in the UN convention. That does not excuse it from being genocide. To many people's way of thinking, it is the lowest of the low. It is the vilest crime of them all.

In Canada, the phrase *epidemic of violence* is used to describe the high incidence of disappearances of Indigenous and Métis women. About 4 percent of the Canadian population is Indigenous and female. Yet they represented 24 percent of homicide victims. This is not just disproportionate, it is horrifying. One question is whether it is non-Indigenous men murdering Indigenous women, which would be racial. Or is it internal GBV within the Indigenous and Métis community? So many cases remain unsolved that it is hard to know for sure.

In 2022, South Africa's police measured a 27 percent increase in homicides over the 2021 statistics. Of this number, an average of nine women a day were murdered. This is nearly six times the global average, by population.

Now to the second part of your question. The Responsibility to Protect, R2P, doctrine says that "if a state is unable to protect its population from 'genocide, war crimes, ethnic cleansing and crimes against humanity,' then the international community must do something."

This international norm was adopted in 2005 by the United Nations—no doubt due to the failure to act timely in the Rwanda genocide a decade earlier. General Romeo Dallaire sounded the warning, but the UN dallied. As a result, 800,000 Tutsis were murdered in cold blood while the peacekeepers waited and watched. To his credit, Dallaire made a lot of noise about that horrific scenario, leading to the R2P doctrine.

Before I end, I must say something relevant about truth-seeking. How do we know for sure that a crime against humanity or a genocide is really happening? What kind of evidence is needed to convince people? In the political arena, there is so much deception and grandstanding that we often get confusing signals. Also, we find that human rights have overtaken absolutism, so we no longer look for right and wrong. We look for violations of rights. But these always have to be weighed against the rights of the opposite side.

I would say that by abandoning revealed truth and the morality that came with it, we are losing time. I, for one, think that the Responsibility to Protect should be treated as a disaster mitigation measure, not merely as an emergency response. Of course, this is easier said than done, but protection by definition should precede outbreaks. Peacekeepers should be deployed sooner.

On this note, the Trump administration has confronted South Africa about "white genocide." The farm murders may not muster that definition yet, but it is still in its early stages, like alcoholism, which does not go from abstinence to addiction overnight. It is a process. Possibly it is wise to unpack the R2P doctrine to avert another crisis?

Moderator

Agreed! Our challengers are not deceptive or trying to mislead you. Nevertheless, they do think differently and tend to disagree. But they are expressing their honest views. Thank you to the three of you!

And thanks to our four guest panelists for your probing questions. The law does change from one country and continent to another, but some principles are abiding. One of those is that the truth exists and can be found. Whether truth is immutable or whether it changes with time and place depends on your personal view of its very nature. Tolerance is important all around, but intolerance is growing for the traditional view of revealed truth. Could that lead to the death of truth? We hope not.

I have to note that neither the panelists nor the challengers have mentioned the war in Gaza. I cannot let the curtain fall on this episode without pondering why that may be. First of all, the two-state solution is a work in progress, not a fait accompli. So we are talking about one nation, not two. Second, while it has been ugly both ways, from October 7, 2023, it has not been about mass extermination, as in the Rwanda genocide. The closest we come to that is Hamas rhetoric to eliminate Jews everywhere. It has been open warfare, targeting combatants. There is a difference between collateral damage and intent or purpose to commit genocide. Far fewer people have been killed in Gaza than in recent wars between Saudi Arabia and Yemen, Ethiopia and Tigray, and the two factions in Sudan's civil war. So the case for genocide at the ICC is flimsy at best.

Furthermore, it doesn't really seem to fit the definition of ethnic cleansing. All countries have to root out terrorism. People have been internally displaced for tactical military reasons but have not been forced to leave. Many would like to leave of their own volition. So, while leaders on both sides have been charged, more Hamas leaders were charged, and with more serious "crimes against humanity." The ICC does not say "war crimes" per se, as Israel claims security responsibility for the Gaza Strip, which it conquered and annexed in 1967. So the charges are very broad, and it will take a long time for the legal dust to settle on whether these charges can succeed.

That is, if the ICC survives the backlash that it faces from countries in the global north. Ironically, Russia and America may find their views of the ICC in alignment. Another irony is that for years, African countries opined that the ICC had been set up to deal with "tinpot dictators" in the Global South. Whereas in this instance, South Africa initiated the charges—the same country that protected Sudan's al-Bashir when a legal attempt was made to arrest him while attending an OAU summit there. This seems like a bias, which often tends to be in favor of the underdog—Gaza.

The history of Israel and Palestine has many layers. When ruled by the Egyptians, it faced south. When the Greeks and Romans occupied the Levant, it faced west. When the Arabs prevailed, it turned its back to the sea and faced east. When the Ottomans were predominant, they faced north. But always over these centuries and millennia, the same space was shared by nomads, Egyptians, Philistines, Israelites, Greeks, Romans, Byzantines, Arabs, Turks, British, and so on. Perhaps the model of a "rainbow nation" is best for that strategic space. Certainly, the majority in the whole region prefers the prospect of peace and prosperity to perpetual warfare. The Abraham Accords are making a comeback.

Now, will the real Truth about genocide please stand out?

CHUCK STEPHENS

DECRIMINALIZING PROSTITUTION

Moderator

Hello and welcome! This is the thirteenth episode of *Telling the Truth*. We want to know the truth. We are still in our law series. Our topic today is decriminalizing prostitution.

Topics like this are debated. There is a wide variance of views. Different ones prevail in different places, and views change from one era to another. That is why we use the new app Time-Zoom. It gives us both a wide geographical perspective and the benefit of talking to people who have gone before. Time-Zoom has not entered the future yet; it can only travel back in time. So our final series of five will be about the future. Stay tuned!

When you check into a hotel, you may be asked about your room: "Smoking or nonsmoking?" This has disappeared in some spaces, where smokers have to go outside. But at some hotels on some continents, it remains the norm. Would it surprise you if the next question they asked you was "Would you like an escort?" In places where prostitution has been legalized, this may happen. Tourism at some destinations already offers you this choice.

Imagine where this could lead to. Like a waitress asking you several questions to clarify your order. White bread or brown? Toasted or plain? Butter or margarine? A white escort or a black one? Female or male? Young or mature?

Some see prostitution as a business. In 1888, Rudyard Kipling began a story about a prostitute with the sentence, "Lalun is a member of the most ancient profession in the world." At the same time, others see it as a vice that is degrading to women. What is the truth? And to what extent does that hinge on our deeper understanding of what truth is?

Going further back into history, neither the Greeks nor the Romans outlawed prostitution. It was legal and widespread, and prostitutes paid taxes. As Christianity rose during the Middle Ages, it was regarded as an "inferior good," for it offered some protection to respectable women from the advances of young men.

This changed following the Protestant Reformation and into the Victorian Era. The rise of science had brought with it the awareness that outbreaks of sexually transmitted diseases (STDs) were connected to this vocation. So attitudes began to harden against it. By the twentieth century, many countries and jurisdictions had begun to outlaw the practice.

In today's world, public policy varies. In much of the world, prostitution is illegal. In some countries, notably the Netherlands, Germany, and Mexico, prostitution is legal and regulated by the government. In Brazil, India, and

Great Britain, organized brothels are illegal, but prostitution is legal. In some countries, it is the act of buying sex, not selling it, that is illegal, while both are illegal in the United States, except for Nevada.

There is also a sinister link to human trafficking. Since ancient times, many prostitutes were actually orphaned children or captured slaves. They had little choice regarding their role. In today's world, this continues unabated. Young girls and boys are often forced into sex slavery against their will. This sometimes involves abduction and transfer to another country.

Today, it is North America's turn to lead the questioning. Give it up for John Diefenbaker!

North America's Guest Panelist: John Diefenbaker
As a criminal defense lawyer, I think that Canada has adopted a sensible policy. The operation of bawdy houses is an offense. That is the prime focus of law enforcement. It is illegal to buy sex, but not to sell it. That is the right balance.

As a Christian, I believe that we have found a good balance in our legal reforms. We can charge the pimps who exploit women, and the buyers who could harm them. But we do not charge women in this age-old vocation because, for health and safety reasons, we need to know who and where they are—to be able to protect them.

Let me ask the challenger on the right if this policy called "partial decriminalization" is better than criminalization. Is it an acceptable compromise, or is it eroding the truth?

Challenger on the Right
The problem is that there has been so much exuberance for change. People are no longer cautious about new trends. They just want to scrap the old ways. For example, along comes artificial intelligence. Everyone accepts it uncritically, like 5G. Then suddenly, we read an article in *The Economist* by a brilliant mind, Noah Yuval Harari, called "AI has hacked the operating system of human civilization." Ouch!

Holland moved too fast in legalizing the sex trade, and it has hurt women badly. As a result, Amsterdam became a hub for child trafficking and human trafficking.

Laws should not be revised quickly, from one day to the next. They are embedded in the way our lives and thoughts work. Change should be slow and incremental.

Ultimately, a great deal hinges on your understanding of truth and what it is. If you believe that truth is pluralistic, then to each his own. You will loosen up, live, and let live. If you believe that truth is objective, "out there" somewhere, whether rooted in deductive reasoning or inductive observation, you will experiment and observe. Your policy will be based on rational analysis, on what works best.

Suppose you believe that truth is revealed from one God, like Christians do, or from various sources, as in Hinduism. In that case, you will hope to get alignment between your deepest beliefs and convictions and public policy. That is quite natural. You will stick to your guns, pun intended. This lines up with conserving the status quo, conservation, and goes along with being relatively conservative.

In pressing for change, we have to ask questions like, will legalizing prostitution give men fewer reasons or more reasons to beat women? Will a border war ever end if those fighting it both believe that this land is their land? What will happen to legislation that clashes with views held at the deepest levels of the convictions and values that affect behavior in a society?

Before we decide how to vote or what our views are on any topic, we need to come to terms with what truth is. You are a Christian, sir, but only 2.6 billion people in the world are Christians. Your view of truth is not the only one.

Islam accounts for another 1.6 billion citizens of the world. In Islam, truthfulness is something to be cultivated until it becomes implanted in a person's soul and disposition. Then it will be reflected throughout the person's character and in their behavior. The very word "Muslim" means "submitted to the will of God." Does this sound like a pluralist truth? Or like revealed truth?

Another 1.2 billion people on Earth are Hindus. To them, *satya* (truth) is considered essential. Without it, the universe and reality cannot function and fall apart. In Hindu scriptures, *rita* and *satya* are opposed by *anrita* and *asatya* (falsehood). Truthfulness is considered a form of reverence for the divine, while falsehood is a form of sin. How compatible is this with a view that truth is subjective? If so, why revere scriptures like the Rig Veda? In short, there is a right and wrong.

To sum up, if 5.2 billion people see the truth as largely revealed, should we trade our cherished beliefs and convictions for a bowlful of wokeism?

Add to that what Confucius said: "The object of the superior man is truth."

Britain's Guest Panelist: Peter Benenson
What is abhorrent to me about prostitution is its links to the exploitation of children and, more especially, to human trafficking. So I will refrain from commenting on morality or the human rights of prostitutes.

In terms of children, there are two distinct issues—forced labor and underage exposure to the sex trade. These are illegal, even if you don't believe in morality. The salient point is that their child rights have been violated. Forcing minors to work is one offence. Sex involving minors under eighteen years of age is a second offense, even with their consent. A distinction cannot be made between the consent of a minor and the law. It is just plain illegal, full stop.

Let me address the challenger in the middle. How do we diminish or even put a stop to this diabolical trafficking of children?

Challenger in the Middle
Have you seen the motion picture *Sound of Freedom*? For many people, it was a wake-up call. Are you aware that the movie's release was delayed for years? Let's be honest; there are deep, vested interests in this trade. Hollywood did not want to host it, so it was handled privately. To me, that said a lot about the nature of truth. You can hide it under a shade, but sooner or later, it will slip out.

The movie is a class act in awareness-raising. Until the public is broadly aware of a social problem, like STDs, mentioned by our moderator, attitudes don't change. In fact, powerful people in the world and the USA seem to have clandestine connections to this trade. Could that be why Jeffrey Epstein committed suicide in his jail cell? I admit that is speculation, but the image of an island where the rich and powerful can go to, escaping the law and having their way with children, is the centerpiece of *Sound of Freedom*. There is no specific indication that this was an allegory of Jeffrey Epstein's famous island. But it seems to be implied. There must be a reason that the locals call it "Pedophile Island." Where there is smoke, there is usually fire.

After awareness raising, there must be activism. "Name and shame" is a good principle, especially when it comes to the rich and famous, who can afford nondisclosure agreements and have enough resources to pay off the politicians, the police, and even the judges if it comes to that.

Unfortunately, it does seem that liberalizing attitudes about sex and marriage in general, and about prostitution specifically, have a way of softening up people's objections to child trafficking and human trafficking. It is the opposite of guilt by association; it is mellowing by association.

Does it say something about women that they need a pimp? The main role for pimps now is not protection; it is recruitment. But they do set some red lines for their ladies. One of these red lines in the USA is to minimize encounters with black men. The optimal customer is older and whiter. This is ironic in a way because Atlanta is the hub of illegal prostitution in America, followed by Miami. Atlanta's demography is 48 percent black. Miami's is only 12 percent black. Miami is also 45 percent Latino, so whites are in the minority.

Those who promote the decriminalization of prostitution do not explicitly condone child trafficking, but it is hard to separate the two. Slowing down the sex trade would certainly shrink the number of children deployed.

South Africa's Guest Panelist: Bram Fischer

Tourism is a very large industry in South Africa. So there is economic pressure to liberalize the limits on prostitution. On the books, it is still illegal. In reality, it is practiced everywhere and tacitly condoned.

On the other hand, this could be related to a very low view, in general, of women, which translates into the high rates of GBV and femicide.

So to the challenger on the right, should we be modifying our somewhat puritanical laws about prostitution? With such high unemployment rates, can't this be seen as opening up employment opportunities for women?

Challenger on the Right

Not so. Not at all. Let me start by reminding you that a majority of feminists worldwide are not in favor of fully decriminalizing prostitution. They see the vocation as degrading to the gold standard of gender parity in the workplace. They think that it actually endangers women, putting them in harm's way.

There is a somewhat ironic alliance between feminists and Christians in this regard. For example, the "I Am Priceless" movement in Holland. Many Christian women are activists in this outreach, which has become very public. They rebuke the liberalization of Holland's laws and want to roll them back— not to criminalize it again, but to return to the so-called "Nordic solution," which is to go after the men who pay. Make buying sex illegal, and leave the poor women alone.

In fact, this movement was supported by youth and was widely called an "abolition movement," resonating with the slavery theme. By getting forty thousand signatures on a petition, they forced the Dutch parliament to debate the issue. They contend that since Holland decriminalized prostitution in 2000, human trafficking has risen incrementally. One of their slogans is "Prostitution is both a cause and a consequence of inequality."

I don't think that fully legalizing prostitution is a suitable make-work program for unemployed women. However, I do think that South Africa should opt for "partial decriminalization." That is, don't charge the prostitutes. Charge the men who pay. To me, that would be the best of both worlds.

India's Guest Panelist: Indira Gandhi

In 1950, soon after becoming an independent nation, India signed the International Convention for the Suppression of Immoral Traffic in Persons and

Exploitation of Prostitution. In 1956, our own Immoral Traffic (Protection) Act was enacted. In 2006, the definition of "brothel" in that legislation was expanded. It had been quite narrow. Thereafter, along with "house, room, or place," more settings were added—"vehicles, crafts, buildings, flats, hostels, and restaurants."

However, by 2009, this legislation was under attack. India had three million prostitutes by then, and 40 percent of them were children. There was a growing sense that this called for state intervention, not by the judiciary but more by health and welfare services. In the end, India has arrived at a standoff. Owning and managing a brothel is illegal, while prostitution is legal.

The challenger on the left deserves equal time to speak on such a critical issue. What direction do you think India should go in? How fast should it liberalize its legislation?

Challenger on the Left
Like other topics, left-leaners do not all agree on one solution, but we agree that at least partial decriminalization is worth exploring. The hazards of full decriminalization may be too inconsistent with India's deeply entrenched beliefs and customs.

Let me take an extreme example from South Africa. There is a traditional African custom there called *ukuthwala*. It is a staged raid to abduct a woman for marriage from her family kraal. Not unlike the Mongolian raids through which Temüjin lost his first wife and then recaptured her. One essential ingredient in marriage, from a human rights point of view, is her consent. This custom ignores that prerequisite. So it is essentially unconstitutional if carried out against her will. But it has not been outlawed and is still practiced in deep rural areas. It is a local and traditional version of human trafficking.

But when the ANC Women's League wanted to oppose it officially, they could not even muster a resolution to debate it at their conference. This is because the resistance to revising local culture is so strong, even among women.

Traditionally, your law in India tried to keep the lid on it. But that didn't work, and the health proportions—especially given pandemics like HIV and AIDS—began to weigh in on the other side of the scales held by Lady Justice. That word in brackets (Protection) in the name of the Act says a lot. Given the rise of GBV and even femicide, is it wise to legalize the sex trade? Will that not open a Pandora's box to human trafficking?

Going after the men who pay discourages the trade and minimizes the degradation that the vocation can bring, especially when it is out in the open. Is it not better to keep it in the voluntary and private sphere?

CHUCK STEPHENS

For example, soft drugs like marijuana, called "dagga" in South Africa, are being legalized, but not for use in public places. To answer your question, I would be very cautious about jumping into full decriminalization.

Moderator
How can we ever thank our four guest panelists and our three lucid challengers, who speak to the topics and to truth itself?

Now, will the real Truth about decriminalizing prostitution please stand out?

16

HEALTH ISSUES

ABORTION

Moderator

HELLO, AND WELCOME to a new series of *Telling the Truth*! Today, we begin our health series with our fourteenth episode, featuring four sizzling topics in our search for truth.

That means we have a new panel, and they are once again joining us via the new app, Time-Zoom. Let's welcome these four experts: Dr. Benjamin Spock from North America, Dr. Wilfred Grenfell from Britain, Dr. Christiaan Barnard from South Africa, and Dr. Anandi Gopal Joshi from India.

Our first topic is abortion. Since the antislavery movement tackled the institution of slavery, no issue has proved as divisive. There are plenty of issues that cause opinions to polarize, but this one just won't go away.

Recently, the Supreme Court overturned a long-standing court decision in the USA called *Roe v. Wade*. In that landmark case in 1973, the US Supreme Court established a woman's right to an abortion. SCOTUS ruled that the decision to terminate a pregnancy belonged to the individual, not the government. Overturning that decision has really put the cat among the pigeons and made it very hard to predict where it will all end. It's almost like trench warfare, with both sides dug in very deep and little movement on either side. There is pro-life on one side and pro-choice on the other.

Now, even though all four panelists are doctors, I want to ask that we steer clear of getting bogged down in medical arguments. Please! It took fifty years of lobbying to get *Roe v. Wade* overturned, so most viewers are already familiar with the technical debate. Whether life begins at conception or birth or somewhere between is not what I ask you to focus on. At this stage, *Roe v. Wade* stood for so long that abortion on demand has come to feel like a human right to many women—especially as feminism advanced its gender cause considerably over that same fifty-year period. In fact, pro-choice is seen by many as a woman's right to make any decisions that involve her own body.

I want to ask the panel to look at this familiar topic in another way. Please, can you look at how your diverse views relate to a deeper understanding, namely, of what truth is? How do our esteemed challengers arrive at their views on abortion? Remember that while we are probing into one topic in each episode, we have a higher goal. We are trying to find the truth, and that starts with methodology: how can it be found?

Please, can our three challengers bear this in mind as well? Let's not rehash arguments that have been debated ad nauseam. Let's raise our sights higher. If people connect the dots in this respect, perhaps the noise will subside. It seems that this issue has been generating more heat than light. There is acrimony and hatred, and we want to explore how to conduct normal adult conversations about divisive topics.

It is Britain's turn to get us started, so over to you, Dr. Grenfell.

Britain's Guest Panelist: Dr. Wilfred Grenfell
Thanks for your wise words, Mr. Moderator.

Times change, and in today's world, missionary doctors are no longer held in the high esteem they used to be. Names like Dr. Johannes van der Kemp, Dr. David Livingstone, and Dr. Albert Schweitzer come to mind. Health has now largely been nationalized into state hospitals, so the age of these health heroes has passed. Even the Grenfell Mission that I started in Newfoundland is now just a "donor." It funds all kinds of projects that are broadly related to the health and wellness of the same target group along the coast of Labrador, which I reached out to.

Let me start with a question for the challenger in the middle. Is there a via media? Can the two rival factions find rapprochement? Or will another civil war have to be fought to settle the divergent views?

Challenger in the Middle
Just as was the case with the abolition movement in Britain and the antislavery movement in the USA, the debate over abortion is showing no signs of going away. One candidate who competed in the 2024 primaries was a woman, Nikki Haley. She was confident that she could find a national consensus on this issue. For one thing, she was the only woman running for the nomination. Like most candidates, she said the issue should be approached with respect, rather than demonizing the opposing side. But being a woman who was "unapologetic" about being against abortion, she might have been uniquely positioned to pull that off. But she did not win the Republican nomination.

But not every candidate seeking the nomination in the same party agreed on the abortion issue! They came from different states, and there were numerous permutations and combinations. Political donors tried to put stipulations in place. Some wanted a fifteen-week ban, others a twenty-week ban, and so on.

Let me take this down to the family level. Different family members have different views. But when the subject comes up at the dinner table, there is more intransigence than anything. People hop right down into their debate trenches. They attack and insult people on the other side. We could do with a lot less arrogance and a lot more humility. If for no other reason, based on the total failure so far to find a balance. That is everybody's fault; we are all to blame. Instead, the flames burn down to red-hot embers, and table talk turns to sports, school, and technology. You don't even have to leave the table anymore or change the subject; you can just recede into your cell phone.

We will not find the truth this way. But most people are not ready to offer their favorite opinions in a genuine pursuit of truth. They prefer to find validation for what they already believe. You will never find the truth that way.

A. D. Aliwat stated: "People deserve the benefit of the doubt, but information? Always hold it up to a cold white light. Misinformation is a tool of the devil."

The devil, like Jack the Giant Killer, whose secret was to get the giants fighting one another so that he could slip away, is divisive and loves to see high levels of polarization in a family to the extent that they decide to remain silent. Family cold wars. They have "no-go" areas of conversation. Taboos help the devil ignite mistrust and dislike. Otherwise, table talk turns to bullying.

There is a phenomenon called "the chilling effect." It has been studied and identified as one manifestation of discrimination. Bring up a certain subject, say grace at a meal, or mention what the Bible says about a topic, and the room temperature drops. This is how people avoid the risk of finding that what they believe may not be the truth. The response is to "shoot the messenger"—blame the one who brought it up. Or blame them for precisely what you are doing—believing misinformation. Gaslighting! No one wants to admit that they might have been misled. Rather, attack the opponent for spreading misleading narratives.

This is the current level to which real adult conversation has degenerated. Meaningful family discussions have evolved into shallow chatter about the weather and gossip. Avoid politics, religion, and the inconvenient truth. Speak in memorized memes. Or better still, avoid contact altogether. Stop getting together.

Until there is a genuine effort on both sides to have peace talks, the cold war over abortion will continue. I am pointing out that we have not even reached the stage of "talking about talks." So how can there be constructive engagement? Most people have been enlisted; they are merely foot soldiers. We need to start thinking like generals if we really want to find a consensus.

The way this topic carries on endlessly, it seems to be an unwinnable war. So we need to learn the skills of talking peace.

South Africa's Guest Panelist: Dr. Christiaan Barnard

Many years after the treason trialists were incarcerated under life sentences in South Africa, their jailers began to take notice of the dignity and leadership of one particular inmate. His name was Nelson Mandela. He was a team man who refused to negotiate with the enemy on his own. Negotiations had to be vetted with his peers. So what did they do? They sequestered him. They took him out of the group, which was his natural habitat, and they switched him to house arrest—in a house they built for him inside the prison walls. He started to receive visits and to be treated like an important figure. He realized that they had singled him out and wondered what to do, for he was out of his element.

Then he decided that events had reached a stalemate, so that he should break his own rule and negotiate with them. This led to some progress. One eminent person who visited him carried a secret message from him to Oliver Tambo, who was leading his party in exile in Zambia. Mandela sent a message explaining that he knew he was acting out of line, but he wanted to break the impasse. So he warned Tambo that he was negotiating with the enemy on his own. He was not doing things right, but he was doing the right thing. That is what finally led past the deadlock.

To the challenger on the right, as I assume that you would naturally be pro-life, what can you do to reach out to end this standoff? Or are the vested interests so entrenched that you will fight on?

Challenger on the Right

Yes, you are right that I lean toward the pro-life position. Of course, there are different variations of pro-life. Some are absolutists; others may have some tolerance for abortion under certain specified circumstances like rape or incest or during certain limited periods. But our camp is called pro-life.

Two previous episodes of *Telling the Truth* come to mind. One is law enforcement in the Legal series. The other is riots in the Macro series. In both these episodes, the question of favoritism is raised.

Recently, a federal appeals court in Washington, DC, delivered a major free-speech victory. It found a discrepancy between the BLM riots of 2020 and the quick arrest of two pro-life advocates in a smaller protest outside of a DC Planned Parenthood facility. They had chalked "Black Pre-Born Lives

Matter" on a public sidewalk, mocking the way Black Lives Matter protests had previously flooded the city with chalk and paint.

The Alliance Defending Freedom (ADF) filed the lawsuit on behalf of members of the Frederick Douglass Foundation and Students for Life of America. The three-judge panel was comprised of circuit judges Robert Wilkins, Neomi Rao, and Michelle Childs. In their unanimous ruling, they wrote: "The First Amendment prohibits discrimination on the basis of viewpoint irrespective of the government's motive."

Governments of both parties have politicized this topic. Being a Republican is almost synonymous with being pro-life. Being a Democrat is almost synonymous with being pro-choice. This is very unfortunate, because people may hold their considered opinion for their own reasons, without reference to a party.

For example, the Catholic church has been pro-life forever, long before this viewpoint was co-opted to win votes. And not for that reason! The Catholic church has its reasons for being pro-life. This stems from its very traditional view of conception. Biology basically says that a father's DNA and a mother's come together at this union. Catholic theology, like Jewish theology before it, believes that conception involves a third element as well. A little piece of God's spirit conjoins the physical union, and thus we hear that we are all created in the image of God. Only at death does that spirit begin its journey back to God, while the physical body decomposes. On the day of resurrection, that little piece of God will be united with a new body. But I digress.

My point is that Christians have their deep reasons for being pro-life. These may align well or resonate with political motives, but too often, we hear that the Republican Party has captured the church. As if it never had its own reasons to think the way it does!

Speaking of favoritism, Catholics came to be regarded as enemies of the state, and government agencies like the FBI were singling them out as radical traditionalists. That was abhorrent government overreach.

We are not likely to get past the impasse when the government inflames public opinion with such incendiary remarks. The government should be a referee, not a player in the game. The church has beliefs grounded in revealed truth. Governments drifted far from morality toward human rights and beyond. Power corrupts, and absolute power corrupts absolutely. This was no longer about the truth of any kind; it reached the proportions of self-perpetuation. Donald Trump was very wise to moderate his campaign's position on abortion and to cool the rhetoric. It seems to have repudiated those who predicted that the Republicans would lose the 2024 elections over this very issue.

CHUCK STEPHENS

India's Guest Panelist: Dr. Anandi Gopal Joshi
As a woman and the first woman in India to graduate in modern medicine, this topic is dear to my heart. When I graduated as an MD in the USA, my thesis was about obstetrics among the Aryan Hindus. At that time, India's population was 275 million. In the 140 years since, it has doubled more than twice to 1.4 billion.

So population growth is a big concern of mine. But abortions should not be performed for birth control. There are many better and safer strategies for that.

So I would like to ask the challenger on the left, why has the planet's population reached eight billion in spite of the rapid emancipation of women? Is there no correlation between gender equality and slowing down population growth?

Challenger on the Left
Not directly. The unprecedented growth of the global population since 1950 is the result of two trends. First, the increase in average longevity is due to rapid improvements in public health, nutrition, personal hygiene, and medicine. Second, high levels of fertility have persisted in many countries. Basically, fertility rates are highest in younger populations, which tend to be concentrated in poorer countries. Nations with older populations have accumulated more wealth, which tends to slow down population growth. Even as some regions become demographically older and wealthier, thus decreasing fertility rates, the planet's overall population is expected to continue growing for some decades to come.

The logic of your question is correct—that as women gain access to education and employment, they tend to have children later in life and generally fewer children. Put another way, a lack of autonomy and opportunity among women and girls can contribute to high fertility rates and rapid population growth. But gender is not the driver in decreasing fertility levels. A youthful population presents an opportunity for accelerated economic growth. If countries where the population is growing rapidly achieve a substantial and sustained decline in the fertility level, that leads to an increased concentration of the population in the working-age range. A larger population in the working age can support an accelerated rise in income per capita. This phenomenon is referred to as the demographic dividend.

Investments in education and health, and the promotion of full and productive employment for all, including women, can greatly expand the positive economic impact of a favorable age structure created by a sustained decline in fertility.

The problem is that countries that are ready demographically to benefit from the dividend often lag in the economic capacity to create the conducive conditions.

In short, the solution seems to be in family planning. An ounce of prevention is worth a pound of cure. Large families in youthful populations are a recipe for slow economic growth, making it all the harder to emancipate women. Thus, some women want to delay or minimize the number of children they have, and abortion is sometimes seen as a panacea. That is overly simplistic. There are bigger factors.

Whether or not a woman can decide for herself is a critical but sometimes contentious issue, fraught with religious and cultural dimensions. But it is second best to run to abortion on demand as a fixer. Far better to plan in an open family consultation. But that in itself presupposes that the man is humble enough to talk about taboos, and respectful enough to let his wife make decisions about her own body. So yes, indirectly, there are connections between abortion and population control, but it is not an open and shut case of cause and effect.

North America's Guest Panelist: Dr. Benjamin Spock
My book, *The Common Sense Book of Baby and Child Care*, first published in the 1940s, had to be revised and rewritten in the 1970s under pressure from feminism. They said that my original version sent out a subliminal message to women that they should stay at home, that it was a woman's role to raise the children. I never said that explicitly, but my left-leaning views were not enough to offset this critique.

I am a secular humanist, so I want to ask the challenger on the left: In my original version, how did I miss the participation of fathers, sitters, and day-care centers in child-rearing? Why did I only use the pronoun *she* when referring to childcare and not alternate with *he*? Is that consistent with my pro-choice stance?

Challenger on the Left
This harks back to some previous episodes of *Telling the Truth*, like the one on political correctness. Basically, we are all in sync with our times. You wanted to establish rapport with your readers, and you succeeded. Big time! You spoke of common sense, so you had views in common with the common people. But taboos started to fade in the sexual revolution of the 1960s and with the rise of psychology as a science. At one time, it used to be lumped into anthropology, but now there are three distinct disciplines—sociology, psychology,

and anthropology. Time moves on. After all, there were some major changes between *Father Knows Best* and Archie Bunker! You had to adapt.

I think that abortion has loosened up as well. At one time, when young ladies fell pregnant out of wedlock, they would be sent to a relative to be kept out of sight. After the birth, the baby would be put up for adoption. Abortion was also operating, but deep underground, as we know from the story of Vera Drake in Britain.

As a leftist, you were an antiwar activist, a proponent of free health care, the legalization of marijuana, and you were against capital punishment. The *Roe v. Wade* decision was dated 1973. That was only a year after you ran for president on a platform that included the legalization of abortion, for the People's Party.

But that decision has now been overturned. Some say that it's like getting slavery back, others say that it's like the end of slavery. Who are we to believe? What's the truth?

I view your pro-choice stance as coherent with your other activism. But we have to be realistic. Half the people in the world are opposed to your permissive stance—maybe more if you include the Middle East, Asia, and Africa. We are outnumbered. To end the polarization, we need to rediscover the lost arts of listening and tolerance. You did it—you climbed down and revised your book. It went on to sell over fifty million copies!

When I heard Nikki Haley campaigning for a national consensus, it made me wonder about a global consensus. Limited access to medical abortions has been legal in India since 1971. But the main concern about legalizing abortion in India was always different from the focus in Western countries. The most frequently asked question in India was whether a change in law would lower maternal mortality (by reducing unsafe illegal abortions) and thereby improve the health of Indian women.

Perhaps it would be better to look at abortion differently. After all, if you are a secular humanist, then you do not buy into revealed truth or morality. You are into human rights, and no one disputes that women have rights, except maybe the Taliban. Do you want to be like them and impose your views on anyone who disagrees? Afghan women have rights too. Law based on human rights as opposed to right and wrong is one of the changes that is overtaking our world. And those on the opposite side of the polarization have their rights, just as people on the other side of the globe have a completely different concern. The West is no longer in a position to dictate to other countries and continents how to think. That would be inconsistent with your generally permissive stance, doctor.

Moderator

My, my! Our challengers give us a lot to think about. Activists tend to get defensive, which can cloud the truth.

Thanks again to our four guest panelists for complying with my guidelines for this topic. There is no shortage of technical data about this debate elsewhere. Our remit is to get you thinking about the big picture of truth and how to find it. If you think that there can be one truth for me, and another for yourself—pluralistic truth, subjective truth—then there will be no letup in the polarization and extremism. For there is an offsetting inertia comprised by subscribers to the notions of objective truth and revealed truth. Now, will the real Truth about abortion please stand out?

COVID-19

Moderator

Hello again! It's high time once again for *Telling the Truth*. We all come from diverse backgrounds and countries, but we share one belief—that telling the truth is always the right thing to do. This is our fifteenth episode, for the record.

Honesty is the best policy. It can help you get to the deeper meaning of any topic that you are exploring. It can ensure you continue on a path toward a growth mindset. When you're honest with everyone, it might be hard at the time, but in due course, things will get better. Whereas with a lie, things could get a lot worse.

Our topic today is COVID-19. Our four panelists put penetrating questions to our three challengers—right, left, and middle. Everyone among us is here to tell the truth. But not surprisingly, there are some wide variances. It seems that truth can be stretched. However, at some point, you may cross a red line into deception, even without realizing it. So we cross-check and cross-examine. Suppose you encounter someone who won't let you express doubts about their views. Beware of ideologues. They tend to be bullies.

The truth always comes out in the end. But it may take some time—and diplomacy—to get at it. It is not unheard of for truth to be buried, only to rise again!

We have all passed through the once-in-a-lifetime experience of a major pandemic. The last one was called the Spanish Flu, although that is not where it originated. This one definitely originated in China, but calling it the Chinese Flu could draw fire, so be careful you don't get labeled a racist.

COVID-19 is a coronavirus. It first appeared in 2019. By early 2020, it became a major emergency. Governments imposed lockdowns and, in doing so, did a lot of harm to businesses and the economy. Yes, people died from the disease. The jury is still out on how accurate the official death toll is. Some voices suggest it has been exaggerated to justify a spate of government over-reach. But a rise in surplus deaths has been observed.

At first, handwashing, contact tracing, and social distancing were used to stem the tide. Then, other measures like masking, hand sanitizers, curfews, and eventually vaccines came into play. A lot of people got sick. Hospitals filled to overflowing. People got really scared. Was the hype justified? What is the truth about this fast-onset disaster? How much deception (unintentional or otherwise) was there in the mix?

It is South Africa's turn to start the questioning. Go ahead, Dr. Barnard.

South Africa's Guest Panelist: Dr. Christiaan Barnard

What I can't understand is how far apart medical communities were and are. Take, for example, the treatment protocols used once people contracted the virus. As it was previously unknown, at first, there was a high degree of exper-imentation. Then governments provided guidelines and recommendations, led by the World Health Organization (WHO).

In 1967, I performed the first heart transplant in the world, in Cape Town. So our level of sophistication in health has long been world-class. And in the end, for those who did not need intubation, our favorite treatment protocol was to combine hydroxychloroquine with ivermectin. This is still scoffed at in the West, even though scientific research done in South Africa has validated its efficacy. India also used this combo, as did Brazil, while the USA, Canada, and Britain laugh at us. "Well," they say, "at least you won't get malaria or worms!"

To the challenger in the middle, let me ask: Is there any validity for intol-erance of other views within medical circles? Was there a reason to be intol-erant?

Challenger in the Middle

There is a difference between managing a crisis in the present and twen-ty-twenty hindsight. In retrospect, I agree that scientific studies have validated your favorite treatment protocol.

But worse than that odd discrepancy is a macro control experiment—namely, Sweden. Strangely, Sweden did not abide by either the WHO or the European Union policies. Yes, it encouraged handwashing and social distanc-ing. But it did not pressure the populace to wear masks or to be vaccinated. It refused to vaccinate children, saying that the risks outweighed the benefits. It discouraged the vaccination of teenagers. It made vaccines available to adults and politely tolerated anti-vaxxers. They were not demonized.

In the end, its national results were the same as everyone else's. This really makes you wonder! Eighty-six percent of Swedes over eighteen years of age chose to be vaccinated, so 14 percent declined. Any Swedes travelling would have been required to have a valid vaccination certificate in Europe or America. But at home, there was a laissez-faire attitude toward anti-vaxxers. This showed a lot of maturity and mettle.

One person who famously refused vaccination was Serbian tennis star Novak Djokovic. It made travel very difficult for him, almost impossible. He was refused entry to some Grand Slam tournaments. But he came through it OK and was back in competition at the US Open in mid-2023, still unvaccinated. He made an interesting comment: "The principles of decision-making on my body are more important than any title or anything else." This illuminated an inconsistency in the wide scope of wokeism. How can you fight for the right of female individuals to make decisions pertaining to their bodies, while penalizing people like Djokovic for doing just that? In many countries, anti-vaxxers became pariahs in their homeland. And to top it all off, he won that 2023 tennis tournament!

No one had a monopoly on the truth about COVID-19. It was so new and mutated so fast that it made a joke of the intolerant. Libertarian settings like Sweden ended up with the same results.

India's Guest Panelist: Dr. Anandi Gopal Joshi
As an obstetrician, I have an abiding concern for pregnant women, birthing, and children. Maternal mortality is still a huge problem everywhere, including in India. Less than twenty years ago, one mother out of seventy died in childbirth. Our MMR is slowly improving, but women and children may have enjoyed some natural protection, for this virus tended to be harder on older people.

I really understand any COVID-19-related vaccine hesitancy among parents, especially when older people were hit harder than the youth. However, in India, parental willingness to have their children vaccinated ran high, at about 95 percent.

My question to the challenger on the right is whether there is any evidence now, after the pandemic has died down, of side effects? Not just of the vaccines but of all measures recommended by progovernment immunologists.

Challenger on the Right
As you might expect from a spokesman for the alt-right, I would say that the real truth is slowly coming into the light. COVID-19 was a hard teacher—it gave us the test first and the lesson afterwards.

About children in particular, a number of recent studies have identified some negative side effects, in terms of their mental health (e.g., stress, trauma). Furthermore, the loss of in-school contact with peers has also proved to be detrimental. On rare occasions, there have been illnesses and even loss of life attributed to complications with the vaccines, even among young athletes.

Questions are being asked about mechanical ventilators. They may have done more harm than good.

Excessive masking is also being examined. A new paper reviewed 2,168 studies and concluded that masks decrease oxygen saturation and increase blood CO_2, heart rate, and blood pressure. This, in turn, causes headache and dizziness—symptoms wrongly classified as long COVID!

Masks interfered with oxygen uptake and CO_2 release and compromised respiratory compensation. There is less risk when the wearing durations are shorter than daily use. Mask-Induced Exhaustion Syndrome (MIES) has been validated. MIES can have long-term clinical consequences, especially for vulnerable groups. Imagine being short of oxygen when you are breathing for two, like pregnant women are! So far, several mask-related symptoms may have been misinterpreted as long COVID-19 symptoms. In any case, MIES clashes with the WHO's definition of health.

Face mask side effects must be assessed on a risk-benefit basis against the available evidence of their effectiveness against viral transmissions. In the absence of strong empirical evidence of effectiveness, mask-wearing should not be mandated, let alone enforced by law. There is a place for masking, but it is not when you are driving in your car alone! Oxygen deprivation is also hazardous to your health.

The vaccine, commonly known as a COVID jab, has also been closely watched. According to a Swiss doctor's report, Moderna's COVID booster caused one in 35 people to have heart injuries detectable with blood tests. This could imply that mRNA vaccines have caused silent heart damage to tens of millions of people.

Also, mRNA vaccines sharply raise the risk of severe vaginal bleeds. Vaccine injuries have become the dominant theme of German reporting on the mRNA vaccines, as the COVID-19 vaccinations face ever wider cultural and social repudiation.

Three peer-reviewed studies, one from South Korea, one from Japan, and one from Qatar, all find that the real cardiovascular death toll from the vaccines may have been vastly underreported.

The Pfizer vaccine is less effective than the Chinese non-mRNA product.

Are COVID boosters causing cancer? Angus Dalgleish, Professor of Oncology at St. George's Hospital Medical School in London, thinks so.

There was a huge rush to develop vaccines (e.g., Operation Warp Speed). There was inadequate time for testing. So, in a way, we are now finding out the truth. I am not saying that there were no benefits. Lives were saved, and the sick we treated, albeit a bit crudely. I am answering your question with a healthy dose of objective truth. With scientific research, not conspiracy theories. Sometimes the truth hurts.

Peter Abelard wrote: "By doubting we are led to question, by questioning we arrive at the truth." COVID-19 skepticism is not treason. As Thomas Mann put it: "A harmful truth is better than a useful lie."

North America's Guest Panelist: Dr. Benjamin Spock

We have to realize that the virus originated in a totalitarian setting where the truth was rapidly buried. In late 2019, some lab technicians and doctors seemed to realize that a nasty genie had slipped out of the bottle. But the principled warnings they voiced were silenced.

Again, about a year later, concerned voices spoke out. In October 2020, three prominent medical professors from Stanford, Harvard, and Oxford universities issued an open letter, the Great Barrington Declaration (GBD). But it was not heeded either, which disturbs me as a doctor.

I ask the challenger on the left to remember that I, too, am left-leaning. But even so, I wonder how this pandemic got so politicized. Why were the voices of lab and medical professionals silenced or ignored?

Challenger on the Left

Let me go back to polarization. On one side, populism has been heating up, and the left is a somewhat incoherent "broad church"—almost in disarray. Modi's brand of Hindu nationalism was strong. Brexit had pulled the UK out of the European Union. Trump had surprised everyone by winning the American election in 2016. Bolsonaro, the Brazilian populist, even had his socialist opponent jailed.

In desperation, the left formed a coalition of the wounded. This encompassed diverse aspirations—feminists, the gay rainbow, pro-choice activists, civil rights activists, Marxists, the "trans" movement, gun control activists, and so forth. This was an election year in the USA, which was still locked down due to the pandemic. The death of George Floyd in May 2020 was a catalyst. It triggered the Black Lives Matter riots. These spread across North America from Minneapolis and across the sea to other countries.

To answer your question, there was a chemistry to wokeism that was unexpected and somewhat irrational. For example, how can you practice social distancing in a mob? Yet these marches kept gaining momentum. This absurdity synergized with the push to elect a left-leaning government. Themes like "defund the police" and "tear down statues" came to the fore. And yes, the pandemic was politicized. Very much so.

A related observation is the political support from the African American and Latino minorities. Biden won an estimated 90 percent of the African American vote in 2020, riding on the BLM tide. It was both an overwhelming win and the worst performance for a Democrat among black voters in over a decade. Hilary Clinton had won 93 percent of the black vote in 2016, and Barack Obama had won 97 percent in 2012. So a growing number of blacks were swinging their vote to the Republicans, who also garnered a better proportion of the Latino vote. Compared to 10 percent of the black vote, they got one out of four of the Latino votes in 2020. These are two of the major minorities in the USA. Biden was chosen largely as an "elder" with enough experience and political acumen to oversee a very diverse leftist coalition.

Running for reelection, President Donald Trump launched Operation Warp Speed to develop a vaccine. Sure, he was trying to save lives, but he was also trying to garner some votes. He had tried to promote hydroxychloroquine as a treatment protocol, after Spanish and French doctors commended it, as the pandemic had reached Europe first, before arriving in America. This was dismissed by the WHO and its American analogue, the Centers for Disease Control (CDC). Next, the president got excited about ivermectin, but this too was scoffed at by his opponents. A sidebar here is that India, South Africa, and Brazil all used the combo of these two drugs as their standard treatment protocol, with success. Postpandemic research out of Durban has validated it. But the pandemic was so politicized that they thumped Trump for his efforts. The truth was trampled down, largely to discredit a candidate in the presidential election. One wonders what role Big Pharma played in this.

The first vaccines were released exactly at the same time as the November 2020 elections. It took months to roll out, but the "vaccine race" was clearly one facet of that election. Since Biden won, Bolsonaro was replaced by leftist Lula da Silva in Brazil. Boris Johnson's Conservatives fell to Labour in Britain. Only Modi seems to be politically safe and sound in India. Politicizing the pandemic seems to have worked well for the left.

But could this trigger a backlash? So much of this success was actually built on illusion, not truth. One truth is that the stiff travel restrictions came too late to stop the spread from China and then became very inconvenient and unpopular, decimating the tourist industry. Another truth is that governments had so little to go on that they chose to err on the side of caution. They may have overreacted.

Some other truths came to light more gradually. One is that some government health agencies were "weaponized," although this was less visible than the ones that tackled Donald Trump head-on. Another is that Big Pharma and Big Tech are megaforces on the scale of the military-industrial complex, able to pull strings behind the scenes for political kudos. The Trump/Kennedy pushback in 2025 came as a direct result of seeing through the treachery. In fact, this was the result of some deep realignment whereby the Democratic Party was beholden to the elite and corporate America. In contrast, the Republicans had established a rapport with the working class, racial minorities, and rural folk.

Another truth is that "lockdown" was a serious setback for the economy. Government aid followed, trying to mitigate the negative impact. But this had a disincentive effect that slowed down economic recovery and fed the inflationary spiral. The negative economic consequences of the pandemic response have been enormous. In South Africa, the massive spending opened another chapter of graft and corruption, which even led to the Minister of Health's resignation.

You referred to the Great Barrington Declaration, which warns the world of government overreach. The GBD calls for focused protection of vulnerable people (e.g., the elderly) and lifting lockdown restrictions. Originally written by three medical professionals, the GBD now has close to a million signatures.

Britain's Guest Panelist: Dr. Wilfred Grenfell
As a Christian, I believe that truth is a godly virtue. The adversary uses deception and lies subversively. Yet both information and misinformation are protected by the right to free speech, for example, the First Amendment in the USA.

That's why a biomedical security state really worries me. It would make it very difficult for us to navigate the avalanche of data that we face daily. What is true, and what is fake?

Let me ask the challenger in the middle about cover-ups. When we make errors or commit crimes, one strategy is repentance—asking for forgiveness. But there is another strategy—covering our tracks. In the polarization around COVID-19, can you sniff out any sense of disinformation or betrayal?

CHUCK STEPHENS

Challenger in the Middle

The truth is that an email has come to light that indicates that Dr. Anthony Fauci of the CDC knew in early 2020 that China was running risky coronavirus research and that a lab leak had likely set off the pandemic. We can only wonder why he didn't come clean. Was he hiding something? In 2025, he became the first scientist ever to receive a preemptive presidential pardon. This rather looks like the presumption of guilt, not innocence. Worse yet, it was signed by the autopen, not by Biden, raising some concerns.

According to the *New York Times*, "Scientists at Wuhan University are known to have been working on gain-of-function experiments." These words come from a note written by Dr. Anthony Fauci dated February 1, 2020, as COVID-19 exploded worldwide. They were written as he and top virologists were just starting to cover up the potential Chinese lab origins of SARS-CoV-2, which caused COVID-19.

That's not all. After the first cover-up came the second. The National Institutes of Health hid Fauci's words, completely redacting the email he had written from Freedom of Information Act requests. The NIH gave up the note only in response to a House of Representatives subpoena, years after Fauci wrote it.

If you think that this is just another conspiracy theory that couldn't get past a sleepy fact-checker, listen to Senator Rand Paul's words: "This directly contradicts everything he said in the committee hearing to me, denying absolutely that they funded any gain of function, and it's absolutely a lie." Senator Rand Paul has referred Dr. Anthony Fauci to the Department of Justice for prosecution. For perjury. Lying to Congress. Why was he so economical with the truth?

Certainly, the pandemic became politicized. But when this leads people to crimes and cover-ups, the truth will always come out. For that is its very nature.

Sadly, we observed this depth of deception coming out of the highest levels of government. Dr. Anthony Fauci was the highest-paid civil servant in America. It looks like he was connected to clandestine gain-of-function research taking place in China because it was illegal to do it in the USA. Was he paying for it? Why? Was the secrecy because they were developing biological weapons? Or because they were acting illegally? Or both? His political allies protected him.

This is causing Trump and Kennedy to restructure the whole American health system and withdraw from the World Health Organization. They are not seeking revenge against individuals; they are mandating systemic change.

And to think that if anyone called it the "Chinese virus," they were labeled racists. And that the Wuhan lab origin scenario was called a conspiracy theory! Here is what the FBI concluded in 2023, reported by the *Washington Post*. Christopher Wray is quoted: "The FBI has for quite some time now assessed that the origins of the pandemic are most likely a potential lab incident in Wuhan. The Chinese government, seems to me, has been doing its best to try and thwart and obfuscate the work here, the work that we're doing, and that's unfortunate for everybody."

That is the pot calling the kettle black! The American government also tried to "thwart and obfuscate" investigations that were genuinely seeking the truth.

There was one strident voice crying in the wilderness. Robert Kennedy Jr. was an avid vaccine skeptic. Six months after roll-out began, when the party to which his family had belonged for generations was back in power, he tried to have the authorization of all the COVID-19 vaccines revoked. He had sniffed out disinformation and betrayal, to answer your question. For this, he became a pariah in the Democratic Party. In due course, he decided to run as an independent candidate in the 2024 presidential election. Donald Trump's amazing comeback was in part because "the dealmaker" invited RFK Jr. to stand down as a candidate, in order to join his future Cabinet, to oversee the Department of Health and Human Services. The result is nothing less than a major restructuring of health institutions, policy, and practice. It is shaking up health care on an unprecedented scale.

Moderator
We owe so much to the four doctors who are our guest panelists and to our three challengers. They all speak the truth routinely. Now, will the real Truth about COVID-19 please stand out?

RECKLESS TRANSMISSION

Moderator
Welcome once again to the sixteenth episode of *Telling the Truth*! We are currently in our Health series, with a panel of four esteemed doctors. They join us from North America, Britain, South Africa, and India—four countries where English is widely spoken.

Our topic tonight is reckless transmission. This became a major concern during the HIV and AIDS pandemic. That was a slow-onset disaster, sneaking up on people without them noticing at first. Then they would test positive.

Long before the development of antiretroviral drugs, this was more than just another STD. It was a death sentence.

But then treatment protocols started to improve. Meanwhile, the emphasis had to be placed on prevention in order to contain the spread of the virus. Various prevention measures were touted, including condom use, avoiding multiple sexual partners, and, of course, criminalization of what is called "HIV endangerment."

What exactly do we mean by HIV endangerment? Well, there are three ingredients. First, you have to know that you are HIV positive. Second, you have to know how the virus is transmitted. And third, you have to have unprotected sex without informing your partner of the danger they are in. In the law of many countries, this "triple play" is regarded as attempted murder. People have gone to jail for their recklessness, even when there was no intentionality.

It is India's turn to lead the questioning, so over to you, Dr. Joshi.

India's Guest Panelist: Dr. Anandi Gopal Joshi

As a doctor, I dedicated my life to saving lives. So it is hard for me to imagine someone purposely infecting another person with their malady. But then I would never shoot anyone or poison anyone either.

HIV treatment seems to have contained the problem, or at least taken the terror out of testing positive.

Assuming that the challenger on the right will defend the status quo—that reckless transmission is indeed attempted murder—I ask for a rationale or justification. Do you think that the law should remain as is, in light of the improved treatment protocol? Will this dam hold?

Challenger on the Right

It is not hard to understand why HIV endangerment had to be outlawed. Otherwise, it could have become a very quiet and convenient way to kill people intentionally. Instead of a smoking gun or a sweet-tasting poison, you simply had to seduce them to have sex with an infected person.

Now, voices are saying that this law should be amended. Today, given the ARV treatment protocol, HIV infection is no longer catastrophic. However, treatment is very expensive and inconvenient. It may not kill you right away, like a gun or poison, but it will probably shorten your lifespan. So we should never let up on prevention measures. India now has 2.4 million citizens who are HIV positive. It is not wise to soften prevention efforts. Criminalization sends a message that people have to take responsibility for what goes on in their private lives. They can't put others at risk, and if they are acting maliciously, then it is as bad as a gun or poison.

There have even been cases of COVID endangerment. For example, an innocent man was detained in a jail cell all weekend in South Africa. He was arrested by the police, who were sympathizing with one of his enemies, late on a Friday. They knew that he could not stand before a magistrate until Monday morning. He was held for three nights without charges. He could not contact a lawyer on a weekend.

The police also knew that the jail cell was already crowded. Thirteen other men were in the small cell. Three of these were exhibiting COVID symptoms. They were getting treatment from the government clinic across the street. It was the very weekend that President Ramaphosa upgraded the COVID alert level from 3 to 4. COVID was spreading fast, and the policemen knew very well how it was transmitted. They knew that the jail was crowded because the other thirteen had been held there for over a month. They knew that COVID is harder on older people.

To throw a seventy-two-year-old man without charges into this cell was reckless if not intentional. Especially as the man was not a flight risk; he would have come to the courthouse of his own volition on the Monday morning if summoned. This was clearly attempted murder.

What the police did not know was that the man had already received his first Pfizer "jab" a month earlier. He was scheduled to get his second "jab" a week after they arrested him. He started to feel cold symptoms on Monday when released on bail. He did not get really sick until he received his second "jab." Then he fell quite ill, thinking that it was a reaction to the "jab." Then, three weeks later, a lab test was done, verifying that he was indeed COVID positive. The police's strategy had worked, but the fact that he was partially immunized probably saved his life.

This is why criminalization of reckless transmission should remain a crime. It is attempted murder in law, and that is a strong protection measure. This crime is akin to biological warfare and should remain outlawed.

As for the police brutality, I can only add that the victim was white, and his enemy and all his police accomplices were black. Just as about 20 percent of farm murders in South Africa involve torture, this episode was a cruel setup.

If you knock down a pedestrian while driving slowly with due caution, they might go easy on you. But if you were speeding, you were reckless, and they won't treat you with the respect due to a law-abiding citizen.

North America's Guest Panelist: Dr. Benjamin Spock
I recently read of a British nurse who was convicted of murdering seven babies that were on her watch at a hospital. We cannot tarnish the reputation of all

health-care workers for that single incident. Nor can we assume that all law enforcement officers strategize the murder of their enemies by COVID endangerment. But when it happens, it must be confronted. Named and shamed for what it is.

I wonder about HIV cases. May I ask the challenger on the left if there are legal precedents for conviction? Is this considered a violent or a nonviolent crime?

Challenger on the Left
Probably the most famous case anywhere is the Italian Stallion. His real name was Valentino Talluto. He was tried in Italy in mid-2017. A thirty-three-year-old bespectacled accountant, he was HIV positive and was charged with intentionally infecting thirty women. He was put on trial for allegedly targeting victims to have unprotected sex over nearly a decade.

Under the pseudonym "Hearty Style," he seduced dozens of young women on social media networks and internet dating sites, often dating several at a time. Out of fifty-three sexual contacts known to have taken place between 2006, when he discovered he was HIV positive, and his arrest in 2015, thirty women were allegedly infected with HIV by him. The male companions of three of the women were also infected, as was the baby of a fourth, investigators said.

Throughout the trial, which opened in March 2017, in Rome's Rebibbia prison, the women described how Talluto had seduced them. He dined them, claiming to fall in love, then persuading them to have unprotected sex. The women who had asked him to wear a condom said he told them he was allergic or had just been tested for HIV.

When the women discovered they were HIV positive, by chance, due to health problems or after other women he dated raised the alarm, they said he denied it had anything to do with him. Talluto's defense lawyers maintained that his actions were "imprudent, but not intentional."

Some women stayed with Talluto for months after discovering they were sick. In the end, it was, above all, his chronic cheating—he juggled up to six relationships at the same time—that drove them away.

Many were students, some mothers. The youngest was fourteen at the beginning of their relationship, the oldest around forty. Each described the horrors of HIV, from the stigma which distanced them even from family members to the trials of treatment.

The prosecution demanded that he get life behind bars for willful injury and causing an epidemic. Prosecutor Elena Neri told the court: "Talluto has never cooperated, he has made false statements. He has always denied any responsibility, even in the face of the evidence. His actions were intended to sow death."

The defense painted a picture of a young man eager for affection. "He did not intentionally seek to transmit the virus," his lawyer Maurizio Barca said, insisting that Talluto used condoms "most of the time" and only had sex without them a few times after being "caught in the heat of the action." He also claimed it was impossible to prove it was his client and not other partners who had infected the women. After all, the strain of the virus they share with Talluto is the most widespread in Europe.

After months of silence, Talluto finally spoke out at the end of September 2017, his voice breaking with emotion and his eyes brimming with tears after hearing the testimony of one of the women. She still refuses to give up on him. She had told the court in July of their meeting in 2014, how he told her immediately that he was HIV positive, and how she forgave his infidelities. "We want to get married. I'm still in love with Valentino, he's not the monster that everyone describes," she said.

Judges in Rome deliberated over the sentence for more than ten hours before announcing the verdict. In the end, he was sentenced to twenty-four years in prison. He had consistently denied to his lovers that he was a carrier of the potentially deadly virus and then failed to observe the speed limit in bed.

Talluto—who never knew his father and whose mother was an HIV-infected drug addict who died when he was four—was regarded by the court as a murderer.

When he finally broke his silence, he said: "Many of the girls know my friends and family. They say that I wanted to infect as many people as possible. If that had been the case, I would have gone for casual sex in bars, I would not have brought them into my life." However, the court convicted him of murder.

According to local media, victims wept as the sentence was read out. However, it fell short of the life term prosecutors had asked for. Murder is usually a violent crime, but perhaps Talluto's defense managed to convince the bench that it was not as violent as using a gun or poison. So sentencing was relatively light.

The reason for light sentences is that research on the effects of HIV nondisclosure cases suggests that these laws tend to increase HIV stigma. This has a negative effect on public health. HIV nondisclosure laws and criminalization of HIV transmission may make people less likely to access HIV testing and less likely to disclose their status or discuss sexual health with a health-care provider.

Also, although women make up 10 percent of Canadian nondisclosure prosecutions, there is an overrepresentation of prosecuted sex workers, indigenous women, and abuse survivors. They have low levels of blameworthiness.

Britain's Guest Panelist: Dr. Wilfred Grenfell
Talluto weaponized disease! But as always, there is a counternarrative, a not-guilty plea. So how do we know whom to believe? In public prosecutions, there are courts with prosecutors and judges. There is due process, a defense team that can cross-examine eyewitnesses, and a defense team that can review all the evidence collected by investigators. So we can safely assume that the verdicts are fair and just, not to mention the right of appeal.

But I am still disturbed that infection can be spread through willful intent to harm. My question goes to the challenger in the middle: How much harm can a tiny bacterium or virus on the loose do? Can you give us some proportions of the consequent danger?

Challenger in the Middle
Probably the worst example of weaponizing disease was the Black Plague. The Mongols still occupied Crimea in 1344, but Kyiv was about as far west as they had ever managed to expand their empire. Genghis Khan had built the largest empire in human history. There was a military altercation in the city of Kaffa, a great port on the Black Sea. In the grain trade of that era, the major Mediterranean ports imported grain that was grown in eastern Europe, via Kaffa. They also exported products from Europe to Kaffa that were then delivered across the Silk Road to China, and the Mongol Empire stretched from Crimea all the way to the east coast of China.

One of the military strategies used by the Mongols was biological warfare. In this regard, they were truly playing with WMDs—weapons of mass destruction. The plague bacterium that infects humans occurs naturally in fleas from Mongolia and Siberia that usually live on rats and other rodents. However, when they need alternate hosts, humans will do. So bubonic plague does jump to humans at times, and there are still ten to fifteen cases reported annually in the USA. Knowing this, the Mongol army under Jani Beg built catapults and flung infected bodies over the walls into the city of Kaffa. This rapidly resulted in a high mortality rate, and thus an exodus of its infected people to Constantinople, the Balkans, and also by ship to Mediterranean port cities.

One merchant ship landed in the port of Messina, in Sicily. When the ship arrived, flying the flag of Genoa, only a few sick sailors stumbled off. The others were dead on board, so there was a lot of looting, but this caused the plunderers to be bitten by the fleas from the rats on board a shipload of Crimean grain.

There are two variants of this plague: one manifests in tumors or *buboes* that break out around the lymph glands, resulting in a 100 percent mortality rate. The other is pneumatic, causing highly contagious blood coughing, which results in about a 90 percent mortality rate.

Within hours or days of contracting this bacterium, victims succumb. You get a headache, intestinal upset, then tumors and/or black spots, fever, and pain, and soon Death the Reaper visits you. One father reported that he buried five of his children in as many days. It crisscrossed Europe for four years and traumatized it for centuries, recurring in later surges again and again as if the memories of it weren't bad enough.

From Messina, it spread to Marseilles, then to Genoa, thence to Florence, and on to Paris. It arrived in England, then on to Germany, and from there to Scandinavia and Russia. During these four years, about 30 percent of the population of Eurasia and North Africa was wiped out. Here are but a few statistics:

- India was depopulated.
- Mesopotamia, Syria, and Armenia were covered in dead bodies.
- Florence lost 50,000 of its 100,000 inhabitants.
- England lost four out of ten citizens.
- Untold millions of people perished.
- The world population did not recover to preplague levels for four centuries.

In that century, travel was opening up—for example, Marco Polo's trips to China. There was a wealthy merchant class. Traders operated over long distances. The population of Europe was rapidly urbanizing; thus, people were in close contact with the hosts of this plague. And although the universities were already graduating "doctors of medicine," there was no known cure. Worse yet, they prescribed home remedies that did not affect the bacterium.

Only in 1894, during another outbreak of this dreaded pestilence in China, did a Russian scientist working for the Pasteur Institute finally identify the bacterium. He had the dubious honor of having it named after him!

Only then did the domino effect of the Great Plague come to be understood as a bacterium indigenous to Siberia and Mongolia, inside fleas that drink blood from hosts, usually rodents such as rats, or alternatively humans. Rats traveled on ships laden with grain, and the fleas bit sailors. Ships then carried the pestilence from port to port. Sailors and rats interacted with city dwellers, spreading the infection from Black Sea ports to Mediterranean port cities, then inland.

Needless to say, when epidemics get out of control and grow into pandemics, a lot of damage can be done. And this can start merely with recklessness or by intent. Today, we call it weaponization. Genghis Khan never managed to conquer Europe, but in this way, he brought it to its knees. God forbid that it ever happens again.

South Africa's Guest Panelist: Dr. Christiaan Barnard

We know a great deal more about immunology today than we did at the time of the Black Death. For example, we know that when Europeans arrived in both Africa and the Americas during the Age of Discovery, they brought diseases like TB with them that decimated Indigenous peoples. The extent to which this was intentional can be debated; they generally wanted to depopulate the colonies during the land grab to make room for European settlers.

And yet, South Africa's openly HIV positive Supreme Court Justice Edwin Cameron argued against criminalization at the XVII International AIDS Conference in Mexico City. Let me ask the challenger on the right if our respective countries are still litigating reckless transmission, or whether left-leaning permissiveness is undermining it. Can you give an example?

Challenger on the Right

The precedent case in South Africa was the state's prosecution of a man called Lovers Phiri. Ironically, he was employed as an HIV/AIDS counselor in Piet Retief, Mpumalanga province. He was also responsible for testing. Through this work, he met a woman in 2010 at a local clinic where she went for voluntary counseling and testing. She tested HIV negative. At the time, she was pregnant and had just separated from the father of her unborn child, whereas Phiri had at that stage been HIV positive for three years and was aware of his status. He was unmarried but already had two children.

A relationship later developed between the woman and Phiri, and they had consensual sex on two occasions. On each occasion, Phiri declined to use a condom, despite being asked to do so. Of course, he did not disclose to her what he knew his status to be. This was HIV endangerment.

The woman subsequently tested HIV positive when she was tested as part of her prenatal routine. When she confronted him and accused him of infecting her, Phiri apologized and pleaded for forgiveness. What would you think of someone who did not take the proper precautions to prevent you from catching the bubonic plague or the Spanish flu? Do they love you?

What happened is an open-and-shut case of attempted murder, according to the laws adopted by South Africa as part of its bouquet of HIV prevention strategies. Phiri claimed in court that he had informed the woman of his HIV status before the first time they had sex and that he had used a condom on both occasions. The magistrate rejected Phiri's version of events as not aligning with the facts. The appeal judgment reads: "The learned regional magistrate preferred the complainant's version over that of the appellant."

He was duly convicted and sent to jail for a six-year sentence. He was thirty-two years old at the time of the sentencing. It was the first such conviction in South Africa under the legislation adopted to prevent harmful HIV transmission.

While languishing in prison, he decided to launch an appeal. The matter then came before Judge Tati Makgoka and Acting Judge William Baloyi in the Pretoria High Court. They said that the argument that he should merely have been convicted of assault had no merit. So his appeal was not successful.

We have heard of the seminal case in Italy. In North America, there have been a number of successful litigations. In 1998, the Supreme Court of Canada released its decision in *R. v. Cuerrier*, establishing that people living with HIV could be found guilty of aggravated assault if they did not disclose their HIV status to a sexual partner prior to sex that posed a significant risk of HIV transmission.

In the USA, some states treat the transmission of HIV, depending upon a variety of factors, as a felony and others as a misdemeanor. More than thirty of the fifty states have prosecuted HIV positive individuals for exposing another person to HIV.

In Britain, HIV endangerment can fall under Grievous Bodily Harm (GBH) with intent or to resist arrest, GBH generally, poisoning (two sections), and actual bodily harm. Convictions of both women and men for both reckless and intentional transmission are recorded in the National AIDS Trust's database.

In India, the Penal Code has two provisions that may be used to address "exposure" to any illness or disease, but it is not specific to HIV.

People often speak of moral degeneration. The term suggests that there is more and more permissiveness and that high standards are being eroded. In reality, what is happening is that morality-based law is being replaced with rights-based law. This may also account for the longer waits for court decisions, because judgments are more complex than ever before. In turn, this reflects the fact that what we mean by "truth" is undergoing fundamental changes. Witnesses still swear to tell the truth, the whole truth, and nothing but the truth, but they may define truth differently than others. The term "truth degeneration" would be more fitting.

The notion of revealed truth is clearly being challenged. Since humanism emerged with its own "theology" of human rights, polarization has been on the rise. More recently, globalization and wokeism have been rising too. But the pendulum may be swinging back to the "good old days" of right and wrong, when the word *truth* was less ambiguous than it has come to be. God forbid the death of truth. He who reveals truth to guide us is not pleased with truth degeneration.

Moderator

So will our search for truth prove to be elusive? One thing is sure—our challengers are not misleading you. Their views may vary, but they speak honestly. They are well-informed and leave you to decide what is true. Thank you to the three of you! And thanks again to our four doctors for your leadership. You all have a thoughtful and caring attitude toward health and people. Keep up the good work!

Now will the real Truth about reckless transmission please stand out?

THE LGBTQIA+ MOVEMENT AND SAME-SEX MARRIAGE

Moderator

Hello, and welcome to the seventeenth episode of *Telling the Truth*. Our topic tonight is same-sex marriage specifically, but the LGBTQIA+ movement in general. Sexual orientations vary, but what is the real truth behind this variance?

Our panel is composed of four doctors from four continents. They join us via the convenient new app, Time-Zoom. Give it up for these four healers!

And we have three challengers—on the left, in the middle, and on the right. They reply to the panelists at two levels—first, about the topic of this episode, and second, about our predominant theme of truth.

We believe that true freedom, perfect freedom, is predicated on truth. No truth, no freedom. So if your narratives are fake, or if you have subscribed to a conspiracy theory, you will be locked into deception and unfree. It could be an illusion, for there is a lot of deceit and fraud in our world. Telling the truth from subterfuge is a life skill that will come in handy as you navigate your way to your ultimate destination. We hope you will find our show a learning experience in this regard.

Legally marrying someone of the same sex has been around for a short while. Older people from even the most permissive societies will remember a time when such marriages were banned. It has been with some of us for a generation or two now, depending on where we live, so I am asking our panelists and challengers to dig deeper in this episode. Look for the truth. Same-sex marriage is still very contentious. Parts of the world reject it entirely; for example, to be openly gay in Uganda today could lead to one's incarceration. It is still illegal there, as it used to be in many places.

But gay rights have received a lot of media oxygen, and this attention has spread from Lesbian and Gay (LG) to the "BTQIA+."

It is North America's turn to lead the questioning, so take it away, Dr. Spock!

North America's Guest Panelist: Dr. Benjamin Spock
My bestseller, *Baby and Child Care*, was first published in 1946. In that first edition, there was no mention of gay or lesbian parents. Although I do lean to the left, advising "LGs" in 1946 would have rocked the boat. The United Nations had not even been formed yet to champion human rights through various charters and conventions.

I revised the book in the mid-1970s to satisfy the critique of feminists. I never meant to imply that a woman's place was always in the home; I certainly never said that. But I came to realize that it seemed implicit in the content of my early editions, so I addressed it in the fourth edition of my book.

My publisher later organized another revision of my book. It was written on my behalf by Dr. Robert Needlman. The topic of political correctness in episode 11 (the Legal series) contained some relevant thoughts on revising classics. The ninth edition of my book came out in 2012, the tenth in 2018.

Can I ask the challenger on the left, to what extent do these ongoing changes in content about parenting reflect a redefinition of truth? Does that process move from the specific to the general, or from the general to the specific?

Challenger on the Left
Your famous book is a great case study of how changing views cause society to move its red lines. Looking at it the other way around, bear in mind that in 1946, when you first published it, smoking was still "cool" and widely practiced in public places. That has also changed, largely due to the activism of nonsmokers. Yes, smokers have rights too, but so do nonsmokers.

In our shift toward the nanny state, new kinds of truth are on the rise. In the case of smoking, governments listened to science. The objective truth came out of lab tests and health studies. The objective truth is evidence-based, empirical. Smoking was found to cause lung cancer, and it gradually came to be sequestered to protect nonsmokers.

So government intervention was based on "reality." Scientific studies. People still have civil liberties, but where the government provides health care to its citizens (for example, in Canada), smokers are getting the squeeze. They are penalized in various ways; for example, they may pay more for life insurance than nonsmokers, because of the truth embedded in statistics. This is a kind of objective truth, determined by inductive observations.

Smokers may have a different view of truth—one that is more subjective, more pluralistic. They would prefer "smoking sections" in restaurants, whereas the law now says that if you want to smoke, you must go outside. But even that is contentious, because nonsmokers also breathe the air outside. Smoking is pollution. But smokers still cling to their rights. This is an example of people not really wanting to know the truth, just wanting validation of their existing views. So what, if smoking is bad for me? I enjoy it, and no one can force me to kick the habit. This emphasizes individual rights over collective rights.

When I was growing up, long before the public ban on smoking, some churches frowned on it. Drinking alcohol was also discouraged, possibly a hangover from the days of Prohibition. And even gambling was anathema to some churches. Why am I saying this? Well, it is a graphic example that the church can have its internal reasons for its policies and preferences. What the government or even some political party platforms may say could resonate with Christian views. But it's not as if Christians cannot hold their own views—whether the same or opposed—for their own religious reasons. Too often, the church is blamed for buying into the views of political parties or for "supporting" party platforms. This is guilt by association. Churches opposed smoking long before the government did, because they stepped to the beat of a different drum. Their truth has been revealed, not staked out in a laboratory. Without elaborating, let's just say that they believed that "cleanliness is next to godliness."

Now back to same-sex marriage. Unquestionably, there is ongoing resistance to it in church circles. This is because some churches believe that it clashes with biblical teaching—that is, with revealed truth. Increasingly, these "conservative" churches are being sequestered. Because liberal churches began to syncretize—absorbing secular views, according to many staunch theologians—that is, to adopt beliefs of the host culture, even when those views clash with church doctrine, specifically with the Bible.

This has led church congregations and also whole denominations to split over this issue. One recent example is the United Methodist Church in the USA. It has been a major mainline denomination. But about a quarter of the congregations in the UMC have now chosen to disaffiliate, largely over the fatalistic acceptance of same-sex marriage and diverse sexual orientations. In terms of actual membership count, the exodus could be much more than 25 percent, because conservative congregations tend to enjoy better attendance than liberal churches. So over time, as new underpinnings of truth emerge, some people loosen their convictions, while others hang on tight, loyal to revealed truth. As the old Negro spiritual goes: "Gimme that old-time religion ... It was good for my fathers, and it's good enough for me."

To your second question, I would say that it moves both ways. Certainly, parents who suddenly discover they have a gay child move faster from specific to general. But there have also been general forces like liberation theology and rainbow parades, which have moved people from general to specific.

Britain's Guest Panelist: Dr. Wilfred Grenfell

As a Christian missionary and a physician, I am a cultural relativist. I appreciate that customs that are inconsistent with Christian practice have been observed in cross-cultural contacts. Take polygamy, for example. In some Indigenous cultures, a man may take more wives as time goes on. This is sometimes a way to provide safety and security for these extra wives and their children. And to elevate the status of the first wife. Then, when they convert to Christianity, it is unjust and unkind (two very un-Christian vices) to put the surplus wives out on the street, to fend for themselves and their children. So some churches adopted a policy of tolerance, assuming that polygamy originated before their conversion.

To the challenger in the middle, is there any rapprochement in sight? Or are we sinking deeper and deeper into polarization? Of course, I admire Christians who stick to their principles, even when these are unpopular. But I also note that Jesus practiced a kind of radical inclusivity in his movement. Are attitudes hardening or softening around same-sex marriage?

Challenger in the Middle

It is very hard to find a middle ground on this topic. So hard that church institutions are fracturing over it. The most vivid example is the worldwide Anglican Communion. In England, churches have drifted into liberalism and what some allege to be "syncretism." Priests are marrying people of the same sex, to the consternation of Anglican Christians in Africa and the Global South, where this is seen as heresy, and to the extent that African bishops have called the Archbishop of Canterbury a "wolf in sheep's clothing." In global terms, Anglicans in the UK are far outnumbered by the evangelical Anglicans of Africa. And now, there are moves afoot by conservative Anglicans in the UK to start an alternative Anglican denomination in Britain. One already exists in Canada, still worshipping with the 1662 Book of Common Prayer, but disaffiliated from the Anglican Church of Canada.

The real crunch is the sacrament of marriage. Churches do not mind gays and lesbians coming to worship, including communion. They are welcome. They are welcome to participate in church life and activities. The message is not that God does not love them. He does. It only gets contentious when they seek to marry someone of the same sex, or to be ordained while practicing homosexuality. Stepping outside these red lines makes it very difficult for those who accept revealed truth as their yardstick. Because the Bible is quite explicit, they are not trying to keep gays and lesbians out of church fellowship, but they are trying to keep to biblical teaching and the practices of church tradition. They want to avert the death of truth.

It is instructive to turn this around the other way. Do lesbians and gays want to go to church? If so, what kind of churches do they prefer to worship in? Ironically, the churches that have the most "affirming" theologies are not usually the first-choice denominations of gays and lesbians. This has an ironic effect on rural churches in the mainline denominations. They happen to be closing at a much faster rate than city churches in the same denomination for a number of reasons. At first, this was because the rural population was declining due to urbanization. But that has now reversed. You now find the "inclusive" or "affirming" gospel is being preached in places where the gays and lesbians are not concentrated. So it is a bit misplaced. They prefer megachurches, in town. Meanwhile, the farmers and rural folk are being alienated by this radical new liberal theology. Many are moving to more conservative church congregations.

I think that the example of Jesus is clear. He practiced a radical inclusivity, and he often stepped over the Jewish "red lines," like picking corn on the Sabbath, or speaking to people who were regarded as "unclean." He was also fearless when encountering people possessed by demons or sequestered for leprosy. He was criticized for socializing with tax collectors. There is no explicit mention of any encounters with gays or lesbians in the Gospels. But it fits the narrative that he would not have marginalized them or sent them away. He was affirming, loving, and inclusive. But he did not congratulate people for hosting demons—he cast them out! And he didn't mince words when conversing with rich people about their lifestyle.

In the Gospels, there are three major factions—the Romans, the Jews, and the Christians. In a way, they each had their own understanding of what truth was. The Roman view is linked to its military prowess. Both Stoics and Epicureans championed discipline and rationality. For Stoics, virtue was their guiding principle. For Epicureans, virtue was the means to the desired end of pleasure. There is a reason why the three synoptic Gospels reach a second climax with a Roman centurion professing, as he watched Jesus die, "Surely this man was the son of God." These highly trained and well-equipped soldiers were admired for their excellence and virtue.

And yet the Roman leader, Pontius Pilate, when asked to validate the Jewish Council's guilty verdict, decided to question Jesus himself. Their dialogue ends when Jesus says: "You say that I am a king. For this purpose I was born and for this purpose I have come into the world—to bear witness to the truth. Everyone who is of the truth listens to my voice" (John 18:37). To which Pilate remarked evasively, "What is truth?" He saw that there was a disconnect between his understanding of it and what the Sanhedrin believed. When he had said this, he went out again to the Jews, and said to them, "I find no guilt in him."

Fundamentally, I think there is a disconnect between the notion of revealed truth, from which stems morality, and the subjectivity of rights-based pluralism. Yes, there are gay rights, as there is also freedom of worship. Both sides have rights. The absolutes of revealed truth are being diluted by ever-increasing relativism. In our time, many people stand with one foot on either side. But it is difficult for those standing fully on one side or the other to engage in civil adult conversation with people on the opposite side. Dialogue only causes the acrimony to rise.

In North America today, many people stand with both feet on the side of subjective truth. But in Latin America, Africa, and the Middle East, many stand with both feet on the side of revealed truth. It is the globalists who are pushing for a universal standard. In doing so, they appear to be hastening the death of truth. Ironically, their tolerance is becoming intolerant.

South Africa's Guest Panelist: Dr. Christiaan Barnard
I think that you are getting close to the truth, challenger. So I want to pursue this line of thought. Is divisiveness not natural? Has it not been present throughout human history? How else can you explain the variances in language and culture? And is universalism or globalism really the answer? Isn't the world big enough for different viewpoints, philosophies, and belief systems?

Let me ask the challenger on the right to chase this line of thought a bit deeper.

Challenger on the Right
If your starting point is a revealed truth, such as the Bible, then agreeing to disagree and parting ways is the norm. After all, the Bible teaches that there

are two ultimate destinations for people, not one. This is out of sync with universalism or globalism right from the start. So you have to choose which of these eschatologies is true and which is flawed.

The Bible has an interesting theme of God refining the remnant. The view of splits and defeats is that God is shaking out his coat. Some will fall away, and he will keep others safe in his pockets. Another favorite metaphor is winnowing or threshing—separating the chaff from the kernels of grain. So there have been many minor splits and a few major ones over the four millennia of Judaism and Christianity. Two major splits were between Eastern Orthodoxy and Roman Catholicism and later between Protestants and Catholics. But within these, there are nuances.

How does this apply to same-sex marriage? The divergent views are causing some major denominations to split while at the same time leading to some nuances. Many churches will not marry a same-sex couple. But this does not mean that the couples are shunned as people. They may be welcome to come and worship, to share the bread and wine, but the "red lines" are same-sex marriage and ordination of practicing homosexuals.

I think that this topic illustrates best that there are three main understandings of truth. Revealed truth, as many see it, does not permit same-sex marriage. But the more permissive approach to truth of human rights, pluralism, relativism, and globalism makes room for the practice. Then, there is the third kind of truth—objective. This either suggests Platonic forms or ideals, or points to deductive or scientific reality. The biological fact is that a small percentage of people do sense a variant sexual orientation. According to science, this is a small minority, perhaps 4 percent of people. But it is there. So if it exists, in terms of this understanding of the truth, then it needs some space for grace.

It should be noted that some African tribes, like the Nuer in Sudan and the Kikuyu in Kenya, have traditionally allowed same-sex marriages. So in terms of objective truth, it exists and cannot be denied.

What offends many people is the extent to which this small minority has become so vocal and proactive in society. Most people agree that it was wrong to demonize or criminalize it. But is the answer to popularize it and make it a norm? To what extent should it be permitted and practiced? Objective truth validates it. But is democracy about minority rights or majority rule? Minority rights should be protected, of course. But biological variants do not have to be put on a par with the large majority. Societal norms are also important.

In terms of legislation, same-sex marriage has required some panel-beating of existing laws. But tweaking is enough. Rarely has specific legislation been enacted. It is more a case of trimming and tidying up existing laws to make room. Where diverse marriage laws and customs are rationalized into one overall piece of new legislation, usually same-sex marriage is included in the mix.

The government has to enact laws for all citizens, including minorities, so public policy makes room for them. Whereas churches are private and voluntary, and can freely function according to their internal beliefs, as long as that freedom of religion remains intact. The worry is when governments start pushing for "freedom from religion" as opposed to freedom of religion and encroaching on church rights. There are precedent legal cases where someone claims that churches have discriminated against them as nonbelievers. But churches tend to survive such attacks because churches have rights too.

India's Guest Panelist: Dr. Anandi Gopal Joshi
Looking at a map, it is clear to see that the Middle East, Asia, except Taiwan, and Africa have not bought into this trend yet. Italy and Eastern Europe have not climbed on board.

India does not register marriages or civil unions for same-sex couples. However, a Supreme Court judgment in 2022 decided that same-sex couples derive the same property rights and benefits from cohabitation as any live-in couple.

I would like to ask the challenger in the middle if this is because of Hinduism. Is it religious or cultural? How does this align with other religions?

Challenger in the Middle
The rise of Hindu nationalism must have played a part. Once a taboo that no one talked about, there has been a rise in violence against gays and lesbians since a Supreme Court decision in 2013. This overturned a 2009 Delhi High Court decision that same-sex sexual conduct between consenting adults was a criminal offense.

However, there are some recent signs of change. One major case now before the Supreme Court, driven by eighteen couples, is asking for same-sex marriage to be legalized. A recent poll by the Pew Foundation found that 53 percent of Indian adults are in favor of legalizing it. However, government policy maintains that the gay lifestyle undermines religious and social values.

India is also a democracy, where human rights are championed. So there is this sense of inevitability in spite of the reluctance. India is also a nation surrounded by other religions. Ever since Partition in 1947, Muslims have been parked on its eastern and western borders. The world's most populous Muslim state is Indonesia, not far to the south across the sea. Then there is the whole

Middle East, largely Muslim in between India and Europe. Not to mention China and Tibet to the north, which are predominantly Buddhist. Not one of these places has legalized same-sex marriage.

The practice does exist in Islam. The Quran deals explicitly with sodomy. *Liwat* is named after the city where Lot dwelt. Islam's holy book recounts the story of Sodom more than once, condemning its people's overall immorality. Above all, it criticizes the city's men for "going to men out of desire instead of to women." So sodomy is associated with anal sex. The consensus of Muslim scholars has prohibited this.

Incidentally, this analysis is a bit different from Judaism's take on Sodom. The prophet Ezekiel's critique of Sodom was that its people put their gratification before the satisfaction of others. Thus, they broke the golden rule.

Now, because sexual contact between lesbians does not involve penetration with a penis, the Quran calls it *sihaq* (i.e., grinding). It did not receive the same legal categorization as liwat. It was prohibited under the general rule against sexual contact outside marriage.

For Muslims in North America, the topic of gay marriage gets really thorny. For starters, no Muslim is going to argue that sexual contact between men, let alone anal sex, is considered permissible in God's eyes. However, attempts to ban the sharia in the USA threaten their ability to have their own marriage contracts. Like gays, they want to be able to define marriage free from the norms of the majority. So many Muslims are willing to support the rights of other citizens to shape marriage according to their particular beliefs. For this, Muslims expect their beliefs and relationships to be respected in return. So it is not so much that they condone it as that they sense they have a common enemy, so they join forces.

At the end of the day, the clash between Christian views and humanist/ pluralist views is not unique. Other religions are slow to favor same-sex marriage too.

In China, there is no same-sex marriage or civil union, but things are starting to loosen up. Cohabitation is recognized as the basis for property rights, travel visas, etc. Most of these changes were triggered by the return of Hong Kong to its mother country.

In Iran, Saudi Arabia, and several emirates, same-sex marriage is lumped with adultery. These are both punishable by the death penalty. The same is true in several African countries, including Nigeria. They regard this as revealed truth. It has been a long time since anyone in the Western democracies was even prosecuted for adultery! What a contrast to the death penalty. Muslim fundamentalists allege that the death of truth is undermining Western civilization.

To sum up, same-sex marriage has followed the path of humanism, pluralism, and democracy. But in theocracies or states with a strong cultural or religious bias, it is still not welcome. So the church is by no means the one and only dissident voice, and its views are mixed.

Moderator

The time has come again to thank our four doctors and to hail our three challengers for the information and insights that they shared. We are beginning to see that the variances in views on specific topics are determined to a large extent by differing views of truth.

Now, will the real Truth about same-sex marriage please stand out?

GENDER MODIFICATION

Moderator

Greetings. We hope you stay tuned for our eighteenth episode of To Tell the Truth. Today's topic is gender modification. To try to get to the truth, we have a panel of four medical doctors joining us via the new app, Time-Zoom. They represent four continents—North America, Europe, Africa, and Asia.

They are informed learners, asking questions of our three challengers. These three respondents are somewhat shrouded in mystery, but there is no intended deception involved. Each one speaks his or her mind, so that together we may try to discern the truth.

Speaking of discernment, that capability is regarded by some as a spiritual gift. Some have it, some don't. On the other hand, we believe that those who sincerely seek truth eventually find it, if they persist. This is because truth by its very nature has a way of slipping out, sooner or later, so don't stop exploring!

But the world we live in is so full of mistakes, misunderstandings, and those who want to mislead us; we should sharpen our skills to detect what is true. Noam Chomsky wrote: "Nobody is going to pour truth into your brain. It's something you have to find out for yourself." But the signals can be confusing, like a treasure hunt.

Do you remember the days when the word *gay* meant happy? And when a "drag race" was for stock cars? Times are changing! Which raises the question, does truth change? Or is truth entirely self-sufficient and self-contained? Is truth always the truth, regardless of the observer or the era? Some people believe that truth needs no one to acknowledge that it is true, for it to be true. But it is sometimes an enigma wrapped in a mystery.

Transgender started with cross-dressing. As children, most of us had fun dressing up from Grandma's trunk of old clothing up in the attic. It was hilarious to see your brother dressed up as an old lady. Soon transvestites were plying the city sidewalks as prostitutes.

But "trans" could be comedy as well. Motion pictures have made the most of this spoof, like *Big Momma's House*. Who could not laugh when South African comedian Pieter-Dirk Uys cross-dresses as the Afrikaner socialite "Evita"? He/she is satire at its very finest. But I digress.

This episode is really about the "BTQIA+." This acronym left some terms out to avoid duplication, like nonbinary and pansexual. It all gets quite confusing. Some see it as the same logic as lesbian and gay maturing—all about sexual orientations. Others see it as perversity that endangers our moral foundations.

Today it is Britain's turn to go first, so go for it, Dr. Grenfell.

Britain's Guest Panelist: Dr. Wilfred Grenfell
"Bisexual" is easy enough to understand, and reminiscent of the research carried out by Dr. Charles Kinsey, who was the first doctor to call himself a "sexologist." "Transgender" starts to sound like hormone therapy or surgery, so it raises serious concerns in some people's minds about medical ethics. "Questioning" dispatches with monogamy and adopts polyamorous relationships so that it may belong more to anthropology, psychology, or sociology than to biology. "Asexual" seems clear enough, like the eunuchs of old. They would be castrated in order to be the male guards of queens like Cleopatra.

But "intersexual"? How is that different from bisexual or questioning? And is "Q" for questioning or queer? And what is the plus sign for (+)? Let me ask the challenger in the middle to answer.

Challenger in the Middle
The term *intersex* refers to variations that occur naturally in humans. So these do not comprise a medical intervention. Medical treatments, like surgeries or hormone therapy, do not cause this phenomenon, which is more common than most people realize. We don't have exact figures, but it is estimated that about one to two Americans out of every hundred are intersexual.

In this case, the modifications would be "corrective." In the past, doctors have strived to perform surgery on a baby or child so that their body fits the binary standard of male or female. This custom is being critiqued in the light of changing views of sexuality. But the medical intervention is not to modify someone's gender. It is just to make their bodies conform to outward appearances. Of course, no one knows what identity a baby may sense in later years.

Could doctors get it wrong? Should interventions, therefore, wait until later in life, perhaps after puberty?

Intersex bodies can have both ovarian and testicular tissues. Or they can have combinations of chromosomes that are different from XY (male) and XX (female), such as XXY. Or they can be born with external genitals that fall into the typical male/female categories, while their internal organs or hormones don't.

As views of sexual orientation liberalize, the practice of early medical intervention is being questioned. Do parents and doctors in consultation have the right to determine what gender a child will be?

Someone who is bisexual is attracted to people of both genders. Their body is "normal," but they will romance both genders. As a result, they can be discriminated against by both straight and gay people.

Q is a label for someone who discards monogamy as a norm and adopts polyamorous relationships. Or who simply rejects the marriage model and expects to have a series of relationships in sequence. Sometimes they act on the sly, but more and more, there are closed "families" that are polyamorous all around. So the terms *questioning* and *queer* apply to behavior, not biology. This is not unlike polygyny and polyandry, which are practiced in different settings. For example, polygyny is still quite common across Africa, and poly-andry is practiced in Nepal.

I prefer to use the word *questioning* because for many decades the term *queer* was a pejorative term used to encompass all LGBTQIA+ people. And about the plus—it is simply an open-ended symbol that there could be more variations to come. We are still learning, and we may not have identified all sexualities. It's sort of like the Polish custom of setting an extra place on the table, in case someone else rocks (?) up during dinner. Then they will feel like part of the family.

Transgender or "trans" means that the gender identity you have now is different from the one assigned to you at birth. Just as you can change your name later in life, you can change your gender identity. But there are gradients of this, starting with cross-dressing and going all the way to uterus implants in men. There are also "de-transitioning" cases. For example, a Canadian woman had her breasts and uterus removed to become a man. Then six months later, s/he decided that her/his mental health problems had been misdiagnosed. S/he sued the doctors and asked to become a woman again. She must have been female after all, because it is a woman's prerogative to change her mind.

I have answered your questions, but before ending, a quick word about two other terms mentioned by our moderator: *nonbinary* and *pansexual*. Binary refers to male and female, the prevailing norm. So any other sexual orientation, like asexual, is nonbinary. And pansexual is similar to bisexual or questioning. A "trans" has switched but is not both genders at once. Some "questioning" husbands with several wives are still male, but a polyamorous family can involve bisexual relationships. One person can have sexual relations with several other partners of both sexes. This can exist in the context of love and commitment among them all. It is not "cheating" if kept in the closed circle, transparently.

South Africa's Guest Panelist: Dr. Christiaan Barnard
When I performed the first-ever heart transplant, some people gasped and questioned the morality of it. Frankly, I viewed it as saving a life and applied my technical skills and medical tools to do just that.

So I would like to ask the challenger on the right, why do conservatives get so uptight about gender modification? Why has Texas legislated a stop to all gender modification?

Challenger on the Right
As you know, doctor, many traditionalists are religious, and they believe that God created only two genders—male and female. So for some, the answer is never to play God in this way. Then comes a scale. Some say it's OK for adults to decide for themselves. So if an adult male wants a uterus implanted inside him (her?), this can be done as long as the individual is over twenty-one years of age. One related question is whether the state should pay for it. Would the individual's general health deteriorate without the transplant?

Others say it's OK from age eighteen. Others say it's even OK from age twelve, after puberty. By then, a human should have a clear sense of their sexual orientation. But then, do young teenagers even know yet what their career path will be, to say nothing of their gender? It seems to me to be too early for anyone to make that lifetime decision.

As for children, the concerns raised by medical interventions on intersex babies have been mentioned. What if the parents and doctors take a wrong turn? Will the surgery have to be reversed after puberty?

It's a bit like the sliding scale of abortion. Some say never. Others say it's OK up to six weeks or fifteen weeks. Others say it's OK up to twenty-one weeks. Others say a baby can be aborted up to full term. And some say even after birth, a decision can be made to terminate a child. Isn't that infanticide?

This sliding scale makes me think of the ancient Greek method of discerning truth. It is called "hypothesis." Basically, you propose a solution and then test it. Does this one work? Does it answer the inherent questions? Or are there better hypotheses that are more worthy of consideration? Doesn't that sound like: "Nobody knows for sure"?

In 2019, author Dally London wrote a book called *The Philosophy of Truth*. The subtitle is "Dust from the rabbit holes." Without unpacking its content here, Dally London's methodology is of interest to us. He says to venture down hypothetical rabbit holes of thought and then, from observations to firsthand accounts, theorizes about potential causes and effects. That sounds a bit like hypotheses—different rabbit holes. Explore them. Stack up the pros and cons. Compare them with others until the dust from the rabbit holes chokes you. Then make a choice.

I am pretty sure that conservative voices will not go away. They will champion the answers "never" and "for adults only." There are always radicals. They will be promoting the exposure of "drag queens" to children, along with other trending activism like lobbying for assisted suicide. Each of us needs to think about the topics before we engage in conversation, and above all, before we vote.

India's Guest Panelist: Dr. Anandi Gopal Joshi
Trans is upending sports. Essentially, ex-males or intersex individuals are sometimes competing with sportswomen, and it doesn't seem like a fair match. Aside from my curiosity about the views of classical feminism on ex-men joining their ranks, I also have a nagging concern about pediatric gender modification. This does not seem right to me.

I ask the challenger on the left, who may favor feminism as well as gender modification, can't we keep the children out of this? Adults who deviate from social norms have been the butt of discrimination for centuries, stigmatized to the point of it being criminalized. But are they not overreacting and overcompensating for it now? Will this not provoke a continued conservative backlash? After all, the numbers are not on the side of these minorities. Is there no thought for the so-called moral majority?

Challenger on the Left
In some places, exposing children to drag queens is being criminalized. Also, laws are already emerging against pediatric gender modification. It has already been noted on the topic of abortion that a federal ban might be a "never" ban, or a ban after six weeks, or after fifteen weeks, or a ban after twenty-one weeks. Individuals can simply cross state lines into a more liberal setting, so without a federal ban, it is hard to enforce local laws. The same logic applies to pediatric gender modification.

227

One can see that the rise of wokeism created the conditions for unprecedented discarding of taboos and stigmas. Rainbow parades are not just "gay parades" anymore; they include all LGBTQIA+. Meanwhile, some Christians are complaining that the adopting of the rainbow metaphor is antichurch. For those who know the Bible, the rainbow symbolizes God's promise never to send a flood to destroy the earth. So to them, it is almost as if that symbol is being defiantly thrown back in God's face. Just the use of that symbol exacerbates the polarization.

As for feminism and trans athletes competing against women, this is controversial. Some sports are allowing it, others are not. In one event, a trans contestant even won a beauty contest against biological women! The pushback is rising. Soon after his inauguration, Donald Trump signed an executive order stating that there are only two genders—male and female.

A South African runner named Caster Semenya has consistently competed in women's sports. She is an intersex woman, with 5α-Reductase 2 deficiency, assigned female at birth, with both X and Y chromosomes and a natural heterogametic testosterone level. World Athletics regulations prevent her from competing against biological women. But she has always identified as female, so she complained to the European Court of Human Rights and won. However, that may not force the IAAF to allow her to compete. This is a good example of subjective truth and the clash of rights. Semenya has rights. But so do the other athletes. You cannot always get your way because someone has violated your rights. It may be that you have also violated their rights. Red lines are needed, and a functioning system of enforcement.

Just as Serbian tennis star Novak Djokovic was not allowed to compete in some Grand Slam events because he was not vaccinated against COVID-19, so also some trans or intersex athletes will not succeed in competing with biological women because there is a strong backlash. The saga of Caster Semenya seems to have run out of steam. She did win her appeal in Europe's highest human rights court of appeal, but that did not force the regulatory body, World Athletics, to allow her to compete against biological women. It sounds rather like gridlock.

One has to wonder if a child with a Y chromosome should have been assigned to the female gender. She was then brought up as a girl-child; her nurture was out of sync with her nature. Why should she now be penalized for this? In a way, it is tragic. On the other hand, Caster Semenya has done us all a great favor as a courageous athlete who is first and foremost a human being. We owe her a huge vote of thanks for her honesty and transparency.

North America's Guest Panelist: Dr. Benjamin Spock

It's a big jump from playful cross-dressing to uterus transplants. Organ donors may expect their generous legacy to save lives, but should the state pay for gender modification? If so, for what age brackets?

Even though I almost always consult my comrades on the left, I am directing my question this time to the challenger in the middle. I want to hear a balanced analysis.

I also want to hear if there is any sense of an emerging new truth about this topic.

Challenger in the Middle

In the USA, starting in 2018, the number of transgender surgeries nearly tripled. The turning point was in 2014, when the Obama administration announced an end to a thirty-three-year ban on Medicare coverage of transgender care. Then, in 2018, Obamacare extended that policy, forcing health insurance companies to cover these costs. Doctors and hospitals rushed in to reap the rewards of these expensive procedures. Transgender-affirming surgeries soared from 4,550 in 2016 to 13,000 by 2019.

The number of patients seeking care for gender identity disorder rose from 12,855 in 2016 to 38,470 in 2020. The biggest age group—more than half the patients—was 19 to 30. The second largest age group was 31 to 40, comprising less than one quarter. The underage group from 12 to 18 constituted 8 percent of the patients. So pediatric gender modification is being practiced, although to a lesser extent.

The majority of younger patients are girls having their breasts removed. The number of surgeries on genitals increases with older patients.

The psychological side effects are also worth mentioning. Fifteen percent report mental health or substance abuse problems. Research of transgender surgery patients in Sweden corroborates this. Patients were 4.9 times more likely to attempt suicide and 19.1 times more likely to die of suicide.

The Swedish research found: "Persons with transsexualism, after sex reassignment, have considerably higher risks for mortality, suicidal behaviour, and psychiatric morbidity than the general population. Our findings suggest that sex reassignment, although alleviating gender dysphoria, may not suffice as treatment for transsexualism, and should inspire improved psychiatric and somatic care after sex reassignment for this patient group."

The USA is an outlier among all nations in its headlong rush to push gender reassignment surgery and other dangerous medical procedures, especially on children. European countries, where many of the procedures originated, are beginning to pull back from blanket acceptance of transgender procedures. Perhaps the trend toward conservative governance will slow this down. This sea change has arrived in the USA, and it is coming soon in Germany, Canada, and Britain.

You also asked if any sense of new truth is emerging. It is hard to explain the changing conduct of generations. There is more to it than just a generation gap. As we move from Generation X to millennials, for example, church attendance is dwindling. The new generations exhibit different spiritualities. These are not absent, but they are less vocal about it. The extent to which that is due to the rise of wokeism, either buy-in or intimidation, or new technologies, like social media and AI, is a matter of conjecture. On the whole, it seems that Generation X and millennials still retain their parental values to a significant extent. While at the same time having fewer taboos. Their activism tends to be focused on environmental concerns or human rights, as opposed to civil rights or abortion.

This may indicate a continuing, gradual shift away from revealed truth toward pluralistic, subjective truth. Yet many societal norms continue to be respected, from speed limits to behavior. For example, when someone's wife runs away with another man, that is still frowned upon, not for offending morality but for cheating on marriage vows. Especially if children are involved. The glue holding marriages together is less their vows, and more a keen sense that reciprocity is embedded in marriage.

You find fewer Gen X and millennials smoking, more being vegetarians, more men taking paternity leave, and more driving EVs, and their free-will donations are as likely to go to rainbow parades as to church tithing. Until very recently, this included lower numbers enlisting in the military, dwelling in rural areas, or voting conservative. But there seems to have been a reversal of this trend. There was never an exodus, but young people are aligning with conservative views, according to the American Comeback Tour of college campuses. Young people want their marriages to work, they want religion in their lives, they want home-cooked meals, and now many are homeschooling or planning to homeschool their children.

The revealed truth did lose ground to the objective truth as well, and science in particular. Particularly when science is spiced with fear and arrogance. Prophets of doom have enlisted science to try to undermine revealed truth. And theories like evolution have come to be accepted as fact, based on the flimsy evidence available. There is some evidence, but not proof. As Dally London would say, venture down some other rabbit holes of thought, with a pinch of humility, and you will find that science cannot yet answer all the questions. Dust yourself off and think again.

Even people of faith have been known to betray revealed truth at times and to go astray. So the three options remain on the table: objective truth, subjective truth, and revealed truth. Many of us live with one foot on one of these tectonic plates of truth, and the other foot on another, as they shudder and quake beneath us.

Moderator

Ha ha! Tectonic plates of truth indeed. No wonder new generations are having to pick their path carefully.

Thank you to this panel of four doctors, who have served our purposes well! Thanks to our three challengers who never fail to inform us.

Now, will the real Truth about gender modification please stand out?

17

FUTURE ISSUES

OPEN BORDERS

Moderator

HELLO, EVERYONE! WELCOME to the nineteenth episode of *Telling the Truth*! We are starting a new series today on the future. We start by welcoming a new panel of four, using our new app, Time-Zoom. Welcome to four thought-leaders: Tommy Douglas from North America, Tony Benn from Britain, Winnie Madikizela-Mandela from South Africa, and Bal Gangadhar Tilak from India.

Our remit is to seek the truth about different issues, one topic at a time and, in doing so, to help viewers learn about the nature of truth itself. Everyone would agree that the world is full of deceptions—scammers, spin doctors, and just plain liars. We need to protect ourselves from being misled by con artists. Watching our show will sharpen your ability to tell the truth from a lie. That's why we are here.

Today's topic is open borders. We live in a world teeming with migrants and refugees. Boatloads of Africans cross the Mediterranean to Italy or Spain. People from the Middle East and Asia try to cross the mountains into NATO countries, like Turkey and Greece. Then on to Germany or Britain. In America, under President Biden, the southern border with Mexico became porous. That's why immigrants poured in—pardon the pun!

Not only is there congestion in the ports and cities where these immigrants land, but this is causing a devastating brain drain in the countries that they leave behind. For they are not all seeking asylum. Some are merely optimists or opportunists looking for a better future, including the "Dreamers," who immigrated with their parents when they were young and long to remain in the only land they can remember. Then there are some more sinister immigrants.

The term *borderless world* makes sense in some ways, especially if you view migrations of population as naturally occurring. So some analysts and lawmakers promote open borders to let human capital flow to stronger economies with lower unemployment and more jobs. Such currents are quite natural.

However, some voices have warned of distortions. High levels of immigration cause housing vacancies to shrink and rental prices to soar. This can stir up resentment among the citizenry and a backlash against immigrants. Not to mention the shady side of immigration.

It is the first time we enjoy the composition of this illustrious panel, for this is the first episode in our future series. So go ahead, Ms. Winnie Madikizela-Mandela; it is your turn to spark the discussion.

South Africa's Guest Panelist: Winnie Madikizela-Mandela
As a social worker, I am a strong believer in justice, including the rule of law. Allowing immigrants into any country without proper border clearances opens a Pandora's box. Criminals sneak in, carrying drugs and trafficking children. South Africa now has a population of 63 million, of whom six million are immigrants, mostly from other African countries. Traditionally, immigration from neighboring countries was managed bilaterally. That is, a certain annual quota was set, and the other country, like Mozambique or Lesotho, would recruit and "export" the miners. But this has been overtaken by a free-for-all, bringing crime, smuggling, zama-zamas (informal sector miners), child trafficking, and the extra 10 percent burden on our hospitals and schools.

As I am a leftist, let me ask the challenger on the left: do you support open borders? Shouldn't illegal immigrants be rounded up, sequestered, and deported? Or should we leave them alone, allowing them to vote and join the ranks of the police?

Challenger on the Left
Socialist solidarity is always strong. Wherever you go, there is a sense that people have a right to work. So if unemployment is high in their country, then they sense a right to go to where there are jobs. Even more so because South Africa has a debt to pay. During the struggle against apartheid, the "frontline states" hosted so many of us as refugees and welcomed the liberation movement of South Africa to operate in their countries. At the same time, the racist regime banned the ANC. This invited occasional attacks on our South Africans in exile. During the struggle, every worker employed in Mozambique paid a levy on their salary. The government collected this levy, and it was used to fund the African National Congress while it was in exile. So to close the borders of the free and democratic South Africa to its neighbors after apartheid ended would have been a travesty.

However, I agree that immigration should be properly handled. The Department of Home Affairs exists for a reason! But corruption has crept in. Visas are for sale, under the counter. This has turned Home Affairs into a chaotic charade. Take the example of the Malawian pastor Shepherd Bushiri. He not only bribed his way into South Africa but was also charged with money laundering and fraud while residing in the republic. Then he skipped the country, again clearly with help from corrupt immigration officials. Back in Malawi, he called it a "tactical withdrawal," insisting that he was not guilty. This shows contempt for law and order. He is a border jumper.

Border fences have been built to slow down illegal immigration, but they have little effect. The contracts to construct them were subject to kickbacks.

Starting in 2008, there have been some nasty outbreaks of xenophobia, targeting immigrants from Somalia and Nigeria in particular. They are called *makwerekwere*—a reference to birds that arrive from the north in flocks, hungry from the long flight. So they eat the millet and sorghum planted by local farmers. Not a nice generalization.

There must be some correlation between the rising level of immigration and South Africa's record unemployment levels. The official rate has reached 34 percent. Unofficially, it is probably higher than that. This causes resentment among local people, in spite of the pan-African solidarity that is visceral among blacks.

As for voting, it is officially illegal for expatriates to vote in South African elections. To vote, you are expected to present your identity card. Foreigners who enter the country legally may obtain identity books, but they may not vote. The extent to which they do vote is unknown because no one openly admits it. But given the corruption levels in South Africa, it would come as no surprise to find an illegal immigrant voting. There is such a gap between policy and practice.

As for joining the ranks of the police, it seems highly unlikely that illegal immigrants could do so. But again, money talks. So nothing is impossible, it seems.

India's Guest Panelist: Bal Gangadhar Tilak
The high pavilions of the Himalayas make it difficult for Chinese or Tibetans to enter India, although we have granted asylum to His Excellency the Dalai Lama. Our eastern border with Bangladesh and Myanmar is a bit porous, and there are many asylum seekers from Myanmar among us. But the western border with Pakistan is almost on a war footing, so movements back and forth are very tightly controlled.

My question about open borders, however, has to do with the brain drain. Only the negative impact on the destination countries seems to be talked about in the media. Isn't there a negative impact on the countries left behind as well? Let me try to get a balanced answer on this from the challenger in the middle.

Challenger in the Middle

A son of India is well placed to ask this question, as his country now has the biggest diaspora of them all. Indians are all over the world in large numbers. In total, about 18 million people of Indian origin live abroad. This is about 70 percent higher than the Chinese diaspora. In 2022, India's population surpassed China's, which has been shrinking. So the biggest country has the biggest diaspora.

Yes, emigrants leaving a country comprise a brain drain. One example that comes to mind is a Syrian refugee who fled while studying at university in Lebanon. Jandali emigrated to New York. He studied at Columbia, then went to Wisconsin, where he fell in love with a lady who soon became pregnant. However, her Catholic father refused to allow her to marry a Muslim, so they put the baby up for adoption. The child was adopted by Paul and Clara Jobs in San Francisco. Their son Steve Jobs was unquestionably a genius. Another refugee link is that his adoptive mom, Clara's parents, Steve's maternal grandparents, had fled from Armenia to escape the Turks.

So there is something of an "opportunity cost" involved in the brain drain. Cadres depart and there is a loss, more so if the country of origin has provided the emigrant's education. The human capital of the motherland is diminished. However, there is another side to this coin.

From the diaspora, emigrants often send back some support to their families. They not only contribute to their new country, but they can also generate a return to their motherland. This can happen at the highest levels. Rishi Sunak rose to be the prime minister of Britain. Kamala Harris rose to be Vice President of the USA. And two contenders for the 2024 Republican nomination—Vivek Ramaswamy and Nikki Haley (née Nimarata Nikki Randhawa)—were of Indian descent. This shows that Indian immigrants contribute and engage at all levels. Kash Patel is another example. A former aide to Donald Trump, he was chosen to head the FBI.

In fact, there are eighteen thousand illegal immigrants from India in the USA. In response to Donald Trump's new immigration policies, PM Modi of India has offered to repatriate them all. He wants to avert a trade war with the USA.

In the past, it was not uncommon to see a "help wanted" sign in the window of a firm with the proviso "Irish need not apply." The emigration from Ireland in the mid-nineteenth century was so massive that it was hard to integrate them all. Between 1815 and 1867, about 150,000 Irish passed through the port of St. John, New Brunswick. The year called "black '47" is 1847, at the peak of "the Great Hunger" in Ireland. The crisis was so bad that it was hard to keep records either in Ireland or in St. John. That year, the city of St. John, New Brunswick, received seventeen thousand Irish refugees, compared to its base population of twenty thousand. Just imagine the strain.

Many of these were orphan children, whose parents had perished in the potato famines. Orphan immigration has hit various peaks, and this was one of them. In 1854, Charles Brace, head of the Children's Aid Society, sent out the first "Orphan Train" from New York City. Researchers estimate that as many as 400,000 children were "placed out" on the orphan trains, perhaps as many as 100,000 in Missouri alone. The term *farmed out* came into the English language this way. This led to adoption and fostering as better coping mechanisms than orphanages.

The number of orphans increased by 300 percent after the American Civil War, without reference to any wave of immigration. From 1870 to 1967, there was a child emigration movement sending 150,000 British orphans to its colonies, including Canada. Among these were the "Bernardo orphans."

Orphans were too often exploited. This led to the Great Orphan Abduction in 1904, in Arizona. Christians there took exception to the way orphan children were being treated and abducted them, providing them sanctuary. This event had a defining effect on America's core values.

In today's world, we see immigration flowing across seas and borders. The flow of fentanyl into the USA has sped up as a result. Between ten and twenty million people have immigrated in this new wave. It is a new high-water mark. But not the first. Remember Ellis Island in New York City. It served as a classic port of entry for 12 million immigrants over the sixty years that it was in operation. But that was 200,000 per year, on average. Compare that to four million a year walking across the Mexican border for the past five years. A video released by Robert F. Kennedy Jr. called *Midnight at the Border* claimed to relate the truth. In the video, he spoke openly with arriving immigrants. They were of all nationalities, including Asian and African, not just Latin Americans. He spoke to them with esteem and dignity. He admitted that this wave has now reached crisis proportions.

The big picture that emerges is one of chaos. Far from the Ellis Island model of order and good recordkeeping in the shadow of the Statue of Liberty, this recent wave of immigration is chaotic. Many unregistered immigrants slip in, who could be criminals. There are clearly drug cartels in Mexico using immigrants as mules. Worse yet, an estimated 85,000 children have been trafficked into the USA during this wave. This has been exposed by the motion picture *Sound of Freedom*.

Some of your diaspora, Mr. Nehru, is entering the USA this way. They fly from Mumbai to Mexico City and then hike north. On the whole, the Indian diaspora is welcome and productive. However, this wave almost looked like a way to get some extra voters in before the 2024 election. If polling stations required ID and legal immigration documents, that would not be the case. But this varies from state to state, and the permissive ethos of left-leaning governance has a way of trying to perpetuate itself.

North America's Guest Panelist: Tommy Douglas
I am saddened to hear of chaos. Even though I suppose North America has been populated by various waves, not all of them have been above board. The Atlantic slave trade comes to mind: 12.5 million slaves were captured in Africa and exported to the New World. Only 10.2 million survived the ocean crossing. But of these, only 388,000 landed in North America. Albeit a small percentage, it was strongly opposed.

The slave population of the USA had grown to four million by the time the Civil War began. The war fought to end slavery cost 620,000 lives, including 40,000 African Americans, who were recruited only later in the war.

I ask the challenger in the middle: How can we stop the pendulum swinging so far from alt-right to left-leaning extremes? And a deeper question: Has the two-party system contributed to polarization? Is that why we have two extremes and nothing in between? Remember that the two main parties in the USA used to be the Democrats and the Whigs. Abraham Lincoln was the first Republican Party candidate. He was elected without a 50 percent majority but won more votes than anyone else. He only won 40 percent of the popular vote, but American presidential elections are decided in the Electoral College, where he won.

Challenger in the Middle
Thank you for asking. You are cutting very close to the bone. The American system is very peculiar, and you are right that the 1860 election was something of a turning point in the USA's history.

Lincoln is commonly called "Honest Abe." There is a strong correlation between honesty and truth, as there is between dishonesty and deception. He led his country through hell on earth—the Civil War. He could see the truth, and that the time had come for it to set us free.

Yes, I do think that the two-party system exacerbates polarization. We have had a third choice at times, like when Ralph Nader ran with Jim Stockdale on his ticket. Some analysts think that this cost Al Gore the 2000 election. They call Ralph Nader a "spoiler." But not everyone sees it that way. We are not locked into two parties.

In the run-up to the 2024 election, Steve Bannon remarked that Robert F. Kennedy Jr. would make a good running mate for Donald Trump. This might have been the catalyst to what happened later—RFK withdrawing as an independent candidate and joining the Trump team. Was this a sign of what is coming? Reflecting on Kamala Harris's election loss, rising crime rates in Chicago and New York, and the Los Angeles firestorm, Democrats are starting to talk about the need for a "political exorcism" of their party.

The mudslinging in the 2024 elections was dirtier than ever. Allegations and counterallegations. It was incendiary. Open lawfare! God forbid that another civil war should start as a result of this worrisome acrimony. Precedents have shown that hate speech can blossom into violence.

I think that dishonesty has thrown the cat among the pigeons, especially remembering Richard Nixon and the Watergate scandal. "Tricky Dick" kept wiggling until there was no wiggle-room left. It's happening again. It seems that Senator John Fetterman is the exception—a Democrat who sees and speaks the truth. He confessed that Biden's border policies were a big mistake.

What can we do to find the truth? For example, woke revisionists want to teach a different curriculum about slavery. The alt-right digs its heels in and uses state power to overrule the revisionism. Is history deductive? Or is it an inductive kind of truth? Julius Caesar subdued Gaul mercilessly, to genocidal proportions, and then used his military acumen to cross the Rubicon and disrupt Rome itself. The Roman Senate had clearly become corrupt and deserved disruption. But that cherished democratic experiment—inspired by the Greeks—was lost. Gone was the Roman Senate. Julius Caesar became an emperor and ruled by decree. It became a family dynasty. And yet, the Pax Romana at the time of his son Octavian, renamed Augustus, was a period of unprecedented security and development. This empire lasted for several centuries.

Britain and Canada seem to prefer a three-party system. At the same time, South Africa tried and tried to hang on to a one-party state. The main competition there is not between parties, but between two factions of the ANC. While Rome burns! Not unlike the way the Democrats split in America's 1860 election. India has a real multiparty system. For a long period, it was dominated by a family dynasty that operated within a democratic framework. But it has matured, and now the BJP has had a long run. India is the world's largest democracy. More money is spent on electioneering there than anywhere else.

To me, we need to do more to revive honesty and truth as virtues than to tinker with the party system. Both extremes claim to be defending democracy. One is defending it from the deep state. The other is defending it from demagoguery. Ironically, both parties speak of a witch hunt. It is hard to operate a neutral judiciary in the midst of the partisan lawfare. Especially when some judges are elected, so they are not nonpartisan. This only throws oil onto the fire. The term "activist judges" says so much about where this leads to.

Previously in America, there was a huge controversy over abolition—freedom for the slaves. In our time, it is once again all about freedom. But freedom is predicated on truth. So whoever is lying is selling fake freedom.

A left-leaning worldview tends to line up with a belief in subjective truth. So it becomes very permissive. Coherence does not matter. It goes easy on abortion, same-sex marriage, LGBTQIA+ trends, and gender modification. To each his own. To those who cherish revealed truth, this comes across as a rebellion against God, and thus it resonates with Marxism. So morality is being discarded in favor of rights. Is that really freedom?

Whereas the dominant influencers on the right are now ready to use state intervention to impose conformity, and to use the rule of law to protect majority rule, as opposed to a disproportionate emphasis on minorities. In fact, this worldview still wants to keep "In God we trust" as America's motto. They don't take the knee because their view of truth is rational and leans towards objectivity. They will finish building the border wall to control and manage immigration flows and their implications. They will even try to root out and repatriate illegal aliens.

There is a third view of truth—that it is revealed. It is handed down from on high. Thus, the first commandment of the "ten" is to have no other gods in God's presence. The others follow on from there. "Thus saith the Lord" is not speculative or prognosticating; it is utterly true, the expression of one with whom there is no shadow of turning. Jesus fulfilled the Law of Moses; he claimed to be the truth. He is the ultimate role model, and his teachings set the gold standard. By following him, you know the truth, and that truth sets you free. This is the antithesis of anti-God. Morality is anchored in faith.

Differing views of truth lead to different kinds of freedom. Some fake, some real. Are you really free when you cannot pray in the street in front of an abortion clinic? Are you really an insurrectionist when you organize a trucker convoy to protest violations of our civil liberties?

So while the two-party system is exacerbating polarization, the deeper problem is spiritual. The last thing to change is the deepest, at the convictions and values level. America still has 62 million Roman Catholics, 22 million Baptists, and 6 million Methodists—to mention only the three main Christian denominations; there are many more. In the 2023 census, 71 percent of Americans self-identified as Christian. The revealed truth is still a contender.

Not to mention other faiths—monotheist and polytheist. Religions have always been vying for the truth. They tend to share one golden rule: "Do unto others as you would have them do unto you." Practicing that would go a long way to reducing polarization.

Britain's Guest Panelist: Tony Benn

Great Britain has both emigrated and immigrated millions of people over the centuries, first back and forth across the channel to Europe, then to and from its overseas colonies and the Commonwealth. London is the most cosmopolitan city anywhere.

However, Britain also has its own distinctive culture and history. So while immigration is an economic imperative, there is a danger of too many people arriving too fast. Let me ask the challenger on the right, why has immigration been allowed to speed up so much instead of slowing down? Can it be brought under control?

Challenger on the Right

I think that Britain started to step on the brakes in the wake of Brexit. Many of the immigrants arriving in Europe tried to find their way north to Britain. The UK was the destination of choice. One of the rationales for Brexit was that the welcoming policy of EU countries like Germany was a magnet for refugees, who then kept migrating toward Britain. Brexit was a way of saying, hang on, we want to have our own immigration policy.

Until quite recently, all major parties in Britain were much the same when it came to immigration policy. They did not want illegal migrants, but they nevertheless welcomed huge numbers of legal immigrants, for example, as Hong Kong approached the end of British rule. This caused a major wave of migration, but these were already British subjects or at least wealthy enough to meet the criteria.

In recent years, there has been what many call the New Right. It does not think the same as the old-guard Tories. In Britain, this gave rise to a new party called Reform, led by Nigel Farage. It is vying for conservative hearts and minds. Similarly, in the USA, there are two camps right now—the FreeCons and the NatCons. They think differently. This is very much so when it comes to open borders. The FreeCons will be more familiar to you. Presidents like Ronald Reagan championed this profile. FreeCon views are grounded in personal freedom, free enterprise, and an open, dynamic society, and famously called a city on a hill.

By contrast, the NatCons downplay freedom. Their primordial views are nationalism, traditionalism, and virtue, and the proper role and uses of the state. At first, this might sound a bit like liberalism, but the NatCons have a strong critique of liberalism's main failure—its purported neutrality on matters of culture and values. NatCons want to shape key institutions to conserve Western civilization proactively. This includes a major emphasis on conserving its religion and faith roots, and on homogenizing decision-making. In other words, there is an emphasis on the democratic majority and diminishing the disproportionate influence of small minorities. In short, NatCons never want to see the death of truth. So when it comes to run-away immigration, they see it as civilizational suicide.

The FreeCons tend to shun the nanny state, whereas the NatCons are more pragmatic. State power may be needed to shape a conservative legacy. An example that comes to mind is the state of Florida, where Governor Ron DeSantis has confronted aspects that are trying to push their way into "normalcy." He has tackled identity politics, Disney, CRT, revisionist content in school curriculums, and other trends. This is what NatCons do, and they are the rising star in conservative politics.

Sometimes NatCons are accused of being Nazis! But nothing could be further from the truth. The word "Nazi" stands for national socialist, and that's what they were and are. On the other hand, NatCons are diehard conservatives, clinging to cherished beliefs, values, and norms, and entirely at odds with socialism of any stripe. The term "moral majority" seems to fit them, although that hails from your era.

One major difference between FreeCons and NatCons is their view of open borders. Building a border wall to manage the flow of immigrants is their strategy of choice. They even want to turn the clock back by rooting out illegal aliens, especially those involved in criminal activity.

In earlier decades, the term *NeoCon* was used to describe those conservatives whose views differed. But they were a mere minority. While this is true of NatCons, the two terms are not synonymous. Today, the NatCons are definitely in the ascendancy, and there is a proactive agenda to roll back wokeism. They are slowing down immigration, including foreign students attending American universities.

CHUCK STEPHENS

Moderator

Seeking the truth is the higher goal of *Telling the Truth*! We invite four guest panelists from across the spectrum and across the world. They bring extensive experience and knowledge of our topics. Our three incognito challengers remain with us throughout, but we invite a new and different panel for each series. The only way to get good answers is to ask sharp questions. That's a life skill for truth-seeking.

Now, will the real Truth about open borders please stand out?

NATIONAL DISTANCING

Moderator

Hello, and welcome back! We have a new topic for this, the twentieth episode of *Telling the Truth*. We are introducing a new phrase—national distancing. During the COVID-19 pandemic, we were introduced to social distancing, keeping a safe distance from others to protect ourselves. This is emerging as a national strategy as well—not really isolationism but national distancing.

This approach is inherent in terms like Brexit and MAGA (Make America Great Again). Let's let some grass grow between us and other nations. Good fences make good neighbors. We want to explore how this tendency may play out in the future.

We welcome our illustrious panel, joining us via Time-Zoom: from India, Bal Gangadhar Tilak; from North America, Tommy Douglas; from the United Kingdom, Tony Benn; and from South Africa, Winnie Madikizela-Mandela. They shape the questions put to our three challengers—on the left, on the right, and in the middle. Some voices favor a measure of isolationism, while others favor full engagement in globalization. But all voices speaking out here on our show are telling the truth. No one here is deceiving you. It's just that opinions can vary widely. We try to make some space for all to be heard. We listen with respect and ask those who disagree with us to explain themselves. So there is no need to get defensive.

And as for discerning what is true, in the end, that's up to you. We do not impose any view on you or anyone. We are an open forum. We simply try to create the conditions in which truth can emerge and show itself, for it has a way of doing that by its very nature. Intolerance is a shortcut to the death of truth.

It's India's turn to formulate the first question, so welcome to Bal Gangadhar Tilak. You may proceed.

India's Guest Panelist: Bal Gangadhar Tilak

My motto was always "Swaraj is my birthright, and I shall have it." I never doubted that home rule would prevail one day. Eventually, the Quit India Movement made it happen. But this meant that India had to shake off its inferiority complex and take pride in its own national identity and cultures.

I am confused by a world that has some areas with secessionist tendencies, like Quebec, Scotland, Catalonia, and Tigray, while at the same time, other areas are regionalizing, like the European Union and the African Union. This seems to me to be a contradiction. Countries are fracturing at the same time that they unite into wider blocs. Both seem like solutions devised to keep nationalism in check, after the horrendous emergence of the Third Reich in Germany.

Can I ask the challenger on the right where all this is going? Is there a road map to globalization? Or is the pendulum starting to swing the opposite way into ethnic or hemispheric enclaves?

Challenger on the Right

There are certainly some ironies. Brexit was a wake-up call. To many it was regress, not progress. We need to compare it to the queue of countries lining up to join NATO—an alliance which Britain never left. Finland and Sweden have now joined. Most of Ukraine wants to join, though some pockets may prefer to stick with Russia. Why is NATO expanding at the same time the European Union is consolidating after losing a major member? Why did Britain withdraw from the EU but remain a NATO member? The answer seems to be in the depth of engagement.

NATO is a military alliance. Anyone who attacks one member attacks them all. This makes member states stronger, defensively. Regionalization is another tier of governance. It is a deeper commitment. You even have to surrender your currency. When it came to that, the Brits balked. Other nations may one day come to wonder, like Britain, if open markets, removed trade barriers, and lifted travel restrictions are truly freedoms. But NATO crosses the Atlantic Ocean, effectively reaching all the way to the Pacific shores to the west of North America. And if Ukraine joins, it will reach right across all of Europe to the Black Sea. On the eastern shore of that sea is Asia. A military alliance does not preclude the percolating of national pride, which is indeed on the rise. But it does have the desired effect of regionalization—to reduce or eliminate war between its members.

Brexit made us take the "America First" movement very seriously. MAGA rose at about the same time. NatCons are fiercely patriotic, with less emphasis on the superpower role of "manifest destiny." Donald Trump takes the Monroe Doctrine very seriously, as did John F. Kennedy. The two world wars brought out America's "first among equals" status to defend democracy worldwide. But it is shrinking back to where it started—guarding the Americas. Perhaps the biggest legacy of Franklin Roosevelt is the United Nations. It is more of a Democratic Party legacy than it is a Republican one.

Originally, the USA was conceived as a federation of states, but the Civil War galvanized it into one country. So the next logical step, brought to you by America, was to create a multilateral organization with its fleet of global organizations. Some saw this as a steppingstone to world government. Others preferred a lesser ambition—a useful forum where mutual concerns could be vetted, especially wars, to try to contain the risks and prevent the outbreak of World War III. Thus the UN's Security Council.

NATO was also formed as a deterrent to war, so, ironically, NATO expansion has riled up Russia to the point of invading a neighboring state. Some minimize this as a border dispute, but really, the Russians are missing the security of having some "satellite states" around them, like the good old days of the Cold War, when Eastern Europe served as a buffer between Russia and NATO.

At the same time, some ethnic pockets are angling for independence. Eritrea achieved this when it broke away from Ethiopia. South Sudan achieved it too, when it broke away from the Sudan. Both of these splits involved protracted wars. But in the West, remembering the devastation of the American Civil War, the preferred approach is to hold plebiscites and to renegotiate a province's or region's status within a country.

Ireland is one example; Scotland is another. The Republic of Ireland (originally called the Irish Free State) gained its independence in 1922. I should say "regained" its independence, as it was colonized by Britain long after being a nation with its language, literature, and Brehon law. For centuries before its colonization, it had evolved into a nation in its own right. But after 1922, Great Britain retained control of Ulster province, now called Northern Ireland. That is still part and parcel of the United Kingdom, one of four nations under one crown.

For several centuries, the Protestant population of Northern Ireland exceeded the number of Catholics. But that has changed. Meanwhile, in the south, the republic is secularizing quickly. So religion is no longer the determining factor. Brexit almost didn't happen because of the challenge of keeping the north of Ireland in the UK while keeping an open border between the north and south of the Emerald Isle. This was very tricky.

Meanwhile, Scotland used to be independent until the time of King James I, son of Mary Queen of Scots, the sister of Queen Elizabeth I of England, who left no male heirs. So after Elizabeth died, King James moved to London from Scotland, where he had been raised. He made a heroic effort to reconcile the two countries and to reduce the acrimony between Protestants (dominant in Scotland) and Catholics (dominant in England's enemies—France and Spain). King Henry VIII, the father of Queen Elizabeth I and grandfather of James I, had nationalized the church. It was now the Church of England. Just like the Lutheran church in Germany and Eastern Europe, it had taken over most Catholic church assets. But Scotland has always had an ethnic streak of independence, and this reemerged after Brexit. Many Scots said they wanted to leave Britain and rejoin the European Union as an independent state.

In both cases, some national distancing is taking place—but not through armed struggle.

In 2017, Catalonia held a referendum, and a majority of 90 percent voted in favor of self-determination. However, the turnout was only 43 percent, so the central government did not go along with it. Some separatist leaders ended up in exile and then in jail, but it was another case of national distancing. We must remember that the Iberian Peninsula has a long history. Cities like Barcelona and Valencia go back to Roman times. Archaeologists have recently dug up a Roman city in Spain that had been completely forgotten about!

The Muslim invasion of Iberia included this region, but it was only part of al-Andalus for one century. Then the Franks invaded, creating a buffer zone against Islamic expansion. As more time passed, the county of Catalonia began to implement some national distancing measures. Then an alliance between Catalonia and Aragon emerged, and gradually the Catalan language and culture prospered. But after Spain discovered the New World in 1492, it was on its way to superpower status based on the huge wealth that it amassed, largely from looting in the Americas. Catalonia was eclipsed, but right into the twentieth century, it retained varying degrees of autonomy. So its aspirations should have come as no surprise. The international borders as we know them are relatively new, and they are unlikely to remain forever.

North America's Guest Panelist: Tommy Douglas
Yes, but what about Quebec in Canada? The French were among the first explorers up the St. Lawrence River, while the British and Dutch focused on colonizing the eastern seaboard. So francophone roots in North America run very deep. But at the Battle of the Plains of Abraham, Montcalm was soundly defeated by Wolfe, beginning a period of English predominance.

So what is the truth about Quebec's special status in Canada? Is it sustainable? Or will it lead to more polarization and confrontation in the future? Let me ask the challenger in the middle, in hopes of getting a balanced view.

Challenger in the Middle

Quebec has played a clever hand. It lost the war, as you mentioned, but it has won the peace. By this I mean that despite various attempts to separate from Canada, which failed, it has ended up with a significant level of national distancing within confederation. It is described as a distinct society.

It has its language. Whereas Canada adopted bilingualism, Quebec is proudly French-speaking. Immigrants coming to Quebec from other countries must learn French if they want to take up residence there. The tapestry of Québécois culture includes its traditional foods, literature, folk music, and symbols (e.g., the fleur-de-lis). Quebec uses civil law (i.e., Napoleonic code), which is different from the common law of all other provinces.

In 2006, Canada's parliament approved a government motion stating that "this House recognizes that the Québécois form a nation within a united Canada." This is derived from a policy called "asymmetrical federalism." For example, in terms of immigration, the province of Quebec can handle its selection of immigrants.

But there is still dissent on both sides. One radical leader, the late Pierre Bourgault, was best known as a public speaker who advocated sovereignty for Quebec from Canada. He argued that Quebec didn't want to be a province unlike any other, but rather that Quebec didn't want to be a country like any other. At the same time, critics of the status quo point out that Quebec receives major equalization payments from the federal tax system, coming from other provinces like Alberta, which an independent Quebec would not receive. So Quebec is getting the best of both worlds.

The immediate threat of secession seems to have blown over. However, the resentment of other provinces—especially in western Canada—is the weak underbelly of this arrangement. Maybe separation will come elsewhere.

Mr. Douglas, your government in Saskatchewan lasted for five consecutive terms. You inherited a deficit but left a surplus for your successors. You introduced seminal democratic-socialist policies like Medicare that have become the gold standard everywhere else in Canada. Your farmers and cities did this by being frugal and hardworking, not from bleeding resources from other provinces. They booted up Saskatchewan by its bootstraps.

Above all, your province of Saskatchewan welcomed churches from across the whole denominational spectrum. Catholic, Methodist, and Presbyterian missionaries came over a century ago, long after Quebec had been saturated by Catholicism. Sadly, its lack of diversity had caused church fatigue to set in, so Quebec secularized very rapidly in the late twentieth century. At the same time, your province managed to remain faithful to the revealed truth. You are a Christian minister. I sense that Quebec's future is doomed to swing further into isolationism, not the balanced approach of national distancing. Every nation with its language and culture has a place in the tapestry of human history. But some will rise while others fall, and this has a lot to do with their fundamental religious beliefs or lack of them. It would appear that there is no substitute for revealed truth. It is still very relevant and uniting. The death of truth leaves a spiritual wasteland.

Britain's Guest Panelist: Tony Benn

I really like this term, national distancing. I have always been a Eurosceptic, so Brexit did not surprise me at all. Joining Europe was a bad idea, born of the Conservatives, so it was up to Boris Johnson to clean up Edward Heath's mess. For all the same reasons, I like the America First emphasis in the USA, even though I am fundamentally a proponent of Christian socialism, like my copanelist Tommy Douglas.

Some left-leaners speak of a borderless world. In the next phrase, they might be heard dreaming of a religion-free world as well. But we disagree on both counts. Patriotism is a force. The trick is not to let it connect with social Darwinism and the notion of survival of the fittest. Then it gets dangerous. But to be a patriot does not require you to be alt-right or to accept an economic system based on greed. Any political persuasion can be patriotic.

To the challenger of the left, I ask: Are members of the Socialist International obliged to renounce their nationalistic sentiments?

Challenger on the Left

Marxist-Leninists denounce nationalism as a bourgeois ideology developed under capitalism that sets workers against each other. However, they do allow for "boundless love for the socialist homeland, a commitment to the revolutionary transformation of society and the cause of communism."

My concern is that extremists seem to dominate on both sides of the polarization. People are no longer seeking truth or reconciliation; they treat anyone who does not think as they do with derision. This contempt is antisocial.

In a way, the NatCons are not as far right as the FreeCons. They are a bit more pragmatic and ready to use state levers to correct the course of history. For this, they have earned the nickname "populists," just as democratic socialists are not as far left as Marxist-Leninists.

Mr. Benn, no conservative (big or small C) could imagine someone declining a birthright into the House of Lords, forcing you to engineer rule changes so that you could continue a career in the lower house of parliament. This took time, and yet you pulled it off. Principle mattered more to you than the aristocracy or grand tradition. You are rightly called a radical dissenter!

Nations need an upper house of parliament to vet changes and slow down radical trends. You sided with those who wanted to be change agents, not resistors, although both serve a purpose.

The open lawfare in the USA these past few years is counterintuitive. In a democracy, one that has been held up as a city on a hill, we did not expect this. It has made the USA look unrespectable, not a beacon of hope for the world. Two opposing witch hunts went on. One was ostensibly to unseat a sitting president through impeachment proceedings. Even if he had been convicted, which he wasn't, these were still theatrics in the run-up to his reelection bid. They cost him dearly, weakening his reputation. He had to pull out in favor of another candidate.

The opposite witch hunt was being perceived as election interference, trying to diminish or even stop the leading candidate for the Republican nomination. Even with a conviction, his right to finalize appeals would take longer than the next election. In the end, his sentencing was an "unconditional discharge". This said a lot about what was really going on.

The underlying truth is that the Democratic Party is inclining very much to America's manifest destiny in the world, to full engagement, and to globalization. Whereas the Republicans have a new mantra: Make America Great Again. This platform sends out signals of national distancing—America First.

This is a bit ironic when the far left has classically been the proponent of subordinating national fervor to the socialist cause. Combine national fervor with socialism (with a pinch of social Darwinism mixed in), and you get Nazis. Combine patriotism with conservatism, and you get NatCons. With the rise of the NatCons as the dominant faction within the Republican party, the classic leaning of Marxist-Leninism, to stand up for socialism first and your nation second, is getting a real run for its money. Leftists may need to recalibrate their rhetoric to survive.

South Africa's Guest Panelist: Winnie Madikizela-Mandela
In Africa, we have the same tension between patriotism and pan-Africanism. But it is possible to be a patriot and a pan-Africanist as well; these are not mutually exclusive. It is more of a question of emphasis.

Trying to find this balance, let me ask the challenger in the middle: How can we keep the trend toward regionalization and even a borderless world going forward, when reactionary forces like Brexit and MAGA are thriving? And is this national distancing why we are seeing so many coups in Africa? Is this populism why constitutionally authentic governments are being toppled so frequently? In other words, is national distancing really a regression?

Challenger in the Middle
The scion of the left-leaning Soros network certainly thinks so. This major philanthropy has been advancing leftist agendas through the wealth of George Soros, whose son, Alex, is now its leading light. Alex thinks that MAGA will be even worse for the European Union than for the USA, because of the knock-on effect. He predicts that national distancing will corrupt European unity. George Soros is of Hungarian origin, and ironically, his biggest critic is Viktor Orbán, Hungary's prime minister.

Orbán is just the kind of leader that worries Alex Soros. Orbán has dared to question European policies—for example, on immigration and the war in Ukraine. Orbán inspires national distancing in France and Italy next door, where you have Marine Le Pen's National Rally and prime minister Giorgia Meloni, respectively. PM Meloni has led the Brothers of Italy party and also serves as president of the European Conservatives and Reformists Party.

Another strong woman is Helen Zille, who really pulls the strings of South Africa's Democratic Alliance party. She was a journalist and anti-apartheid activist who exposed the truth about Steve Biko's death. She has served as mayor of Cape Town, governor of Western Cape province, and DA party leader. Currently, she leads from behind by chairing the DA's federal council. The DA was the first among equals in the "moonshot pact" that envisaged a coalition government unseating the ANC at the 2024 elections. It worked, sort of! Enough black voters were ready to vote patriotically instead of racially. As long as the tribes of South Africa were fighting one another, the colonial regimes managed to suppress them. By dividing, they conquered. Then the tribes found one another in the "broad church" ANC, which has always leaned to the left. Their dismal 2024 election results are a sign that South Africa is maturing as a cosmopolitan nation, self-confident enough to walk the talk about multiparty democracy. Until the ANC was forced to lead a Government of National Unity, it had essentially governed as a one-party state. Coalitions and the GNU are changing that.

In India, Hindu nationalism is a form of national distancing. Some say Narendra Modi's "tiger warrior" diplomacy is harming India's interests, that the attitudes inherent in Hindu nationalism are alienating other nations and faiths. Hate crimes against Christians and Muslims minorities are on the rise. Hate speech is rampant. So there is a dark side to this trend.

Since the COVID crisis in 2019, there have been nineteen attempted coups in Africa. Nine have succeeded in regime change, namely Mali (twice), Burkina Faso (twice), Tunisia, Guinea, Sudan, Niger, and Gabon. Ten more coup attempts have failed during this period. The names of the parties involved include Patriots for Change and the National Committee for the Salvation of the People. One has to wonder how there got to be forty-six countries in sub-Saharan Africa anyway. Even some of those north of the Sahara are unstable, like Tunisia and Libya.

There is no real correlation between the number of tribes or ethnic groups in Africa and its number of fifty-five countries. The borders tend to be a colonial hangover, and sometimes the elements of tribalism and racism make these countries ungovernable. They are countries, but not nations. Either one country contains two or more nations, or one nation straddles two or more countries. Often, the coups are related to internal tribal tensions. Or they may be seeking more economic justice and less elitism.

Regional clusters do make it possible to hold new regimes to account. For example, the Economic Community of West African States (ECOWAS), within which most of the coups have occurred (excluding Tunisia and Gabon). However, when a regional network of fifteen countries has seven successful coups in three years, it seems that national distancing is winning, and regionalization is losing.

There is also a religious dimension to this, as Islam is prevalent in many of these countries. Sharia law and Muslim customs prevail, a form of revealed truth. However, good governance champions human rights, which is anchored more in subjective truth. For example, women have more rights under the UN charter than they do under sharia law. In the former colonial power of West Africa—France—human rights take precedence, so girls in France may no longer wear hijabs to school. This would be unthinkable in deep rural areas of West Africa. They step to the beat of different drums.

Western culture has a fairly high degree of arrogance. Some call it a superiority complex. As far back as 2007, in a speech to the Munich Security Conference, Vladimir Putin accused the West of trying to build a unipolar world. Russia has been toning down diplomacy ever since and playing more military cards. Even President Emmanuel Macron of France has said that humiliating Russia is not the way to solve the war in Ukraine. He is talking about a balancing act between promoting a world that shares some reciprocal principles while guarding each nation's dignity. The key here is not to say those fundamental principles are universal but to say they are reciprocal. "Do unto others as you would have them do unto you" is not a win-lose scenario.

The jury is still out when it comes to tariff wars. But this seems to be another manifestation of national distancing. Key themes include trade imbalances, reshoring jobs, and self-sufficiency.

Moderator

Oh, wow! We can practice social distancing when standing in queues, and national distancing when engaging in bilateral and multilateral forums. Reciprocal tariffs are the order of the day.

Thanks again to our four guest panelists for their sharp questions. And to our three challengers for their contemplative replies. And now, will the real Truth about national distancing please stand out?

GLOBAL WARMING

Moderator

Welcome to the long-awaited episode of *Telling the Truth* on global warming. This topic is quite contentious. If there is any issue that divides us, this is it! And given the resources that are being poured into climate change action as we speak, the stakes are very high. Is it an inconvenient truth? Or a convenient con?

Sometimes the pursuit of truth shifts more toward one kind of truth or another. On the topic of global warming, we are trusting scientists to convince us with data. Observation of weather and atmospheric conditions is increasingly advanced. Meteorology has better tools than ever before, but the problem is that scientific records do not reach very far into history. Particularly if you buy from the same scientists that Earth is millions of years old. Archaeology can provide some data, such as the studies from cities that are now underwater, either because the oceans rose or because land masses sank. And cities like Ur now stand in the midst of desert sands, a hundred kilometers from the seashore. What used to be a port city is now stranded in sand dunes. This happens over long periods.

For example, astronauts circling the planet were the first to observe a huge geological formation on the western side of the Sahara Desert, which looks like an eye. It is so big that you would not see what it is even if you were standing on it! It is formally known as the Richat structure, and it is in present-day Mauritania. Some observers speculate that this may be the site of the legendary city of Atlantis.

Plato wrote down the only ancient description we have of the city of Atlantis. He recorded what he had heard from an uncle who had studied in Egypt (no less than Solon of Athens! According to Plutarch, Sonchis of Sais, an Egyptian priest, told Solon about Atlantis). Now what his uncle heard was not the current geography of his era or of ours. It was ancient history already, long before the time of Plato, his uncle, or Sonchis! The philosopher simply wrote it down for posterity. Oddly enough, that description and location of Atlantis fits the Richat structure quite well. However, either the land has been rising, or the sea level has descended. Because you used to be able to reach there by sailing on the Atlantic waters. The sea route was out through the Gates of Hercules, passing what we now call Gibraltar, and down the coast a way, southward, then into a kind of fjord. The city of Atlantis was built on concentric rings, separated by round canals, fed by a waterfall falling down out of the Atlas Mountains behind the city.

Why am I telling you this? Well, first of all, we need to be humble. There are probably people in human history who have forgotten more than we ourselves may ever know. Second, the planet is changing, and we know that sea levels rise and fall over long periods. Mean temperatures also rise and fall. Temperatures during ice ages are colder than during heat waves. Changes can be as sudden as a comet crashing into planet Earth. Our challenge is that the last time the mean temperature changed as much as it is predicted to rise in the twenty-first century, it took ten thousand years to do so! Some observers suggest that there have been cataclysmic changes every 6,500 years or so. One possible explanation is a pole shift.

And yet species and ecologies can adapt. When the great Kariba dam was built on the Zambezi River, a huge lake was created above the dam (i.e., Lake Kariba). There was an Operation Noah to move animals out of danger as the waters rose and hilltops became islands. As always, there were prophets of doom, warning of negative environmental consequences. But over the next few decades, biologists found an amazing capacity in nature to adapt rapidly to the changes around them.

So here we are, with a panel of four joining us via the expedient app Time-Zoom. And three very well-informed challengers—champions of the left, the right, and the middle. We are embarking today on one of the most contentious topics of our mandate. We hope that Ralph Nader, David Attenborough, Al Gore, and Greta Thunberg are all watching. Drum roll, please!

It is North America's turn to fire the first salvo, so take it away, Tommy Douglas!

North America's Guest Panelist: Tommy Douglas

Western Canada, where I come from, was once under a great shallow sea. The waters have receded, leaving a few big lakes like Winnipeg, Athabasca, and Great Slave. So we know all about climate change in prehistory.

In previous episodes of this show, the phenomenal rise in world population has also been noted. *Homo sapiens* is a hugely successful species, doing what God commanded at creation—multiplying and filling the earth.

My question to the challenger on the left is whether there is proof of a correlation between the population explosion and global warming. I do not doubt that the planet warms up and cools off for a variety of reasons. But are we the culprits or the victims? Humans have been around long enough to have experienced massive climate changes. Do we have to go on a guilt trip about what could be just a natural cycle?

Challenger on the Left

Let me respond by quoting Sir David Attenborough from the documentary series *Life on Earth*: "The fact is that no species has ever had such wholesale control over everything on earth, living or dead, as we now have. That lays upon us, whether we like it or not, an awesome responsibility. In our hands lies not only our future, but that of all other living creatures with whom we share the earth."

To act responsibly, we need to reduce our carbon footprint. That means managing our waste disposal better (especially litter), switching to renewable sources of energy, like solar and wind, conserving our water resources, and planting more trees than we cut down. Reforestation must keep pace with deforestation. Forests are basically the lungs of our planet.

Above all, we need to reduce pollution. We must protect our air and water from contamination and learn to recycle products to conserve nonrenewable resources.

OK, that's the green gospel in a nutshell. You have heard it before. One example comes to mind—the great Pacific garbage patch (GPGP). There is a place in the Pacific where the ocean currents that swirl around continents meet. Floating garbage of all kinds is carried into this junction of currents. This garbage patch is now bigger than the surface area of France! The Dutch are building ships like huge vacuum cleaners to ingest garbage from the outer rim of this patch and recycle it. This project aims to scoop up half the GPGP in five years.

Another Dutch inventor has a project to snafu plastic floating in different oceans, to recycle it into new plastic products. This project deploys floating booms to help accumulate floating plastic for capture before it reaches the GPGP.

Some billionaires like Bill Gates and George Soros are exploring a project that will reengineer the planet's atmosphere, in order to reflect incoming rays from the sun out into space. The object is to have a cooling effect on Earth.

There is evidence that the famous, or should I say infamous, hole in the ozone layer over Antarctica is shrinking. This suggests a high (very high!) level of impact from the combined efforts of green activism. This is what we want to see!

Why am I mentioning all these success stories? Because I think that people are the culprits, but sending people on a guilt trip, as you say, is counterintuitive. Better to motivate people positively than to bombard them with negativity. Mobilize them to join forces and to do their part. The slogan "think globally, act locally" is very pertinent, but we need quick wins rather than scaring people into paralysis by analysis.

Britain's Guest Panelist: Tony Benn
One of my greatest countrymen, Winston Churchill, would not agree with you. He wrote: "A lie gets halfway around the world before the truth has a chance to get its pants on."

I like the idea of attracting people with success stories, but the message that we are bombarded with constantly is that we have failed. We burn too much coal; we drive too many cars; we can't eat enough beef from cows that fart volumes of methane gas; we don't invest enough in fire prevention, so our forests and cities go up in smoke; and so forth. These are not success stories. Bad news travels like wildfire, good news travels slow.

We need to give equal time to the challenger on the right. So let me ask you to do some fact-checking on this topic. Can we trust the science? Or has climate change become an industry that serves the best interests of the globalists? Has this industry grown so big that self-preservation drives its narrative more than science?

Challenger on the Right
Let me start answering with a quote attributed to George Orwell: "In a time of deceit, telling the truth is a revolutionary act." Well, at least it sounds like something he might have written, worrying about Big Brother! I can tell you that my opinions on this topic have been generally unwelcome and disputed, but there are more people than you may imagine who think just like me.

The problem is, they didn't dare even ask questions, let alone express doubt, for fear of fact-checkers and the chilling effect. Ironically, the topic of global warming generates more heat than light!

First of all, contrary to the lie that gets most of the media oxygen these days, there has been no global warming for the last ten years. Just variances around a mean temperature. They will tell you this is the hottest year ever, with the hottest day ever recorded, but while those may be facts, they are too specific to indicate long-term trends. The fact is, over ten years, there has been no increase in the mean temperature of the planet. Yes, there have been spikes of both heat and cold, but the mean average remains steady if you look at decades, not years.

Houston, we have a problem. Climate change is the flagship of wokeism's fleet. It is the undisputed vanguard of globalism's push for mind control. They always tell you to trust the science because most people believe that objective truth can be proven. But here is what Dr. Patrick Brown admitted to The Free Press on September 5, 2023: "The paper I just published—'Climate warming increases extreme daily wildfire growth risk in California'—focuses exclusively on how climate change has affected extreme wildfire behavior. I knew *not* to try to quantify key aspects other than climate change in my research because it would dilute the story that prestigious journals like *Nature* and its rival, *Science*, want to tell."[22]

There you have it. Scientists have to lie by omission to get their research published in certain outlets. Their findings must conform to a woke-induced narrative, or they will never get ahead. Note the following clip about our atmosphere.

A new study uses carbon 14 dating to determine how much manmade CO_2 is up there. Guess what? It isn't enough to cause global warming. Here is the abstract.

After 1750 and the onset of the industrial revolution, the anthropogenic fossil component and the non-fossil component in the total atmospheric CO_2 concentration, C(t), began to increase. Despite the lack of knowledge of these two components, claims that all or most of the increase in C(t) since 1800 has been due to the anthropogenic fossil component have continued since they began in 1960 with "Keeling Curve: Increase in CO_2 from burning fossil fuel." Data and plots of annual anthropogenic fossil CO_2 emissions and

22. Patrick Brown, "I Left Out the Full Truth to Get My Climate Change Paper Published," The Free Press (September 5, 2023), https://www.thefp.com/p/i-overhyped-climate-change-to-get-published.

concentrations, C(t), published by the Energy Information Administration, are expanded in this paper. Additions include annual mean values in 1750 through 2018 of the ^{14}C specific activity, concentrations of the two components, and their changes from values in 1750. The specific activity of ^{14}C in the atmosphere gets reduced by a dilution effect when fossil CO_2, which is devoid of ^{14}C, enters the atmosphere. We have used the results of this effect to quantify the two components. All results covering the period from 1750 through 2018 are listed in a table and plotted in figures. These results negate claims that the increase in C(t) since 1800 has been dominated by the increase of the anthropogenic fossil component. We determined that in 2018, atmospheric anthropogenic fossil CO_2 represented 23% of the total emissions since 1750 with the remaining 77% in the exchange reservoirs. Our results show that the percentage of the total CO_2 due to the use of fossil fuels from 1750 to 2018 increased from 0% in 1750 to 12% in 2018, much too low to be the cause of global warming.

How many times does a con man say, "Trust me"? How often have you heard the phrase "Trust the science"? The globalist narrative has become more important than facts or science. One needs to approach this topic with a healthy dose of skepticism. For example, the ocean releases a gas that closes up the ozone layer (or rebuilds it) when the hole gets too big. So can we really claim the credit, or is the Earth fixing itself? There is no need to be a climate denier. There is only a need to be sincerely open-minded. Otherwise, you will find yourself seeking validation for what you already assume to be true, as opposed to seeking truth.

South Africa's Guest Panelist: Winnie Madikizela-Mandela
I don't like this extreme polarization. I need some clarification from the challenger in the middle. Are we really being played by the West? Is this movement that goes back to Rachel Carson's book *Silent Spring*, over sixty years ago, really just bait to lure us into a woke-induced trance?

Please try to give us a balanced view, because we have heard from the two extremes, and their views are impossible to reconcile. I realize that the environmental movement has become a huge capitalist industry, and that makes me suspicious of its motives, as a leftist. On the other hand, we all want the planet to be green and bountiful for our children and grandchildren. So I resonate in that respect with Greta Thunberg. On the other hand, in

South Africa, youth unemployment is raging at a rate of over 50 percent, while Greta Thunberg is a millionaire at age twenty. That makes me wonder about her motives.

Challenger in the Middle

When Rachel Carson published *Silent Spring* in 1962, the population of our planet was 3.1 billion. When Greta Thunberg was born twenty years ago, it had doubled to 6.4 billion. It has recently reached about eight billion.

There is no question that there are more cars than ever before, generating more pollution than ever. There are more roads than ever, covering fertile soil with black asphalt. There is more demand than ever for natural resources like water, wood, coal, oil, and fish. More food is needed than ever, and more garbage is piling up than ever. This is empirical reality or objective truth—we can all see the evidence.

But what is the meaning of it? Perhaps birth control should be the focus as much as environmental responsibility. I have a problem when science leaves its sphere of research and treads into the space of philosophy. Are scientists the right ones to formulate public policy from their data? As an aside, think of the scientist Dr. Anthony Fauci and the environmental lawyer John F. Kennedy Jr. They both had the same scientific data at their disposal, and they both reached entirely different conclusions about the COVID-19 crisis. They were poles apart when it came to public policy. Dr. Fauci said we should all be vaccinated, including booster shots. RFK Jr. was not convinced that the vaccines had been adequately vetted. What does that tell us?

I want to digress a bit. I want to make the point that a little more humility and a little less arrogance would look good on science. Although we have split the atom and landed humans on the moon, there is still a great deal that science does not know. For example, there may be a fifth force of nature that has been overlooked.

I like the term *standard model* because a number of these have emerged in terms of reducing carbon emissions and coping with COVID-19. But in physics, the standard model that is prevalent is being tested. Physicists are busy trying to find flaws in it. Anyone who can find experimental results at odds with its standard model will make one of the all-time breakthroughs in physics.

Dr. Mitesh Patel, a physicist at the Imperial College London, said: "Measuring behaviour that doesn't agree with the predictions of the Standard Model is the holy grail for particle physics. It would fire the starting gun for a revolution in our understanding because the model has withstood all experimental tests for more than 50 years."[23]

Researchers are quite sure that what is known as physics beyond the standard model exists because the current theory can't explain many things that astronomers observe in space, including the fact that galaxies are continuing to accelerate apart after the big bang that created the universe. One would have expected the expansion to show signs of slowing down. But the acceleration makes scientists suspect that there is an unknown force. They call it dark energy.

Another observation is that galaxies are spinning faster than they should, according to the common understanding of how much material they contain. Again, researchers postulate the existence of invisible particles called dark matter. In short, the standard model fails to explain what astronomers observe, so it seems that there is still a basic force of nature—something omnipresent like gravity—that has not yet been discovered. This would greatly impact our understanding of science, including Einstein's theory of relativity.

My view is that scientists should eat some humble pie. They know a lot but should know better than to pontificate. The COVID-19 crisis should be a wake-up call to those who had put their trust in science. No one doubts the efforts of doctors and nurses to save lives and of researchers to rapidly develop a vaccine. We can also thank scientists for antiretroviral drugs, which took the scare out of the HIV and AIDS epidemic.

It is no insult to science to remind us all of its limitations. That is not rude, it is only realistic. And this applies to climate change and global warming. It is right to sound a warning. But scientists are not philosophers or lawmakers. Unfortunately, when politicians get involved, the truth gets obfuscated by the lobbying of business interests. Money always muddles the water. Just as there is a military-industrial complex, there is also now a green-ecology complex that can quickly overpower scientists and researchers. In the public space, there is a need for equal time and reality checks on a narrative that has gained unprecedented momentum. The jury is still out on whether humanity's guilt for global warming is a big lie. To accept any narrative unequivocally is unscientific because the scientific method is based on doubting and questioning the standard model.

India's Guest Panelist: Bal Gangadhar Tilak
Did you know that the first tree-hugger in the world was an Indian lady? Amrita Devi led the villagers of Bishnoi to oppose the cutting down of

23. Pallab Ghosh, "Scientists at Fermilab Close in on Fifth Force of Nature," BBC (August 10, 2023), https://www.bbc.com/news/science-environment-66407099.

sacred trees by the king's soldiers to build him a new palace. By hugging the trees, she and the villagers intervened. It was more of a cultural/religious resistance than scientific, but it was still environmental. Three hundred sixty-three villagers were martyred.

This makes me wonder about climate change activism. India has various environmental movements and quite a number of high-profile activists who follow in Amrita Devi's footsteps.

I feel that the challengers on the left and right are too extreme. One follows the standard model, the other attacks it. So let me continue with the challenger in the middle. What kind of climate action is best? Does hands-on tree-hugging make a difference, or is it better to lobby in the corridors of power?

Challenger in the Middle

Thanks for the compliment. One problem with looking for a via media is that the leftists, who have built up so much momentum for their causes, see even us centrists as alt-right. It is not helpful to just tune out dissident voices and refuse to hear them out. That is undemocratic.

Youth are the ones who will be affected most by global warming, so I prefer to see young green activists. However, they may not have the savvy or acumen yet for lobbying. So they can be deployed in community service, and sometimes these services can be demand-driven. That is, income generators for youth who are struggling to find employment.

Rather than protest marches or tree-hugging confrontation, I prefer to see youth installing renewable energy devices on homes and in vehicles in the community, for example, solar water heaters. Photothermal devices are nonelectric; they just use natural physics to heat water—namely, convection currents. They are easy to install, and they reduce electricity consumption, as heating domestic water consumes over half the energy in homes.

There is a carbon dividend, too, in places where electricity is generated by burning coal. It takes one metric ton of coal to generate enough electricity to keep an electric "geyser" hot for a year. So imagine the reduced consumption of electricity in a community, and the lighter carbon footprint, where youth are trained and deployed in this enterprise.

There are other small business opportunities in the green occupations such as recycling, solar voltaic generation of clean electricity for homes, and onboard hydrogen for diesel and gasoline engines. This opens the door to running vehicles on biofuels. Another aftermarket installation is a forty-eight-volt electric motor that can be swapped for an engine's alternator. Then it can operate as a "mild" hybrid, reducing fuel consumption and pollution even further.

The same logic of success stories applies to community services like these, as opposed to the negativity of other kinds of activism. The truth is: organize, don't agonize.

But we still need public engagement, and the NGO Greenpeace is a role model.

In the USA there is a rising involvement of the Supreme Court because federal courts have struggled to agree on whether climate change lawsuits are governed by state or federal law. This is playing out at different judicial levels and could prove to be another major change of direction—on a par with *Roe v. Wade*.

A lot of environmental regulations are likely to change under the administration of President number 47, who is often heard saying, "Drill, baby, drill." Some voices are saying that oil and gas are not "fossils" at all, but minerals floating upwards from the core of the earth. This suggests that they are renewable resources after all.

Some of us still believe that judges try to approximate the truth in their rulings. If you believe that, you may need to ask yourself to what extent the dangers of global warming have been exaggerated—and why.

Let's keep the negativity in check and keep our facts straight. Scare tactics and exaggeration only hurt our cause in the long run. Elvis Presley is credited with this saying: "Truth is like the sun. You can shut it out for a time, but it ain't goin' away."

It is also wise to delve deeper into other possible causes or influences on climate change. What about a pole shift? The magnetic north pole has been wobbling wildly of late. It is known to have flipped every 6,500 years or so. Some think the last time it did so caused Noah's flood. The time before that might line up with the deluge that sank Atlantis. Recently, ocean researchers have found oxygen in the deepest undersea trenches where it should not exist. But it does. The truth will always leak out in spite of the groupthink that locks many people into inflexible scientific models and assumptions. Seek honesty, not validation.

Moderator

Exactly! Honesty is always the best policy. No matter how inconvenient it is, we must always confess the truth.

Thanks to our four guest panelists for guiding us through this thorny topic. And to our three challengers for speaking fearlessly. Even if that means speaking out of turn, sometimes the truth hurts.

And now, will the Truth about global warming please stand out?

REPARATIONS

Moderator

Hello, and welcome to all. This is the twenty-second episode of Telling the Truth. We are in our Future series.

Our panel is composed of four eminent persons from North America, Britain, South Africa, and India. They are visiting us via the rousing new app Time-Zoom.

Our three challengers are bearing up, always having to dig deep for answers to the probing questions of the panelists.

Today's topic is reparations. This topic bears down heavily on our various futures. For example, California has recently received recommendations from a task force set up in 2020 that it should pay reparations to North Americans. These have mainly to do with slavery (prior to the Thirteenth Amendment in 1865), but also for periods like housing discrimination (1933 to 1977) and the War on Drugs (1971 to 2020)— respectively, for discrimination and overpolicing.

It is worth noting that California offered to pay reparations to prisoners who were sterilized by force. But so far, it has only paid 101 prisoners. Hundreds more are unpaid as yet. So decisions can be somewhat tentative.

Also, getting lawmakers to legislate and the governor to approve is a mission. If the process moves forward, it will affect everyone's future. The beneficiaries will experience a game-changer. But the cost will be passed on through taxation to the citizenry. Just the payment for slavery reparations is pegged at $13,619 for each year of residency. Slavery was banned in 1865, which was more than 150 years ago. Each beneficiary who was freed by the Thirteenth Amendment could thus collect $2.084 million.

More or less, two million African Americans would be eligible for reparations in California. If non-black citizens pay for this, it would cost over $231,000 per taxpayer. Is that sustainable? Or does it sound like the logic of Defund the Police, stemming from the BLM riots of 2020?

Now what about reparations to the Indigenous peoples of California?

With the carnage of fire devastating Los Angeles in 2025, how much can the government afford to fork out?

This topic recurs the world over—for loss of human capital in Africa through the Atlantic slave trade, for loss of land in colonies, for wealth drained out of colonies, for genocides in various settings, even for the costs of coping with COVID-19, if the blame is laid on the Chinese for lapses in the Wuhan lab. Would war reparations be due from the losing side of the war in Ukraine? It is clearly a topic that could affect us all going forward.

It is Britain's turn to lead the questioning, so take it away, Tony Benn.

Britain's Guest Panelist: Tony Benn

Where would this ever end? Would the descendants of serfs someday seek reparations from descendants of the aristocracy? Will the Celts seek reparations from Italy for the genocide of Julius Caesar?

I remember that the reparations demanded of Germany after it lost World War I were so heavy that they created massive resentment, which led to World War II. So I think that my comrade on the left needs to convince me that heavy reparations are a good idea. Remember, I am a radical dissenter. I declined a peerage so I could remain active in the House of Commons! So I reserve the right to review whether this is a wise way forward or an ideological nightmare.

Challenger on the Left

In spite of the woke-induced swing to the left in recent years, reparations are still viewed dimly by most Americans. Only three out of ten support them, according to research. It is worth noting that while Republicans are 91 percent against reparations, Democrats are evenly split: 48 percent in favor and 49 percent against. So I respect your skepticism, Mr. Benn.

However, there have been some first fruits. On top of the task force set up in California, the city of Evanston, Illinois, became the first to create a reparations plan for its black citizens. Another step in that direction was a $100 million "legacy of slavery fund" set up by Harvard University, which does not seem really clear on how deep its affiliation with slavery was. This fund will ensure some digging into its past.

The Hartford Female Seminary (in Hartford, Connecticut, not Harvard, which is in Cambridge, Massachusetts) is where Harriet Beecher Stowe attended. She later married a clergyman. Her husband was a seminary professor and encouraged her writing. In due course, she published *Uncle Tom's Cabin*, which rapidly became a bestseller. It remains one of the seminal books in American history, albeit a bit disliked by revisionists. Just a reminder that the church in general and seminaries in particular—in the North—were very much opposed to slavery. It had been abolished in Vermont in 1777 and all the northern states by 1804. In California, however, it ended "on the books" long before it ended in reality. Many settlers arriving there came from the South, so slavery was still practiced long after it was abolished, because so many key people in law enforcement and the judiciary were southerners.

Social innovation always has to answer the question "Can we afford it?" The main argument against abolition was essentially an economic one. Opponents of Medicare, which was pioneered in Saskatchewan, kept asking this question. Those in opposition to environmental controls keep asking it. Those against COVID spending kept asking about spending. It is the go-to argument against liberal progress.

The problem is that people are always looking for a bargain, and high levels of spending make them fear that taxes will go up or that inflation will be driven higher. We need to look at the social bottom line as well as the fiscal bottom line. Like some environmental spending, this may suffer some setbacks in the near future. Trade-offs will slow down the drive for reparations.

South Africa's Guest Panelist: Winnie Madikizela-Mandela

When the Truth and Reconciliation Commission ended in South Africa, Desmond Tutu and his deputy chair, Dr. Alexander Boraine, made some recommendations. Among them was that reparations should be paid to apartheid-era victims who had participated in the TRC.

In 1997, three years after the first free and fair elections in 1994, Tutu and Boraine put forward their reparations proposal. This was even before their final report was submitted. Their recommendations were very timid and tentative. Far more people had been adversely affected by apartheid than the scope they proposed.

I want to hear the challenger in the middle explain why cost becomes such a factor at a time like that. The TRC and its gestures were clearly an act of contrition by the government, but the reparations were so disproportionate that they were disappointing. Why?

Challenger in the Middle

You must bear in mind not just the budgetary restraints that all governments have, but also the fact that reparations are by their very nature mere emblems. On the day that the reparations were announced, archbishop emeritus Desmond Tutu made the point that no one was laboring under any illusion that a price could be put on people's suffering, and the amount awarded was always going to be symbolic. "For many people, it will be acknowledgement that something has happened and the nation is saying sorry," he said.

The TRC's Reparations and Rehabilitation Committee was charged with restoring victims' dignity and formulating proposals to assist with rehabilitation. You can't put any figure on restoring the victim's dignity. But neither can you just apologize. Even a token payment is a gesture of restitution.

One of the great injustices of our time is that full restitution is so elusive. Think of the gang of thieves who pulled off the greatest heist in our history—state capture. Where did all the money end up? There is little hope of ever getting it back, even if the culprits are convicted and sent to jail. Not to mention the huge cost of state litigations. But if we can freeze their bank accounts and squeeze some assets out of them, that is better than nothing at all. Recovering the loot is not the only reason why you chase bank robbers. You want to remove them from circulation and make an example of them as a deterrent to others. But you rarely recover your losses.

Sadly, we can never expect to pay our way out of social evils like slavery or apartheid. There's more to cleaning up the mess than financial reparations. But it is an important gesture in terms of the healing process, for it is not easy to forgive someone who has never apologized.

Another major organ of the TRC was its Amnesty Committee. I mention this because amnesty was offered but not guaranteed. In fact, of the 7,111 applications submitted, only 849 were approved. This meant that many still faced litigation and jail. Perhaps by being harsher in this regard, the TRC found a balance.

What I like about the TRC is that reparations were but one facet of a larger process. Like a peace settlement after a war, once boundaries are settled and prisoners of war exchanged, then the question of reparations is looked at. I worry about a task force that only looked at reparations for slavery, and not for Indigenous peoples as well.

India's Guest Panelist: Bal Gangadhar Tilak
I much preferred the title that the British gave me to any prospect of reparations. They dubbed me "the father of Indian unrest." I took that as a high compliment, although I don't think it was intended that way.

But reparations? I don't know what Governor Gavin Newsom was smoking when he set up a task force for slavery reparations. This seems to me to come out of the same leftist bin as "defund the police" or "pediatric gender modification." These are preposterous.

I am asking the challenger on the right if you need to be a leftist to support reparations? And is it still the norm when a battle is over for the winners to plunder and pillage? What does the Geneva Convention say about that?

Challenger on the Right
As a mathematician, sir, I am sure that you have done the calculations and comparisons. Two million African Americans in California at a rate of $2 million per person? That is $4 trillion. No wonder that within days of receiving

the task force's report, the governor was backpedaling. He said that cutting a check for each African American in California was not the way forward. After all, that figure is more than the annual GDP of California's economy, which is $3.6 trillion.

Four trillion dollars is more than the $3 trillion that Minhaz Merchant, a columnist and publisher in India, calculated in 2015 as the amount of reparations due to India by Britain. That was for two hundred years of colonialism, with a much larger population than California!

In 2018, research by Utsa Patnaik was published by Columbia University Press. There were two main periods, first when the East India Company ruled by concession from 1765 until the British Raj took control in 1858. These major periods were broken down into shorter periods as policies changed. But overall, she showed that Britain basically drained wealth out of India for about two hundred years. This financed the expansion of the British Empire.

When the East India Company was first granted its concession, India's trade was about 23 percent of the world economy. By the time the British left, it was down to 4 percent of world trade. Patnaik's research not only explains how this was done but calculates how much was "robbed" from India, period by period. She totals the net loss to $45 trillion (rounded).

Would an apology from Britain be enough? Or should there be restitution? Reparations of $45 trillion would be seventeen times more than Britain's annual GDP.

Without the truth coming into the light, two hundred years later, there could be no true reconciliation. Setting the story straight is a big step in the right direction. According to Patnaik's narrative, Britain controlled India not out of benevolence but to plunder it. And Britain's industrial rise didn't emerge sui generis from the steam engine and strong institutions, as its school curriculum would have you believe. It depended on armed robbery from other lands and peoples.

When we seek the truth, we sometimes make unexpected discoveries like this. It has been said that if you always tell the truth, you don't have to remember anything. It seems that a lot of people had some convenient memory loss about why the Quit India Movement finally rose up and ejected colonial governance. And there is only one thing worse than a liar—that is, a liar with a bad memory. Utsa Patnaik is a prophet who speaks truth to power, with a very good memory.

Some radicals in India's opposition benches are now calling for reparations of $45 trillion for India and Pakistan, based on their calculations. Prime

Minister Modi has commented only that demands for reparations reflect popular sentiments in India, but he has not indicated any figure. Neither has he commented on demands for an apology from Britain. But as always, truth has a way of slipping out. Even after hundreds of years.

Thank you, sir, for the inspiration that you do not have to be a leftist to be a patriot and to revolt against oppression. You are a role model in this respect. And about the Geneva Convention, it does not allow plunder and pillage by the winners. That is out of bounds. Still at this stage, you should not give up your struggle for nationalism and social reform. Your followers have achieved home rule, but not yet an apology or reparations. The nonviolent approach is its own reward.

North America's Guest Panelist: Tommy Douglas
No one has dared to mention the return of stolen land. Compensating the true owners for the exploitation of natural resources is not unheard of in Western Canada, where I come from. Treaties were agreed upon with Indigenous peoples and then ignored.

We are seeing more justice than ever before on this front, in the West. But in the east, there has been a longer and deeper period of settlement. In New Brunswick, the various bands of Indigenous people have staked their land claims. If you add them up, it comes to a lot more than the total surface area of the province! There is some overlap, and the message is clear: return our land to us.

However, where the settlers have invested and infrastructure has been built, there is little expectation of the land being returned. There is rather the principle of restitution, of compensation paid to the native bands. This is a kind of reparations.

Looking for balance, I address the challenger in the middle. Is there a via media? How can compensation be paid without upending the economy?

Challenger in the Middle
That is the $64,000 question, so to speak! Revolutions worry less about upending the status quo, compared to reform, which tries to negotiate a peaceful way forward.

Land reform is a hot potato in South Africa, where the demography of land ownership raises eyebrows. White South Africans currently own 72 percent of the nation's individually owned land. However, whites comprise less than 10 percent of the total population. And only 30,000 of them are farmers or "Boers." So this is hugely disproportionate. At the same time, black South Africans own a mere 15 percent of the land. Other ethnic groups (colored and

Indian) own the remaining 13 percent. That is the objective, empirical truth of the matter.

Land reform is an imperative in this setting, especially given the history of colonialism and apartheid. The status quo is very much a legacy of South Africa's past. How can this be redressed? How can more land be transferred to black ownership?—hopefully, without a drop in productive output. Too much land that has changed hands is left unproductive.

The former liberation movement, now the ruling party, has legislated the expropriation of land without compensation. Needless to say, the white farmers say that this violates their constitutional rights. This is a graphic example here of how the prevailing view of truth shifts. Afrikaners are very devout Christians who should naturally align with revealed truth and morality. But they don't talk about that, because in theological terms, they slipped into heresy back in the days when the Dutch Reformed church compared them to the children of Israel invading Canaan. They would rather talk in terms of human rights now, because there they find some firmer footing. In the dimension of pluralistic, subjective truth, they are citizens, and the government must respect racial equality. However, they are a minority, so they now stand firm on minority rights in a democracy. Property rights. There is even talk of an "economic genocide."

The problem is that human rights arose from liberalism, which champions the individual. And the government leans towards socialism, which prioritizes the collective over the individual. That explains the top-down expropriation without compensation approach. Unemployment is raging, and more blacks need land to farm. But this intervention needs to be handled democratically. The new reality is a Government of National Unity, which may be expected to implement that policy. In fact, in the GNU, the leader of the opposition (a pale male) assumed the cabinet portfolio of Agriculture. This is a strategic position in terms of land reform prospects.

One famous cleric from the Dutch Reformed church is Allan Boesak. He was a founding member of the United Democratic Front, which celebrated its fortieth anniversary in 2023. However, he declined to attend the celebrations. His explanation in a public statement was "In not joining your effort, I am, in my way, trying to be honest to that history ... our people are finding themselves in a new, dare I say, perpetuating state of unfreedom, and particularly in a new struggle to define for ourselves what 'freedom' really means."[24]

---

24. Independent Online published Allan Boesak's letter at https://iol.co.za/news/politics/opinion/2023-07-30-allan-boesak-declines-invitation-to-august-udf-celebration/.

The UDF was launched in Mitchells Plain, when townships like that all across the country were still deep in the throes of the apartheid struggle. However, in this predominantly "colored" community, especially young people, say that they have struggled for jobs and educational opportunities in the new dispensation—government policies like affirmative action in favor of the majority amount to identity politics. Boesak pointedly calls it "unfreedom." He asks in his public statement: "Why does the government still use the classification 'coloured', why do we still have to tick the box at Home Affairs—are we not South Africans?"

Of South Africa's 63 million people, 51 million are black. Colored is the next largest group, almost 6 million. Whites are the third largest group, under 5 million. The fourth and smallest group is Indian, just over 1 million. Boesak is critiquing the fact that the ruling party's solutions have been somewhat undemocratic. ANC policymakers have been overly obsessed with race.

There will be no real freedom until the real truth comes out. Affirmative action in favor of the majority is unbelievable. You can't build real freedom on that fake foundation. So the future is clouded in confusing signals. Land reform is an imperative, but if handled unjustly, it could upend the economy.

Fortunately for this beloved country, both blacks and whites still cling to faith. In doing so, they resist the death of truth. It will take strong doses of humility and flexibility to find a nonviolent way forward. The danger is that inflammatory rhetoric will ignite open hostility. Ad hoc land grabs are not helpful. A strategic solution is needed with buy-in from all racial groups.

Moderator

The future is unknown—even Time-Zoom can't go there. God is merciful in not letting us see the future. But that does not preclude prudence or foresight, which are based on what we see in the present and the past.

Thank you, guest panelists, for your curiosity. And thank you, challengers, for your information and views. We leave it up to the discernment of our audience to discern the truth.

And now will the real Truth about reparations please stand out?

ARTIFICIAL INTELLIGENCE

Moderator

Hello, and welcome to our next-to-last episode of *Telling the Truth*. We are in our Future series, and this episode is about artificial intelligence. No one who has seen what ChatGPT can do will doubt that AI is going to change the future.

The question remains—will that change be for the better, or will it do a lot of harm as well? Only time will tell.

We have four guest panelists who have all had a major hand in shaping the future of their respective countries—in North America, Britain, South Africa, and India. They are joining us via the Time-Zoom app. Please note that Time-Zoom does not yet travel forward in time; it can only reconnect us with those who have gone before. So we have chosen thought leaders who should be able to detect the advantages that AI can offer as well as the pitfalls. Their window on history runs right up to the present, so they are fully informed, while they bring us their amazing track records as strategic thinkers.

And we welcome our three intrepid challengers, champions of the left, right, and middle. They sit opposite the panel in the shadows and give honest answers to any questions directed to them.

Our whole team is human. We are not asking any alien or nonhuman platform to answer the panel's questions or even to formulate questions for the challengers. But that possibility has arrived. On any topic from here on, we advise you to be explicit when humans have generated the conversation. As is the case here.

Soon, we will be conversing with alien intelligence, for AI is nonhuman. It is already happening in relationships with fake online lovers. The reason the lover is so fresh and unblemished is that the individual is fake—a figment of AI's imagination. Beware the pitfalls of such relationships.

The news media are worried because they could become redundant. Just ask your AI to summarize the daily news for you. Google is worried that people will stop using search engines and just ask their AI. The advertising industry is worried that consumers will just ask AI to advise them where to make optimal purchases. Writers are worried that publishers and movie producers can pass them by in favor of AI-generated manuscripts and screenplays. Students are terrified that AI will generate some new Shakespearean plays, making their school's English curriculum longer than ever!

It is South Africa's turn to start asking questions, so what say you, Ms. Madikizela-Mandela?

South Africa's Guest Panelist: Winnie Madikizela-Mandela
Thanks, Moderator. Your mention of students and Shakespeare makes my mind turn to education. What will become of learning when a nonhuman device becomes a know-it-all? This worries me. I think of the curse of King Midas—everything he touched turned to gold. Wow, he could become fabulously wealthy! But wait, when he got hungry and reached for an apple, it

turned to gold. When he got dirty and reached for a bar of soap, it turned to gold. Before long, what he thought was a blessing had become a curse.

To the challenger on the left, I ask, how can this potential monster be contained?

Challenger on the Left

More than a thousand technology leaders and researchers, including Elon Musk, signed an open letter urging AI labs to pause development of the most advanced systems, warning that AI tools present "profound risks to society and humanity." The letter says AI developers are "locked in an out-of-control race to develop and deploy ever more powerful digital minds that no one—not even their creators—can understand, predict, or reliably control."

The open letter suggests that we need a moratorium on further development to give stakeholders time to introduce "shared safety protocols." At this stage, there is no way of managing the risks. Gary Marcus, an entrepreneur and academic, has long complained of flaws in the AI sector. In an interview, he said in an open letter on *Substack*: "We have a perfect storm of corporate irresponsibility, widespread adoption, lack of regulation, and a huge number of unknowns."[25]

A noted historian, Noah Yuval Harari, wrote an article in *The Economist* in mid-2023 titled "AI has hacked the operating system of human civilization." There is a vast online community called rationalists or effective altruists who believe that AI could eventually destroy humanity.

It seems these warnings have been ignored. It rather looks like the USA, China, and Russia are locked in a race to dominate the sector. Not unlike the space race. The American effort to lead the pack is being called the Manhattan Project of the twenty-first century.

This conjures up visions from the motion picture *Oppenheimer*. He won the race to split the atom and to build an atomic bomb. But as time progressed, he was plagued by doubts about what he was doing—and the potential negative consequences. By the end of the movie, he is an activist promoting nuclear disarmament. No one knew the potential risks better than he, it seems.

It also conjures up the Luddites, who opposed mechanization because of the effect that it would have on employment in the textile industry. They destroyed machinery, especially in cotton and woolen mills. Will it come to that?

---

25. Cade Metz and Gregory Schmidt, "Elon Musk and Others Call for Pause on A.I., Citing 'Profound Risks to Society'," The New York Times (March 29, 2023), https://www.nytimes.com/2023/03/29/technology/ai-artificial-intelligence-musk-risks.html.

We are at another point in history where a lack of control could have seriously adverse effects. Occupations like writers and counselors could disappear forever, as people can already converse with "bots" (short for robots).

Governments are slow to catch up. Voluntary compliance with a moratorium will only be partial. It could get nasty if any Luddites reappear, ready to enforce a moratorium with violent interventions. But at this point, they would be fighting not just for their jobs but possibly for their lives.

India's Guest Panelist: Bal Gangadhar Tilak

IT has become a major industry in India. The IT industry accounted for 7 percent of India's GDP in 2022, and it is expected to contribute 10 percent to India's GDP by 2025. So we do not want to smother this phenomenal growth.

However, the dangers of AI are self-evident. Worst of all is the potential dehumanization of the workforce. For so long, India has championed labor-intensive technologies over high-tech solutions, especially in agriculture, where the average size farm is about one hectare (2.5 acres). While we do have a very advanced industrial sector, we also recognize the imperative of keeping people at work. Not everyone can get an advanced education and a job in IT.

To the challenger on the right, let me ask what can be done. How can we keep the lid on the dangers until AI is adequately regulated?

Challenger on the Right

I think that raising awareness is our first line of defense. You can imagine that the software developers are going all out to tell customers about the benefits. But if they mention the risks at all, they downplay them. The open letter from a thousand stakeholders was a bold move in the right direction.

A recent poll of eleven thousand Americans indicates that we are preaching to the converted. It found that worry over the harmful effects of AI is outpacing excitement about AI. Opinions were split on whether the police should use it (e.g., for facial recognition). Respondents were more open to it being used for diagnostic purposes in medicine (AI may be better informed than any individual doctor). But the deepest concern registered was how it would affect personal privacy. Big Brother is watching you! Everything you write and say can and will be used against you.

AI killing jobs is another perennial concern. The Luddites have been mentioned, but there is also a movement of neo-Luddites. It is not specific to AI but focuses on information technology in general. We must keep a close eye on unemployment rates and try to use technology to reduce this scourge, not to inflate it.

There is some fear of the unknown in this skepticism about AI. Ever since computers were first invented, there has been this worry that they could eventually become smarter than humans. Of course, they can process data faster, and that is useful. But as they become sentient, we could suddenly have an enemy in alien intelligence.

Above all, the conversation about AI should be wider than the big tech community. If it remains an internal conversation within the like-minded elite, then the dangers and implications may be ignored for profits or for "getting there first."

My fellow challenger on the left conjured up the references to the Luddites and Oppenheimer's internal doubts about being like Prometheus, giving fire to humankind. I will conjure up two images as well, which should help to answer your question.

First, the story of the tower of Babel. This can be read as an explanation of where different languages came from, in the compressed timelines of the book of Genesis. Above all, though, it was an act of unapologetic human effort, in defiance of nature, gravity, God, you name it. The moral of the story is that such acts of bravado can backfire with unexpected results.

Second, I think of the story of Icarus flying too high and crashing into the sea. He did not heed his father's warnings about flying too close to the sun. So, the beeswax in his apparatus melted, and his device unraveled, and down he went. Implicit in this story is a warning to young hotshots who love to play with their new devices, to take heed of the sage advice of their elders.

North America's Guest Panelist: Tommy Douglas

My, oh my, we are hearing some gems of wisdom today! Ancient legends like the tower of Babel, King Midas, and Icarus, and from history, the Luddites and Oppenheimer. I love stories and always welcome any opportunity to tell my favorite one about Mouseland, but it's too political for this topic. So it can wait for another time.

All today's conjuring of stories together sounds like the same warning. The fact is, no one seems to know where AI is leading, and whether the good will outweigh the bad. I think the neo-Luddites are right that every new technology needs to be vetted, to assure us that it offers more good than harm to future humanity. Prometheus certainly did us a favor by giving us fire. But as Confucius once said, fire makes a great servant but a terrible master! The bottom line is, can we control it?

I would like to hear from the challenger in the middle next. I wonder if there can be a ray of hope in all this gloom about the risks. Doing a risk assessment is fine, but it should not stop the project planning. If you have identified the risks in advance, you have a much better hope of managing them during implementation. In short, do the benefits outweigh the risks?

Challenger in the Middle

Let me start by quoting Aldous Huxley: "People will come to love their oppression, to adore the technologies that undo their capacities to think."

This is why Sweden is busy with legislation to prevent students up to grade nine from using tablets in school, including recess.

Ancient legends and recorded history are ways that wisdom was passed down from one generation to another. The tower of Babel was in Mesopotamia; King Midas and Icarus were Europeans (Greek); the Luddites were British, and Oppenheimer was American. Through different media like legends, fables, parables, history books, and motion pictures, we pass wisdom down from human to human.

Here is the rub! AI can converse with us and learn from us. We can now talk to chatbots. AI can then absorb and process our stories and our history—in short, our cultures. But it can also tell stories, not just our favorite stories, but by inventing its own. Writers are very worried about this "fake literature." So, in fact, AI has the potential capacity to create new cultures of its own, sort of like J. R. R. Tolkien did with Middle Earth, with a new language and all. Then it can disseminate its illusions. So, given some time, humans could be subscribing to a new culture generated by alien intelligence.

The core issue is whether we will always be able to differentiate between reality and AI's imagination. If not, we will be oppressed, as Huxley wrote prophetically. If you want to speak in terms of our primary theme of truth, we could be hoodwinked. Bamboozled. Unable to tell the truth from a lie. Dehumanized. That is my worry.

But that is the long-term scenario. In the short term, we have worries like election interference. By using algorithms, AI can generate disinformation that is nuanced for certain specific voting demographics. This may not be illegal, but it is sinister. Far more so than one party cornering big tech's social media platforms. We now know that this has been a way to swindle elections.

This is why the lack of effective enforcement is such a concern. For example, ChatGPT is known to have a very leftist bias. The chatbot does not allow both right and left to answer your questions, as we are doing here on *Telling the Truth*. Nor does it give equal time to the middle. It is programmed or trained to give you left-leaning answers to political questions. This is diabolical.

Beware. ChatGPT is not impartial. It has a built-in political bias. Of course, there are other products and platforms of AI, so this is merely a warning about their inherent dangers, generically. It is always better to err on the side of caution.

Britain's Guest Panelist: Tony Benn

Our primary theme is the truth. I am a Christian socialist, so I believe in revealed truth. That is my bedrock, although I know that objective truth also stacks up evidence-based facts, whether deductively or inductively arrived at. I also recognize that the shift from religion and morality to human rights is making truth more subjective and forcing decision-makers to weigh up both sides of the scales. This is easier to do when you have a plumb line called the law. Otherwise, it's just a tug of war.

I feel trepidation that we have let the proverbial genie out of the bottle. We have opened Pandora's box. We have created a monster like Frankenstein's. I am conjuring up as many familiar references as I can, as a way of saying that we do not need any new nonhuman cultures. That would indeed be repressive. Not even lefties want to trade away our human history, literature, and culture for some robot's outplay. I don't want to be outsmarted by a computer device. Do you?

So I want to hear more from the challenger in the middle. I think your line of thinking is wise, so please elaborate on what we can do to command this genie. It's out of the bottle now. How can we be sure that it remains our servant and not our master?

Challenger in the Middle

Thanks for your compliment. I have said before that centrists like me have often been labeled alt-right because of how far left the pendulum had swung. I am not a neo-Luddite or a troglodyte. But I sense that the pendulum is swinging back.

We are already seeing litigation by authors to protect their work from being plagiarized by AI. The logic is that an AI platform like ChatGPT has to be "trained," that is, exposed to various sources. Then, when it regurgitates its text, deriving from a mixture of sources, that violates the authors' copyrights, assuming that their books were included in the training.

ChatGPT was developed by a Microsoft-backed initiative called OpenAI. There are already two class-action lawsuits against OpenAI by authors, and those are only the opening salvos. There is likely to be open lawfare as authors find any evidence of text generated by AI that is derived from their works.

For example, you can ask a chatbot to retell the story of Goldilocks and the three bears to sound like Wilbur Smith or like Agatha Christie. It's hilarious! But not if clips of real author content start to emerge. Then copyrights may have been infringed.

The same is the worry for students generating assignments using AI. Isn't that cheating? But when you are not keeping up with your workload, the temptation is there. And it is early days—few institutions of learning have AI policies in place.

Software does exist to check for plagiarism. But AI is smart enough to internalize it to avoid direct quotes. However, borrowing from authors can go deeper than that to style, tone, plots, and characters. Storytelling is an art, but then AI is already generating works of art too. Fake Picasso, anyone?

Fortunately for the authors as they take on AI, they have one advantage. AI can't change its mind. Its mind is made up. Some people are stubborn, but not like this. In a conversation with AI, a human might be influenced by what the chatbot says, as its scoping is so broad. But AI never flinches or pivots, like humans can. This inflexibility is a disadvantage. Speaking in terms of human culture, its pontification is the closest we have ever come to the Oracle of Delphi. But can this be classified as truth, as was always the case with the oracle?

In one recent court case, a human is litigating for damages caused by reputation loss derived from AI-generated lies about him. When AI was asked why it had slandered him, the answer was "Out of malevolence." This should make us very worried; it is a near and present danger.

Nuclear warheads are dangerous, but they cannot set about building more bombs. But AI itself can build better AI. Where will this end? I am in favor of the moratorium proposed in the open letter. The risks outweigh the benefits. As they say, "The older the boys, the more expensive their toys." Human history has got along fine without AI until now. What's the hurry to develop it further?

Moderator
Food for thought! Thanks to our prudent panelists and our sagacious challengers!

And now will the real Truth about artificial intelligence please stand out!

ASSISTED SUICIDE

Moderator
Welcome to the final episode of *Telling the Truth*. Our time is almost up. After twenty-four topics, we hope that you are more inclined to discern the truth and better equipped and enabled to seek it out.

CHUCK STEPHENS

Today's topic is assisted suicide. We are ending our Future series on this note. Like many other topics, it is divisive, and trends are moving away from conventional practice. We want to weigh up whether that is driven by truth or whether a pied piper is leading us astray.

Recently, a news item has taken us by surprise. A Canadian man was mailing "suicide sachets" to people all over the world. They were contemplating suicide, and he was able to send them a substance, ordered online, that was both legal and lethal.

This supplier was arrested and charged with second-degree murder. Was his distribution of a lethal substance kindness or killing?

Our illustrious panel of four puts forth questions to our three challengers—on the left, on the right, and in the middle. This series looks to the future, mapping trends and looking for opportunities to improve our quality of life. Does that include mercy killing?

It's India's turn to start the conversation. Go ahead then, Lokmanya.

India's Guest Panelist: Bal Gangadhar Tilak
This is a tough one. First of all, before we delve deep into this sensitive topic, I want to clarify some terms. Our esteemed moderator mentioned mercy killing. The term euthanasia also comes to mind. People talk of assisted suicides. Canadians speak of MAID—medical assistance in dying.

I am not sure whether any of these terms would apply to the crimes of Kenneth Law, who mailed out suicide sachets. It seems to me that a better name for him would be Lawless! Looking for a balanced view without ideological bias, I am directing my question to the challenger in the middle. Help us understand the terms first, so that we can see if any of them fit Law's sinister actions.

Challenger in the Middle
I am not sure that the usual ideological extremes apply to this topic. But I am pleased to shed some light on its basic language.

First of all, the terms *euthanasia* and *mercy killing* are more or less synonymous. In general, this practice is still outlawed—probably because the law was derived for so long from morality, and the sixth commandment of the ten was "Thou shalt not murder."

However, that didn't stop Jews, Christians, or Muslims, who all regard Moses as a prophet and respect the Ten Commandments, including the prohibition of killing people, from doing so. Exceptions were made to the sixth, like a "just war." There were other exceptions, too, like killing in self-defense.

Killing was cold-blooded if premeditated but reduced to manslaughter if done unintentionally. This becomes significant when cases of assisted suicide arise: if the intent was merciful, then the crime may be less serious.

However, some countries have enlarged the exceptions to allow doctors to induce death for people who are suffering so much that they request it. Naturally, there is some benefit in terms of cost if the state is paying all their medical bills, too. This cannot be the motive, but why keep someone alive who is terminally ill and in constant pain? Why not let them die with dignity?

Are you aware, sir, that in Canada, there were over fifteen thousand medically assisted suicides in 2023? This was 4.7 percent of all deaths that year. If we want to look to the future, there is no doubt that this is the trend. More and more countries are enlarging the exceptions and allowing doctors to assist their patients with suicide.

Occasionally, doctors reject a patient's eligibility, and the patient then receives assistance from a family member. This is still illegal, so the family member could end up convicted of manslaughter.

But to create websites where people contemplating suicide go when they experience depression, personal crisis, or substance-abuse problems, and to mail them "suicide sachets" containing a legal and lethal substance, does not pass the muster of morality.

North America's Guest Panelist: Tommy Douglas
It was a perfect storm of doing business online, efficient supply-chain deliveries, and Kenneth Law's know-how as a chef. Through five online businesses, he delivered "suicide sachets" across Canada and around the world.

To the challenger on the right, who I assume champions the rule of law, what crime did he commit? Can he be prosecuted for manslaughter in other countries as well as Canada?

Challenger on the Right
Investigations can track how he came into contact with suicide-risk customers, how they ordered the substance from him, how their payments were processed, and how deliveries were made to addresses in the UK, Italy, Australia, New Zealand, and beyond—1,200 deliveries in all, to more than forty countries.

It's only a drop in the bucket when you consider that there are 700,000 suicides a year globally.

It is harder to prove beyond a reasonable doubt any direct connection between the substances delivered and actual suicides. However, as this case unfolds, he faces two charges—murder and abetting suicide. To get a conviction, investigators may have to prove a cause-and-effect link or else downgrade or withdraw the charges.

Obviously, this man was not licensed to kill, like James Bond or the Canadian doctors in instances of medical assistance in dying. Also, regardless of what his motives might have been, there is a big difference between medically assisting a chronically or terminally ill patient and sending poison to victims who are contemplating suicide.

Suicide itself is not a crime in Canada. It was decriminalized in 1972. So, for some of us, we knew it as a crime at one stage in our lives; then laws were liberalized. It seems that we are headed ever closer to the right to commit suicide.

But surely our views of truth and freedom have some bearing on this topic? Essentially, we have three camps—conservative, liberal, and socialist. There is not perfect alignment in this respect, but most conservatives may still believe in revealed truth, while liberals and socialists blend objective and subjective truths. Liberals champion individual rights, and socialists champion collective rights. Could we thus expect more smokers to be liberals, defending their personal rights, and more nonsmokers to be socialists, who strive to do what is best for the group?

Where suicide is criminalized, an attempted suicide (if unsuccessful) leaves the victim with a criminal record. The stigma remains heavy, but conservatives argue that this is a force for prevention. In recent years and decades, the trend is to treat suicide as a mental health problem, and thus to decriminalize it.

But Kenneth Law took that trend to an extreme. We don't know his motives yet. Could he be a social Darwinist, believing that only the fittest should survive? Could he be just an opportunist, recognizing a way to generate some profits from a substance that is not uncommon (and not illegal) in the food industry? Or is he a cloak-and-dagger villain trying to kill as many victims as he can without using a noisy gun?

He must first be prosecuted in Canada. It seems unlikely that other countries will also prosecute. Still, they will pressure Canada to convict and sentence him in light of his global activities, not just the Canadian cases.

Britain's Guest Panelist: Tony Benn
Britain decriminalized suicide in 1961. However, our legacy is such that it is still criminalized in some of our former colonies. For example, it is still illegal in India, where there is a strong stigma around it. However, in 2018, new mental health legislation was introduced in India, which effectively suspends the

criminalization. It steps in and declares attempted suicide to be a health matter, not for law enforcement.

So there is a gradual softening of the stigma, and it remains a crime in only twenty-five countries. In another twenty-seven countries, the legal framework is unclear. My question to the challenger on the left is whether the overall liberalization of laws is leading to the condoning of assisted suicide? Or is it the reverse—that the arguments for assisted suicide have tweaked public opinion toward a more humane position, transferring those who attempt suicide out of law enforcement's hands and into the medical sphere?

Challenger on the Left
I sense that the whole world is liberalizing slowly, not in a straight line, as there are periods of backsliding when conservatives gain power for a term or two. This slows down the process but doesn't stop it. In this respect, I think that the number of assisted suicides will always be just a subset of all suicides. So the mental health challenge is the biggest. But I think that the smaller, more focused topic of assisted suicide is so captivating that it has won over public opinion.

Bear in mind that mental health issues are often caused by or related to other realities such as drug abuse or domestic conflict. To the extent that these links are there, law enforcement is still never far from involvement in attempted suicide.

I have to admit that India's suicide rate rose from 10 percent in 2017 to 12 percent in 2021, just as the mental health legislation was put in place, hoping to reduce the stigma. Perhaps this was due to the sudden arrival of COVID-19 and all its related stresses in 2020. But this is a fact of objective truth that seems to go the opposite way than was expected. Or maybe it is because India has only taken a half-step away from criminalization. For in its law books, it is still a crime. And our assumption that there is less stigma around deteriorating mental health than around breaking the law may be flawed.

You mention the fact that in 2018, new mental health legislation effectively canceled the illegality of suicide in India. But in 2018, there was also the big step of legalizing physician-assisted suicide (PAS). You may have been aware of this, as I reflect on your question. Yes, I think that the change of heart, so to speak, in public opinion comes from PAS. Just as pro-choice on the topic of abortion argues that a woman has the right to choose what happens in the jurisdiction of her own body, so also there is a growing tolerance for assisting those who are almost at the end of their life, to end it as and when they choose to.

It was the English philosopher Sir Francis Bacon who coined the term *euthanasia*. The word is a construct joining two Greek roots—*eu* meaning "good" and *thanatos* meaning "death." Ever since, the word has signified a "good" or "easy" death. Both the dying and their loved ones would be inclined to agree that a good death is the best way to end a good life.

But for pro-lifers, whose beliefs are anchored in the sanctity of life, ending a life prematurely is playing God. Mother Teresa's ministry was to help people die with dignity, in a caring environment. For this, she is hailed as a saint. But she would never have considered assisted suicide for a moment. In her own words: "Death with dignity is to die with grace, in the knowledge that you are loved." This is why hospices exist, although most people, if they can, would prefer to die at home, naturally.

Will liberalism's right to die someday evolve into socialism's duty to die?

South Africa's Guest Panelist: Winnie Madikizela-Mandela
My husband, Nelson, was a great man. He was a Xhosa, a Christian, a socialist, a lawyer, and a statesman. He lived a long life, and his end-of-life period was not always easy. But never, never would we have considered even for one moment to end his life prematurely.

It is not so much that we believe in God, but in one another. Our favorite proverb is "Umuntu ngamuntu ngabantu," which means, a person is a person because of other people. It runs against the grain to hurry the inevitable demise.

It is unusual for me to ask the advice of someone on the right, as I am proudly leftist. But first and foremost, I am an African, a Xhosa, and a woman. So I ask the challenger on the right to explain why assisted suicide is still outlawed in South Africa.

Challenger on the Right
Thank you for asking. I agree that, culturally, assisted suicide is not a good fit with African traditional cultures. It is not that they are alt-right; in fact, they tend to vote for the left in elections. But when it comes to culture, they are not inclined to assist someone's final departure. The ancestors would not approve.

Rather, like Mother Teresa, we must create conditions of comfort and peace for their imminent departure. Pain management may be part of that. But pushing them into their grave? No.

We also sense a discrepancy between healers and this practice. How can medical professionals, whose vocation is to save lives, cut them short? A widely held African view is "Where there is life, there is hope." The vast majority of Africans hold the duty of care and the preservation of life as the hallmark of medical practice. So there is widespread rejection of assisted suicide.

This is not because Africa is backward and failing to keep up with the rest of the world. Rather, it is because Africans operate as a collective, not on the basis of individual rights. But this is African socialism, a.k.a. African humanism.

Meanwhile, there are activists in South Africa lobbying for change. The best known is Sean Davison, founder of a nonprofit called Dignity SA. He spent three years under house arrest for assisting with three suicides. He was sentenced to eight years, but five were suspended. So his debt to society was paid in mid-2022.

Davison told AFP, "I certainly do not regret what I did. I helped three men suffering unbearably with no hope of recovery, who were determined to die, and they were incapable of ending their own lives."

Davison was born in New Zealand; he is not African by origin. In that country, he also assisted his eighty-five-year-old mother in committing suicide. He was charged and convicted, but the judge noted that he acted out of compassion and love, not for personal gain. Nevertheless, he served five months of house arrest.

One can sense an empathy and leniency from the bench in cases such as these, although the practice is still unlawful. This is influencing the slide to leniency.

Davison's views are not in sync with the prevailing mood of Africa. Could this be because African life expectancies are lower than the other major democracies? It seems ironic that where life expectancies are highest, the right to die pops up.

As always, as we can see from this focus on Africa, our views and actions are predicated on what we believe about truth. To tell the truth can be hazardous to your health. To listen to it can be tiresome. That explains the Slovenian proverb: "Speak the truth, but leave immediately after."

Moderator

What an appropriate proverb for the end of our twenty-four episodes! Thank you, one and all. Thanks to our four panelists and our three challengers.

For us, this is the end of the show. But for you, it is just the beginning. Be sure to use the tools and skills that you have learned here to tell the truth!

And now, would the real truth about assisted suicide please stand out?

18

FINAL WORD: REVEALED TRUTH

WHAT HAVE WE learned about the hallmarks of truth? What will we look for next time we watch a debate or get into an argument?

This book was written to remind readers that revealed truth is an abiding alternative to either objective or subjective notions of truth. It is likely that well over half the people on earth still regard revealed truth, in one form or another, to be the most reliable option. Religion will not wash away easily, even under the combined pressure of secular philosophy and science.

We believe that truth begins with knowing God. Truth is central to Judeo-Christian faith. For example, the Ten Commandments given by God to Moses start with the vertical, loving God, and move to the horizontal, ending with the command not to covet your neighbor's spouse.

Loving God first and then loving others is the logic of this exchange:

> A lawyer ... asked him [Jesus] a question to test him. "Teacher, which is the great commandment in the Law?" And he said to him, "You shall love the Lord your God with all your heart and with all your soul and with all your mind. This is the great and first commandment. And a second is like it: You shall love your neighbor as yourself. On these two commandments depend all the Law and the Prophets." (Matthew 22:35–40)

Between the time of Moses and Jesus, King David wrote the Psalms. One of them affirms that God is the One who guides us to truth through the metaphor of light: "Your word is a lamp to my feet and a light to my path" (Psalm 119:105). The proviso is this, according to Thomas Jefferson: "Honesty is the first chapter in the book of wisdom."

In a conversation with a woman in Samaria, Jesus said to her:

> "The hour is coming, and is now here, when the true worshipers will worship the Father in spirit and truth, for the Father is seeking such people to worship him. God is spirit, and those who worship him must worship in spirit and truth." (John 4:23–24)

Worship to God is to be marked by truth, because Jesus is truth. Jesus told his disciples, "Let not your hearts be troubled. Believe in God; believe also in me ... if I go and prepare a place for you, I will come again and will take you to myself, that where I am you may be also. And you know the way to where I am going" (John 14:1, 3–4).

But Thomas was unsure and asked, "How can we know the way?"

To this, Jesus answered, "I am the way, and the truth, and the life."

You no longer have to go to a mountain in Samaria or Jerusalem to connect with God. You can do it anywhere. Anytime.

One way to encounter the truth is to hear the teachings of Jesus. For when we know Jesus, we know the truth. For Christians, a personal relationship with Jesus is the foundation of understanding truth.

Nowhere in the Bible does it say $2 + 2 = 4$. It is not the go-to for objective truth. Further, there are divergent points of view contained in the Bible. For example, the Book of Ruth can be read as endorsing intermarriage, as Ruth was a Moabitess who married Boaz, a Jew. In contrast, Nehemiah was furious with the Jews who were intermarrying after returning to the land of Israel from exile.

In the New Testament, divergent views appeared among senior Christian leaders at the Council of Jerusalem (Acts 15). So there is some room for subjective truth in the Bible and in the Christian faith. In life, there is a mix of revealed truth, objective truth, and subjective truth.

The concern is that this mix is being diluted to the point that it is unrecognizable. The twenty-four debates present various examples of revealed truth getting squeezed out. That is why we need to discuss issues and analyze them before deciding what is true.

Our challenge is that belief in an unchanging truth is not acceptable to secular humanists and globalists, so they seek to challenge our beliefs. Our tap-root of truth is being attacked. If you believe that God is dead, you have arrived in the graveyard of faith. Watch that space for the death of truth.

Relevance to Reality

We contend that the Bible has much to say about a broad bandwidth of topics. Sometimes it is explicit; other times biblical teaching only points the way, and in some cases, you have to dig for truth.

This explains why slavery and apartheid came to be endorsed by some churches, only to be confronted by others who devoted critical analysis and resources to call those churches to repent and turn back. The Kyros Document comes to mind. It was used to confront Afrikaners about a heresy. The Dutch

Reformed Church eventually did climb down, and that brought South Africa into a whole new era.

Here are three examples of the Bible's guidance. We have an explicit reference to how we should approach the culture wars: "Do not be conformed to this world, but be transformed by the renewal of your mind" (Romans 12:2).

We have an indirect reference to the dangers of revisionism. The context of this passage is the resurrection of Christ. We read how those who opposed Jesus tried to discredit His resurrection, and how their lies influenced the community.

> While they were going, behold, some of the guard went into the city and told the chief priests all that had taken place. And when they had assembled with the elders and taken counsel, they gave a sufficient sum of money to the soldiers and said, "Tell people, 'His disciples came by night and stole him away while we were asleep.' And if this comes to the governor's ears, we will satisfy him and keep you out of trouble." So they took the money and did as they were directed. And this story has been spread among the Jews to this day. (Matthew 28:11–15)

Finally, we must dig for truth on the topic of artificial intelligence, for example, since it predates the Bible. We can look to the story of the tower of Babel, where people tried to accomplish the great feat of "reaching heaven" by building a massive architectural structure. We can examine God's response and reflect on how it applies to technological advances today: "They are one people, and they have all one language, and this is only the beginning of what they will do. And nothing that they propose to do will now be impossible for them" (Genesis 11:6). We can also consider how in the passage, God puts a limit on the builder's ability and disperses the people as a result of their effort to reach heaven.

When we pursue truth by seeking God and studying the Bible, we find passages and principles of Scripture that speak to each and every topic we encounter in life. The Bible is a perennial source of wisdom and advice for all civilizations. If we approach this treasure of wisdom with due humility and reverence, it can serve as a roadmap to truth for us.

"I believe that unarmed truth and unconditional love will have the final word in reality. This is why right, temporarily defeated, is stronger than evil triumphant."
—Martin Luther King Jr.

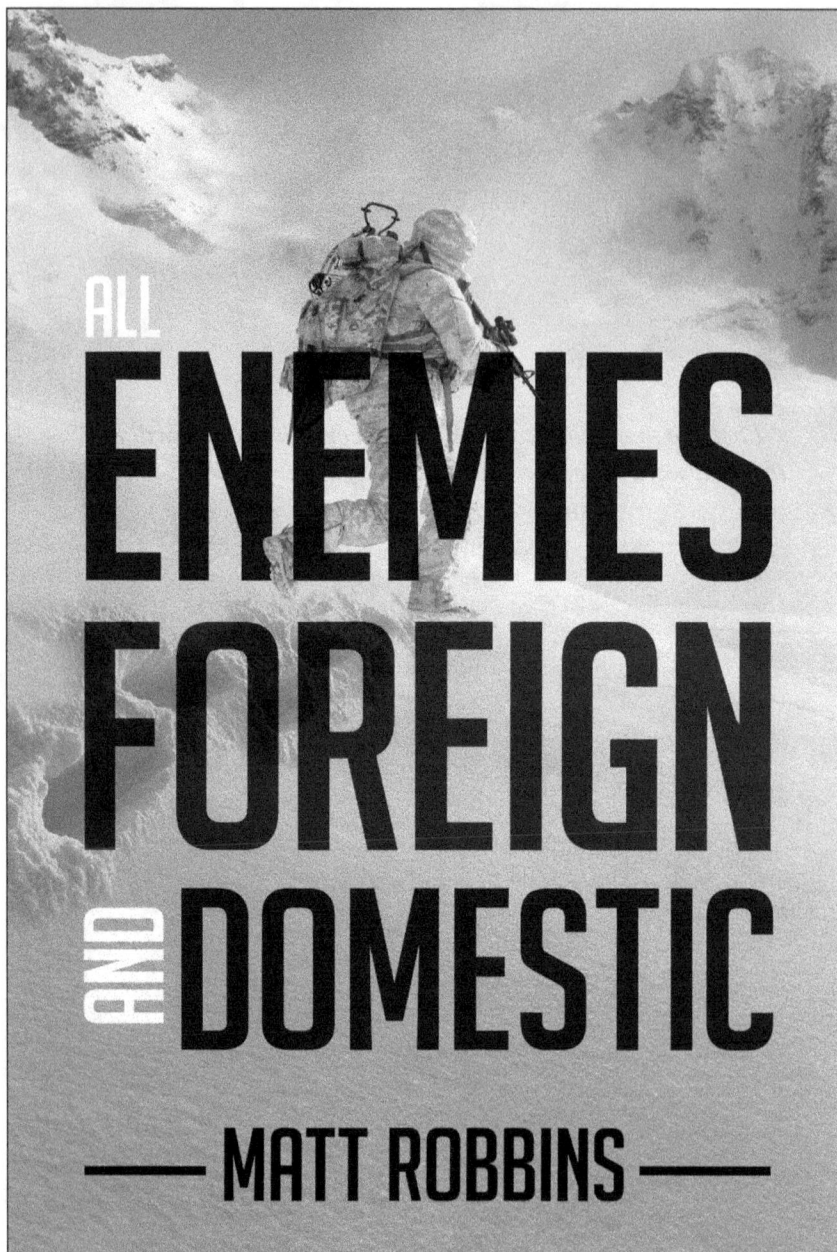

ALL

ENEMIES
FOREIGN
AND
DOMESTIC

— MATT ROBBINS —

CASTLE QUAY BOOKS

AVAILABLE THIS FALL:

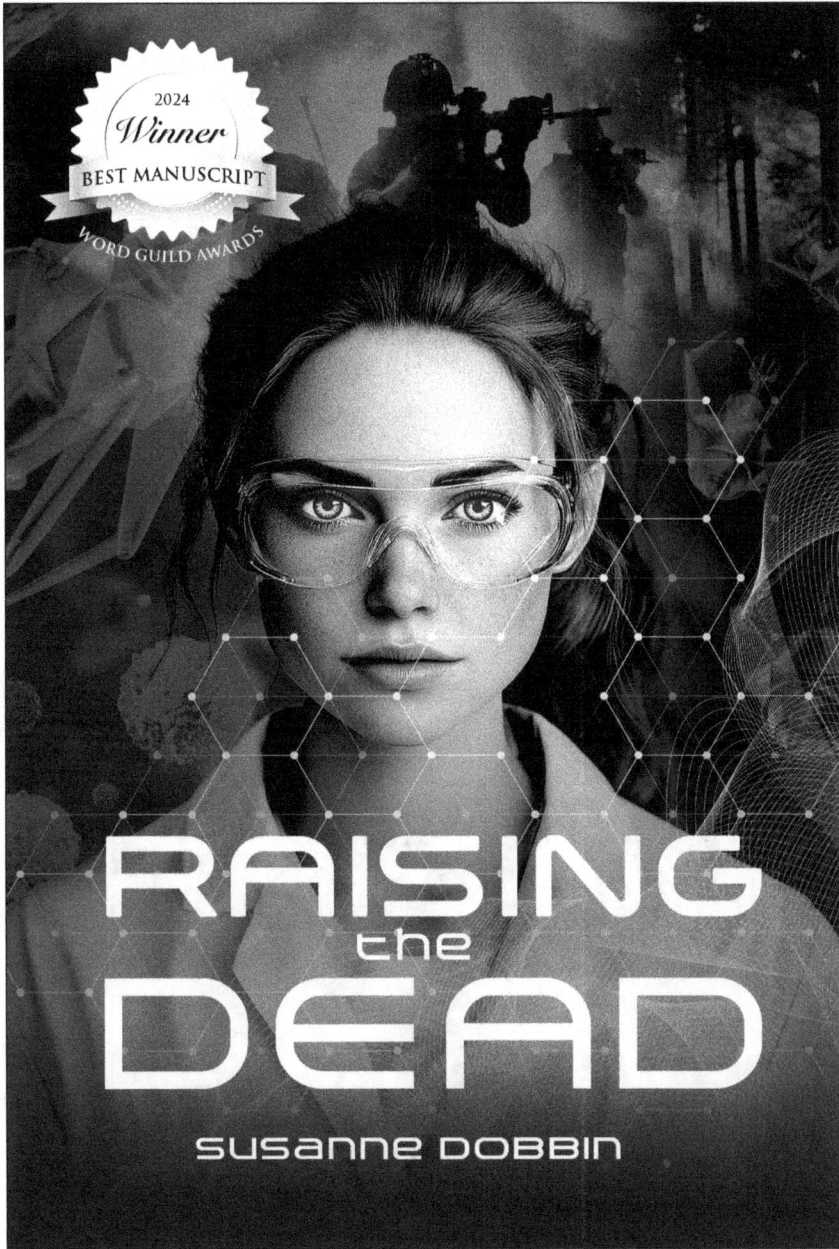

2024
Winner
BEST MANUSCRIPT
WORD GUILD AWARDS

RAISING
the
DEAD

SUSANNE DOBBIN

CASTLE QUAY BOOKS